The Political Economy of Local Cinema: A Critical Introduction

Anne Rajala / Daniel Lindblom / Matteo Stocchetti (eds.)

The Political Economy of Local Cinema: A Critical Introduction

PETER LANG

Bibliographic Information published by the
Deutsche Nationalbibliothek
The Deutsche Nationalbibliothek lists this publication in the Deutsche
Nationalbibliografie; detailed bibliographic data is available online at
http://dnb.d-nb.de.

Library of Congress Cataloging-in-Publication Data
A CIP catalog record for this book has been applied for at the
Library of Congress.

This publication has been funded by the following institutions :
A.F. Lindstedts och Svenska Handelsinstitutes Fond för Handelsutbildning,
Fonden för Teknisk Undervisning och Forskning, and Svenska
Kulturfonden.

Printed by CPI books GmbH, Leck

ISBN 978-3-631-79951-2 (Print)
E-ISBN 978-3-631-81330-0 (E-PDF)
E-ISBN 978-3-631-81331-7 (EPUB)
E-ISBN 978-3-631-81332-4 (MOBI)
DOI 10.3726/b16846

This publication has been peer reviewed.

www.peterlang.com

Preface

This volume is the third book-length publication of the research programme Media and Education in the Digital Age (MEDA), after *Media and Education in the Digital Age. Concepts, Assessments, Subversions* (Peter Lang, 2014) and *Storytelling and Education in the Digital Age. Experiences and Criticisms* (Peter Lang, 2016).

MEDA is an interdisciplinary programme whose main goal it to coordinate, collect and circulate research on the disparate domains in which the development of new technologies has an impact on education.

Launched in 2012 at Arcada University of Applied Sciences (Helsinki, Finland), the main mission of MEDA is to support critical education and pedagogy. Based on the epistemic coordinates of critical theory and social constructionism, MEDA includes several projects inspired by a variety of disciplinary and methodological approaches. In addition to the epistemic coordinates, these projects have two common tasks: to identify the important challenges to critical education and pedagogy and to suggest the contours of adequate responses.

One of the main projects in this programme is MEDA-Cinema. This project originated from the desire to improve the education of Swedish-speaking Finnish filmmakers by looking at the impact of globalization and digitalization on cinema. The main research questions of this project focus on two dimensions: the relationship between cinema and cultural identity and the political economy of local cinema.

The essays in this collection focus on the second dimension or, more precisely, on the organization of material and immaterial resources necessary for local cinema to endure as a valuable and vibrant alternative to other forms of cinema. In line with the mission of applied research, the main normative goal inspiring our project is rather practical: to support local cinema and the education of local filmmakers in addressing the cultural effects and challenges brought about by globalization and digitalization. The essays in this collection pick up particular aspects of these challenges and invite the reader to problematize local cinema as a cultural form that is both vulnerable and valuable.

The publication of this volume has been made possible also thanks to funding provided by the following institutions (in alphabetical order): A.F. Lindstedts & Svenska handelsinstitutets fond för handelsutbildning, Fonden för Teknisk Undervisning & Forskning, Svenska Kulturfonden.

More information of MEDA and MEDA-Cinema are available at https://rdi.arcada.fi/meda/en/

Contents

Notes on Contributors

Abdulrahman Alghannam is a PhD candidate at the University of St Andrews, United Kingdom. He completed his Master of Arts in mass communication at the University of Central Missouri, United States with a research on ethical practice in documentary films. His current research focuses on the development of film industries in the Arab Gulf States in the period of 2004–2017. His research interests include political economy of film, film policies, Khaleeji cinema, and film industries.

Ignacio Bergillos is Lecturer in Media Studies at CESAG – Universidad Pontificia Comillas. He holds a PhD in Audiovisual Communication and Advertising from the Autonomous University of Barcelona. He is interested in media technology and innovation, the changing logics of media industries and the relationship between audiences and professionals within the framework of participatory culture. His work has been published in the *Journal of Computer Mediated Communication, Observatorio (OBS)** and *Journalism Practice*.

Natàlia Ferrer-Roca (PhD) is Adjunct Professor at the Department of Organization, Business Management and Communication at the University of Girona (Catalonia). Her research is interdisciplinary, connecting political economy, media policy, cultural industries and destination branding. She is also a freelance researcher and advisor having worked with the European Broadcasting Union (EBU, Geneva) and the Government of Catalonia. Moreover, she is Associate Director (Research) of The Place Brand Observer (http://placebrandobserver.com). Her research has been published in the *Journal of Media Business Studies, Place Branding and Public Diplomacy, Media Industries* and *Studies in Australasian Cinema*.

Terje Gaustad is Associate Professor and Associate Dean for Creative Industries Management at BI Norwegian Business School. He holds a PhD in Strategic Management from the same school. His main research interests are in institutional and organizational economics applied to the entertainment industries. Among his latest publications is a chapter on "How Film Financing Shapes Project Strategy" in P.C. Murschetz and R. Teichmann (Eds.) *Handbook of State Aid for Film: Finance, Industries and Regulation* (Springer); and an article on "How Streaming Services Make Cinema More Important" in *Nordic Journal of Media Studies*.

Anne-Britt Gran is professor at BI Norwegian Business School and director of BI Center for Creative Industries (BI:CCI). Her main research interests are digitization of the culture and media sector, cultural policy, culture consumption, post colonialism, and theatre history and management. Among her latest publications are "A Digital Museum's Contribution to Diversity – A User Study" (in *Museum Management and Curatorship*, 2019), and "Digital Infrastructure for Diversity – On Digital Bookshelf and Google Books" (in *The Journal of Arts Management, Law, and Society*, 2019).

Heidi Grundström is a PhD candidate at Aalto University's School of Arts, Design and Architecture's Department of Film, Television and Scenography in Helsinki, Finland. She is currently working on her doctoral dissertation "New Cinemas and Changing Audiences in Finland. Understanding the Role of New Technology in the Encounters of Audiences and Films". Her research interests are film and television audiences and film industry/production studies. Her research work focuses on the application of social practice theory for conceptualising contemporary film-viewing practices.

Xiaofei Han is a PhD candidate at the School of Journalism and Communication, Carleton University, in Ottawa, Canada. From her previous experience as a marketing communication professional in Beijing, Xiaofei has developed a keen interest in the emergent and evolving commodification models of major Chinese platforms, which connects different modes of production from online to offline locally and globally. Xiaofei holds a MA in Communication from Hong Kong Baptist University and an Honours BA in Communication Studies from Carleton University with a specialization in Media Industry and Institutions.

Benjamin Lesson has a PhD in Information & Communication studies. Lesson is a member of the laboratory PASSAGES XX-XXI, in Lyon. Lesson's researche focuses on film exhibition economy and on contemporary spectator theories & practices. His study of media practices combines aesthetical, ethical and political point of views. He also teaches social sciences at Sciences Po (Institute for Political Studies) Lyon. His main publications are: "Singularité cinéphilique" in *L'économie de la cinéphilie, Cahier des Champs Visuels*, 2017, "L'ex-spectation. L'écriture comme (une) pratique cinéphilique chez Stanley Cavell", *Revue Textimage*, Varia n°4, printemps 2014, «*(Hi)story telling: un* *nouveau partage du sensible...*». "Transmedia Storytelling", *Terminal*, n°112, Paris, L'Harmattan, Hiver 2012-2013.

Daniel Lindblom is a research assistant in the research programme Media and Education in the Digital Age – MEDA, at Arcada University of Applied Sciences. He is also a candidate to the Master program in Journalism at the University of Helsinki, a freelance journalist and a screenwriter.

Argelia Muñoz Larroa is a postdoctoral researcher at the Center for Research on North America at Universidad Nacional Autónoma de México. She has studied the sustainability of cultural industries as an overarching analytical framework to guide policy-making. Within the field of political economy, she is interested in cultural industries' distribution as a key factor to enhance regional economic development and intercultural relations. She has a PhD in Management from Victoria University of Wellington, New Zealand, a MA in International Affairs, and a BA in History from Universidad Nacional Autónoma de México. She has published in the *International Journal of Communication*, *Media Industries Journal*, *Studies in Australasian Cinema*, *Norteamérica*, and *Estudios sobre las Culturas Contemporáneas*.

Anne Lill Rajala is a research assistant in the Media and Education in the Digital Age (MEDA) research programme at Arcada University of Applied Sciences, Finland. She holds a bachelor degree in Culture and Arts (film & television) and is currently completing a master degree in social sciences (University of Helsinki) with communication as main discipline. Her BA thesis dealt with documentary film as a form of truth-telling and she continues exploring the topic further in her master thesis. Rajala has been involved in artistic productions for more than 15 years through, for example, theater, photography and filmmaking. Additionally Rajala has a strong passion for music, and pursues her artistic ambitions in the critically acclaimed theatrical metal band Lost in Grey.

Matteo Stocchetti (PhD) is Docent in Political Communication at Åbo Academy, Docent in Media and Communication at the University of Helsinki and Principal Lecturer in Critical Media Analysis at Arcada University of Applied Sciences. He is the initiator and main coordinator of the program Media and Education in the Digital Age – MEDA. Among his recent publications, (2018), "Invisibility, Inequality and the Dialectics of the Real in the Digital

Age". *INTERAÇÕES: SOCIEDADE E AS NOVAS MODERNIDADES* 34: 23–46; Stocchetti Matteo (2017), "Digital Visuality and Social Representation. Research Notes on the Visual Construction of Meaning". *KOME. An International Journal of Pure Communication Inquiry* 5(2): 38–56; Stocchetti Matteo (2017), "Persona and Parrhesia: Research Notes on the Dialectics of the Real". *Persona Studies* 3(1); Stocchetti Matteo, (2017), "Re-making the Truth in the Digital Age. Parrhesia and Human Interest". *Comunicazioni Sociali. Journal of Media, Performing Arts and Cultural Studies* 3: 405–414.

Øyvind Torp is currently an advisor at the Norwegian Ministry of Culture, but worked as associated researcher at BI:CCI until 2019. At BI:CCI his work centered around the economics and digitization of the creative industries. He contributed to a number of reports, including two for the Norwegian Ministry of Culture released in 2018 and 2019 identifying economic digitization-effects in the value systems of the Norwegian film and music industries.

Matteo Stocchetti

Critical political economy and local cinema: An Introduction

Abstract Cinema is an influential form of storytelling that depends on myths, capital and technology to perform sense-making and reality-building functions. In this chapter, I argue that local cinema is both important and vulnerable. As ideology is an inherent part of cinematic reality, local cinema is an important form of storytelling because it depends on and narratively reproduces myths and ideologies significantly different from and often antagonistic to those of global and national cinema. Compared to these, however, local cinema is a vulnerable form of storytelling because it cannot rely on an established apparatus and its narratives are often disruptive of established myths. While globalization and digitalization foster the commercial competitiveness of global and national cinema and the visibility of their 'realities', local cinema faces 'market censorship' and the risk of a market-driven extinction. A critical political economy of local cinema is an analytical approach that can help analysts, practitioners and educators to appreciate and support local cinema. At the end of this chapter, I present the main features of this approach and the contributions of the essays in this volume.

Keywords: Critical political economy, local cinema, storytelling, global cinema, globalization, digitalization

Introduction

The main point of this collection and the message throughout its chapters can be summarised as follows: *local cinema is important and vulnerable*. In this chapter, I address three preliminary questions concerning the reasons why local cinema is important, the nature of the challenges and perhaps opportunities facing local cinema in the age of globalization and digitalization, and the main features of an approach that can effectively address these challenges and support the social role of local cinema. Each of these questions connects to widespread debates, a wide variety of perspectives, approaches, concerns and ultimately insights that is impossible to summarize here in all their articulations. In this introductory chapter, therefore, I will not report these debates in all their facets. What I will try to do, however, is to offer the reader the main conceptual coordinates and arguments than provide reasonable grounds to address these questions from the standpoint of our normative goals. In other words, I describe these debates to argue the case for the importance of local cinema, for the need to address the challenges it faces and for a critical approach to the political economy of cinema that could help in addressing these challenges.

What is (local) cinema and why it matters? Storytelling, ideology and reality

A look at dictionary definitions gives an idea of the elements of complexity involved in the concept of 'cinema'. With this word, we design a place, a particular kind of text or 'moving images', an industry, a business and, in its broadest meaning, an institution. As an institution, the notion of cinema includes not only movies (fiction, non-fiction, documentary cinema, etc.) but also organizations, formal and informal rules, conventions, interests, expectations and, most importantly, social functions. It is important to look closer at these functions to appreciate the importance of cinema in general, and of what we refer here as local cinema in particular, and to understand why the processes of globalization and digitalization present distinctive challenges that, in our view, cannot be ignored.

For our purposes, *cinema is an immersive, complex and expensive form of storytelling* that:

- absorbs the attention of its audience through the sensorial involvement (or the 'sensorium') of multimodal narratives;
- is dependent on a complex technological infrastructure (or 'apparatus');
- is also uniquely dependent on capital for the material and immaterial resources necessary for the production, distribution and consumption of the texts it produces.

Compared to other forms of storytelling, cinema has at least two common and two specific sets of features. In common with other forms of storytelling, cinema performs fundamental functions of sense-making commonly referred to in terms of the narrative construction of reality (Bruner 1991; Gottschall 2012). Furthermore, and again as other forms of storytelling, cinema is ambivalently participating to arts and industry: a form of artistic expression and a business. As a form of art, cinema engages with meanings and the symbolic construction of reality as, for example, in myths. In this capacity, cinema has the potential of consolidating or undermining the relations of meaning that constitute the social world and the relations of power that are associated with them. As an industry, cinema is bound to the 'laws' of production. In capitalist societies, the most influential of these 'laws' are the 'self-regulating market' and capital accumulation. Specific to cinema, however, is its influence on viewers and its dependence on capital and technology. The influence of cinema rests on its distinctive capacity to connect the viewer to the myths evoked through immersive storytelling. This influence, however, depends on process (e.g. production, distribution, and consumption) and resources (material like money, and immaterial, like the talent of scriptwriters) that ultimately makes cinematic storytelling distinctively dependent on capital and technology.

The 'power' of cinema reflects the importance of its functions. Here in this chapter, I will discuss these functions in terms of sense-making, reality-building and interpretation (or hermeneutics). Before that, however, I would like to point out that because of its 'power', cinema is also a social institution that is worth competing for. In a critical perspective, the 'politics of cinema' is a notion that describe the competition for the control over the influence of cinema. In the same perspective, the political economy of cinema is the competition for the control over the organization of the resources and functions necessary for the production, distribution and consumption of cinematic texts.

One of the main aspects of sense-making consists in connecting and organizing disparate elements of our experience of the world into a system of causes and effects so that, simply put, whatever happens, happens for a reason. In this process, myths (a Greek word that means 'story') play a key role as stories that, from ancient times, influence the way we make sense of the world and have become established as part of culture and cultural identity.

The study of myths has received scholarly attention from a wide range of approaches and disciplinary domains, such as philosophy, linguistics, theology, social sciences, psychoanalysis etc. Even in our digital age, the importance of myths, and the study of myths, is far from obsolete. Vincent Mosco, for example, interpreted the idiosyncrasies and the perils relating to the 'digital sublime' and the 'myths of the cyberspace', relaying on the works of classics, such as Claude Lévi-Strauss, Roland Barthes and Alisdair MacIntyre (Mosco 2004). As Mosco observed, referring especially to Barthes, the interpretative functions of myth are not politically neutral. Quite contrary, for Barthes "myth is a type of speech" (Barthes 2000 (1957), p. 109), which in a bourgeois or capitalist society takes the connotation of "depoliticized speech" that performs fundamental political functions:

> Myth does not deny things, on the contrary, its function is to talk about them; simply, it purifies them, it makes them innocent, it gives them a natural and eternal justification, it gives them a clarity which is not that of an explanation but that of a statement of fact. (Barthes 2000 (1957), p. 143)

In film studies, scholars such as Martin Winkler, Irving Singer and Sylvie Magerstädt have studied the importance of myths and myth-making in contemporary cinema.

For Winkler, "the mythic patterns of classical antiquity have worked themselves into the very marrow of the cinematic skeletons that support plot, action,
and characterization" (Winkler 2001, p. 33). By interpreting these 'mythic
patterns' from different approaches, Wingler argued that the main intellectual
traditions in film studies can provide unique insights into important aspects of
our social world:

> The psychoanalytic approach (Bruno Bettelheim, Sigmund Freud, Philip Slater) stresses
> the parallels between myth and dreams as a radically narrative means of dealing with
> what society defines as unacceptable desires and fears. The structuralist approach
> (Lévi-Strauss) offers both a methodology for grasping the grammar, so to speak, of these
> peculiar narratives and an account of their function, that is, to overcome unresolved
> intellectual contradictions in a spurious repetitive spiral of narrative mediations. Finally,
> the overtly political, historical approach (Malinowski, Karl Marx) stresses the role of
> myth as a self-interested source of validation for actual social and political institutions—
> in short, as ideology. (Winkler 2001, p. 300)

For Irving Singer, "myths are work of art that convey a significant level of insight
about the world and our concrete involvement in it" (Singer 2010, p. 2). Singer
argued that myth participates in cinema

> …as components in the meaningfulness conveyed through cinematic techniques and
> therefore pertinent to the philosophical importance that films of merit may achieve.
> (Singer 2010, p. 4)

Pointing to the interpretative saliency of cinema, Magerstädt contented that film
is "part of a system of ideas that enables human beings to understand their world,
be in mythological, religious, philosophical or cinematic terms" and "cinema
itself … a way of continuing the ancient human endeavour of creating universal
myths and idea – positive illusions." (Magerstädt 2015, p. xii). This function is
particularly important in time of crisis and, relying on a conceptual framework
which combines Friedrich Nietzsche, Siegfried Krakauer and Gilles Deleuze,
Magerstädt analysis of cinema sought to "examine how postmodern feeling of
insecurity and uprooting (…) relate to our age of globalization and electronic
networks" (Magerstädt 2015, p. xiii).

   In these and other contributions, the role of myths and myth-making in
cinema is a topic that promises rich analytical opportunities as it construes the
role of cinema as an interpretative bridge between the practices of imagination
and reality-building. Through its myth-making function, in other words, cinema
is the tool that contributes to the social construction of reality.

   In this perspective, cinema is at the centre of an interpretative relationship
quite similar to Anthony Giddens' "double hermeneutics" (Giddens 1984).

In this relationship, the cinematic text is both a tool to interpret reality and is itself the object of interpretative processes – a text to interpret. Inherent in cinema, in other words, is the possibility of offering narrative interpretations of salient aspects of the human world and, in addition to that, the possibility of a systematic reflection on the nature of knowledge associated with these same interpretations (Casetti 1999).

In film theory, the possibility of a reality ontologically autonomous or existing independently from its representations, is discussed in relation to the 'myth of total cinema'. For André Bazin, the invention of cinema itself was the result of a myth inherent to the culture of the nineteenth century:

> The guiding myth, then, inspiring the invention of cinema, is the accomplishment of that which dominated in a more or less vague fashion all the techniques of the mechanical reproduction of reality in the nineteenth century, from photography to the phonograph namely an integral realism, a recreation of the world in its own image, an image unburdened by the freedom of interpretation of the artist or the irreversibility of time. (Bazin 1967, p. 21)

In the twentieth century, this myth was undermined by the idea that reality cannot be given for granted. Not a solid and immutable 'bedrock' against which one can assess the value of different representations but an elusive and evolving process whose nature and features are influenced by our representations of it. The elusive nature of reality, and the implications of this elusiveness for the relationship between the individual and society inspired, and was aptly captured by, the frame theory of Erving Goffman. Following William James, Goffman argued that the important question to ask is not "what reality is" but rather "under what circumstances do we think things are real?"

For Goffman:

> The important thing about reality (…) is our sense of its realness in contrast to our feeling that some such things lack this quality. One can then ask under what conditions such a feeling is generated, and this question speaks to a small, manageable problem having to do with the camera and not what it is the camera takes pictures of. (Goffman 1974, p. 2)

The metaphoric reference to the camera and its picture is interesting because it points to the ambivalent role of image making. It suggests that the nature of reality depends on the tools rather than on the artefact, in other words, on cinema more than on what cinema is supposed to represent.

From the perspective of communication studies, James W. Carey argued that reality is a 'scarce resource' fundamentally imbricated with power.

Like any scarce resource it is there to be struggled over, allocated to various purposes and projects, endowed with given meanings and potential, spent and conserved, rationalized and distributed. The fundamental form of power is the power to define, allocate, and display this resource. Once the blank canvas of the world is portrayed and featured, it is also pre-empted and restricted. Therefore, the site where artist paint, writers write, speakers speak, filmmakers film, broadcasters broadcast is simultaneously the site of social conflict over the real. (Carey 1988, p. 87)

The relationship between cinema and reality can thus be interpreted in terms of representation on condition that one keeps in mind that, as Anne Norton argued, "a representation preserve things in their absence ... it is once itself and another, a sign of presence and a sign of absence" (Norton 1988, p. 97). Thus, the paradox here is that cinema contributes to the social construction of reality not despite, but by virtue of its distinctive relationship with the imaginary. In addition, this relationship acquires an important political connotation if one looks at the role of ideology. In film studies, this role is core in the tradition of 'contemporary film theory' that draws from the works of Karl Marx, Louis Althusser, Jacques Lacan and others to study the ideological functions of cinema. Although some fundamental tenets of this tradition has been criticised (Allen 1995), the reason I want to mention it here is that it helps to understand an important dimension of the 'power' of cinema and why local cinema is a valuable form of storytelling. If we consider that cinematic storytelling consists of immersive representations of relationship between individuals and their conditions, then the close relationship between cinema and ideology is effectively summarised by Louis Althusser when he offered his famous definition of 'ideology': "ideology is a 'representation' of the imaginary relationship of individuals to their real conditions of existence" (Althusser 2008 (1971), p. 36).

For our purposes, this definition is useful because it is a simple formulation of a complex problem. The key part of this definition is "the imaginary representation of real conditions". This suggests that ideology performs social and political functions by offering the imaginary as a standpoint to engage and, for all practical purposes, to make sense of reality. In this perspective, cinema is an important institution that participates to the Ideological State Apparatus on its communicative and cultural dimensions (Althusser 2008 (1971), p. 17). Its 'power' reproduces or subverts reality, depending on its relationship with ideology or "the imaginary representation of real conditions".

Cinema is thus an influential institution through which ideology (in the meaning of Althusser), and the imaginary become part of reality. Through cinema and its representations, the imaginary participates to the efforts of making sense of the world and ideology, as a particular form of representation, participates to the social construction of reality.

The social relevance or the 'power' of cinema, in this perspective, is rooted in the representational claim of a reality that, in Goffman sense, does not exists independently from the possibilities of its representation and, following Carey, is the fundamental stake of the competition for power.

Starting from Deleuze idea that "cinema produces reality" (Deleuze 1995, p. 58) and Žižek claim that "ideological fantasies constitutes our reality" (Rushton 2010, pp. 155 156), Richard Rushton argued most explicitly that cinema's reality-building functions are inherently associated with ideological functions:

> Against the idea that films are abstracted from reality and can thus only offer a deficient mode of reality, I instead try to see films as part of the reality we typically inhabit, as part of the world we live in, as parts of our lives. I argue that films help us to shape what we call 'reality'. It is this attempt to acknowledge the reality of film that I call filmic reality. (Rushton 2010, p. 2)

Rushton use of Žižek is particularly useful for our purposes as he argues that "from Žižek's perspective, reality is inherently ideological; it is only by way of ideological fantasy that reality is structured, defined and experienced. (…) As such, all reality is ideological". (Rushton 2010, p. 149). The role of ideology is crucial because "filmic reality is always already ideological" and "there is no way of identifying a reality of film that might reside beyond ideology". Reality, however, is not the Real, and

> filmic reality is itself separated from the Real. This means that if there is a Real of film, then this is not something that can be specified, identified or spoken about. Rather, a Real of film is something that can only be alluded to by way of filmic reality. (Rushton 2010, p. 150)

The sense-making, myth-making, reality-building functions of cinema are interdependent with its technological and industrial dimensions. In a critical perspective, this interdependence needs to be looked at and assessed in relation to the ideological dimension of cinema that, as I have argued, is constitutive of the way in which cinema 'produces reality'. Once reality ceases to be the unchanging and objective bedrock of cinematic representation to become a result of ideological interpretation and sense-making, the 'power' of cinema appears in all its ambivalence as a form of storytelling that can enforce or subvert the credibility and thus the authority of alternative realities.

For our purposes, this double dependency is relevant because the forces that control technological development and capital can in practice, if not in principle, control the 'power' of cinema: the way in which 'cinema produces reality' through sense-making, myth-making, reality-building and ideological interpellation.

The politics of cinema and the challenges of globalization and digitalization

To understand the importance of local cinema one must understand the 'power' of cinema and to reflect on the idea that the control of this 'power' is an important stake in a competition for the control over the social construction of reality. This is, in essence, an ideological competition: a competition between alternative imaginaries and the possible realities relating to them.

In this line of reasoning, and simplifying a bit, even assuming that most of early cinema was pretty much 'national cinema' in the sense that the 'power' of cinema depended mostly on resources (notably myths, capital and technology) associated with the nation-state and its ideology, in the age of globalization and digitalization, however, the situation is far more fluid. The 'power' of cinema is sought from at least three very different ideological standpoints and the notions of global, national and local cinema are perhaps useful simplifications to discuss the main features and ideological connotations of these standpoints. Global cinema is the cinema of globalization or, more precisely the form of storytelling expressing the myths associated with the neoliberal imaginary of a world unified and ruled through and by the self-regulating market. National cinema is the cinema that depends on and seeks to revitalize national myths, imaginaries and ultimately the reality of the nation-state from the risks of erosion associated with globalization and in response to the discontent with the effects of globalization itself. The notion of local cinema is a generic label to describe a radical alternative to global and national cinema: to the totalizing aspects of global and national ideologies and the socio-political imaginaries associated with them.

As I will argue in a moment, the driving force of globalization and digitalization is the ideology of the neoliberal project. While the effects of globalization and digitalization on cinema and elsewhere are complex and in many respects contradictory, consisting of challenges but also opportunities for local cinema, one should not overlook the common ideological connotation of these processes. In this perspective, globalization is yes a multidimensional process, as many have argued (Hjort 2005, p. 25), but one in which the influence of neoliberalism and the 'self-regulating market' utopia is at the core of it and hegemonic throughout its dimensions.

By 'global cinema', thus, I do not mean the cinema of "all moviemaking nation" (Seibel and Shary 2007, p. 5) nor "a competition between different national cinemas" or "a struggle of small independents to survive in a field dominated by a relatively small number of major firms" (Barthel-Bouchier 2018, p. 315). If the notion of 'global cinema' is used to indicate a competition instead as one of the party in this competition, we miss the ideological aspects of globalization and the ideological aspects of cinema reality-building functions.

With this notion of global cinema, I intend to describe a distinctive outcome of globalization and *the cinematic form of storytelling that reproduces globalization, its ideology, its myths and its hegemonic relations.* If globalization is in essence one expression of the neoliberal imaginary – and I argue it is – global cinema is the cinema that make sense of reality and constructs the world in accordance to it.

In the last two decades or so, scholars in film studies have introduced new concepts of cinema (e.g., global cinema, transnational cinema, small nation cinema, small cinema, peripheral cinema, etc.) to address the challenges associated to globalization and digitalization. Danish scholar Mette Hjort, for example, argued that

> The New Danish Cinema is in many ways a small nation's response to globalization, an instance of globalization, and a dense and complicated site for the emergence of alternatives to neoliberal conceptions of globalization or cinematic globalization on a Hollywood model. (Hjort 2005, pp. 8–9)

For Hjort the concept of small nation in film studies is useful to look at "the ways in which subnational, national, international, transnational, regional and global forces dovetail and compete in the sphere of the cinema". (Hjort / Petrie, Introduction 2007, p. 2)

Hjort seeks in the cinema of small nation, in national imaginaries and institutional resources the grounds to conceive of a globalization resistant to a neoliberal imaginary:

> Small nations have a lot at stake in ensuring that alternative imaginings take hold, and it is not surprising, then, that globalizations resistant to a neoliberal imaginary should be emerging in such contexts. The challenge is to pinpoint the ways in which the neoliberal conception—one favorable to global capital, to corporations governed by narrow strategic rationalities, and to the priorities and putative entitlements of the United States— itself can become the engine for alternative conceptions while agents in specific contexts mobilize the institutional resources of a local situation and effectively yoke them to some of the salient features of a globalized world. (Hjort 2005, pp. 26–27)

After more than a decade since this formulation, the idea of seeking the grounds of resistance to the challenge of neoliberal globalization in national cinema seems both appealing and dangerous. Appealing because, as the rise of nationalist and populist movements in Denmark, Europe and elsewhere has proved, there is a growing discontent with the socio-economic and cultural aspects of globalization. Dangerous because the response of national cinema to the insecurities and the selective effacement of difference of globalization relies on myths and ideologies that are historically related to ethnic discrimination and violent exclusions. In a broader perspective, to suggest that global cinema revives national cinema reminds Karl Polanyi's "double movement" and the idea that this revival is as good a response to the disruptions of globalization as fascism and socialism were as "measures which society adopted in order not to be, in its turn, annihilated by the action of the self-regulating market" (Polanyi 2001 (1944), p. 257).

Another tradition that seeks to problematize the cultural and economic effects of globalization but from conceptual grounds alternative to those of national cinema is that of 'transnational cinema'.

For Elizabeth Ezra and Terry Rowden,

> The transnational comprises both globalization – in cinematic terms, Hollywood's domination of world film markets – and the counterhegemonic responses of filmmakers from former colonial and Third World countries. The concept of transnationalism enable us to better understand the changing ways in which the contemporary world is being imagined by an increasing number of filmmakers across genres as a global system rather than as a collection of more or less autonomous nations. (Ezra / Rowden 2006, p. 1)

For Milja Radović transnational cinema is a notion that helps in exposing the ideological and cultural limitations of national cinema by pointing out

> three aspects… that frequently overlap and are often interdependent: transnationalism as a theme, … transnationalism as a transformation of identity and locality, and transnationalism as a cross-cultural exchange. (Radović 2014, p. 136)

In some instances, transnational cinema is a notion used to describe a mutation in small nations' cinema, like for example, Finland, resulting from the efforts "to find a balance between maintaining national identity and economic viability, through creating a variety of transnational networks at all levels of its activities" (Bacon 2016, p. 12). More broadly, however, for Steven Rawle, "the study of transnational cinema grapples with a range of both hegemonic, culturally dominant forms and counter-hegemonic, marginal ones." (Rawle 2018, p. 3). Some of these issues are addressed by the chapters of Alghannam and Han in this volume.

While the transnational approach seeks to transcend national cinema but also to include both global and national cinema, in the tradition associated with the notions of 'peripheral' and 'small' cinema the focus is more explicitly on the "… multifarious debates by foregrounding a body of cinematic practices, traditions, and texts often overlooked in dominant histories" (Iordanova 2010, p. 5).

Discussing the notion of 'cinema at the periphery', for example, Dina Iordanova argued that

> The driving concept is the exploration and theorization of cinemas and practices located in positions marginal to the economic, institutional, and ideological centers of image making. Our emphasis is on the vibrant periphery as it manifests itself in a variety of contexts worldwide, be it within a national, regional, or global framework, and our focus on contemporary filmmaking. (Iordanova, Introduction 2010, p. 5)

Janina Falkowska and Lenuta Giukin proposed the notion of "small cinema...as one which is new, appears for the first time on the world stage, and is an emerging star. It offers a new look into the affairs of the country it comes from, is innovative, and uncompromising" (Falkowska and Giukin 2015, p. vii). Tracing the history of his notion from the 1960s to 2000s, they observed that:

> ...the concept of small cinema is used in a wide variety of situations, from avant-garde, experimental, and independent cinemas, to any small-scale productions, small audiences, small-budget films (all genres), small distribution, or small national cinemas. Through extension, it became an oppositional term to Hollywood, as well as large or nationally funded productions. (Falkowska / Giukin 2015, p. xiii)

Finally, an older notion that in the debates of the last two decades has been neglected but that is useful to address the challenges of globalization and digitalization to local cinema is that of Third Cinema. Coined by Argentinian filmmakers Octavio Getino and Fernando Solana (Getino and Solanas 1969), the concept of Third Cinema describes a form of cinema alternative to the hegemonic forms represented by Hollywood, or the First Cinema, and by European cinema or Second Cinema. However, as Mike Wayne pointed out, "First, Second and Third Cinemas do not designate geographical areas, but institutional structures/ working practices, associated aesthetic strategies and their attendant cultural politics" (Wayne 2001, p. 13).

According to Anthony Guneratne,

> Third Cinema theory is the only major branch of film theory that did not originate within a specifically Euro-American context. No other theory of cinema is so imbued with historical specificities, none so specific in its ideological orientation, and yet none so universal in its claims to represent the highest aspirations of a post-colonial world in the throes of resisting Neocolonialism. (Guneratne 2003, p. 7)

In the years of the Cold War, this notion was often used to designate Third World cinema. In the post-cold war era Third Cinema "designates a body of theory and filmmaking practice committed to social and cultural emancipation" (Wayne 2001, p. 12) that seeks to resist the global influence of Neoliberalism as this infiltrates national cinemas in Europe and elsewhere. On theoretical grounds, Third Cinema is based on the work of Karl Marx, the analyses of the relationship between cinema and ideology by Walter Benjamin, Georg Lukàcs, Louis Althusser, Jacques Lacan, and the experiences of Sergei Eisenstein, Dziga Vertov and Berthold Brecht (Wayne 2001, p. 25). Despite its strong historical and intellectual roots (Stam 2000; Pines and Willemen 1991; Marzano 2009), Third Cinema theory is nowadays a neglected tradition: one that, as Guneratne lamented, "does not appear to merit even a dishonorable mention" (Guneratne 2003, p. 4). Discussing the grounds for this state of affairs, Guneratne argued that

> ...the fundamental causes of neglect have more to do with Eurocentric critical perspectives and philosophical impositions than with the internal disputes within Third Cinema theory. Perhaps the most salient of these factors is that film theory as a whole is not merely Eurocentric but almost exclusively Anglo-Francophone in outlook and in orientation. (Guneratne 2003, pp. 9–10).

In addition to suffer from the effects of the "exclusionary practices of First World Cinema" and "its own critique of and challenge to Eurocentrism" Third Cinema theory "is further disadvantaged linguistically and ideologically in that its initial exposition took place far away from the metropolises of theoretical discourse" (Guneratne 2003, p. 10).

For our purposes, however, and despite this ostracism, the tradition of Third Cinema is relevant for at least four reasons. First, because it is one that most systematically addresses the discontent with hegemonic forms of cinema (the 'system') at both global and national level (Hollywood and European national cinema). Second, because it helps unravelling the ideological dimension of the challenges to local cinema. Thirdly, because through the example of films in its tradition, it suggests alternative theoretical grounds and cinematic practices to engage with hegemonic challenges from the distinctive standpoint of 'local' cinema. Finally, because it offers conceptual grounds to construe globalization as neo-colonialism and digitalization as a form of technological development mostly supportive of the influence of global cinema.

In the debates about the impact of digitalization, this role is sometimes seen as supportive of non-hegemonic cinema. For Ezra and Rowden, for example, "Digital technology in all its aspects has enabled a growing disregard for national boundaries as ideological and aesthetic checkpoints by a range of legal and extra-legal players". Digitalization "has functioned to disrupt and decentralize the forces that have heretofore, maintained strict control over the representational politics of cinematic public sphere" and supports transnational cinema to the extent it "fundamentally compromise the effectiveness of all types of state or official censorship" (Ezra / Rowden 2006, p. 6).

For Iordanova digitalization increases the visibility, and therefore the cultural influence of small cinema by connecting the cinematic text with its audiences. To the extent that new technologies offer the opportunity for a more personal and direct connection, Iordanova saw digitalization as having positive effects on 'small cinema':

> Today, the bulk of cinematic outputs of small national traditions are increasingly becoming available online (…) Entire national cinemas are on the Internet, especially those of small nations. Copyright holders, on the one hand, may not be happy with a situation that they cannot control, but on the other must recognise that films now gain a wider exposure than ever, especially beyond the borders of their respective countries. (Iordanova 2015, p. 266)

The idea that the affordances of digitalization are supportive of small or peripheral cinema is problematic as it neglects the broader role of these affordances and the social change associated to them (e.g., the commodification of culture). More theoretically, this perspective seems to neglect the influence of corporate capital and ideology in the selective actualization of the affordances of these technologies. Ezra and Rowden, for example, argued that:

> The global circulation of money, commodities, information, and human beings is giving rise to films whose aesthetic and narrative dynamics, and even the modes of emotional identification they elicit, reflect the impact of advanced capitalism and new media technologies as components of an increasingly interconnected world-system. (Ezra / Rowden 2006, p. 1)

Globalization and digitalization are not separate processes but are intertwined and sustained by the logic and interests of corporate capitalism, as technological development since the 'information revolution' has been far from revolutionary but has rather contributed to strengthen the power of corporate capitalism (H. I. Schiller 1980; Beniger 1986; D. Schiller 1999; Curran, Fenton, and Freedman 2012; McChesney 2013). As Pierre Bourdieu (1998) argued, "the globalization of financial markets, when joined with the progress of information technology, ensures an unprecedented mobility of capital". The capitalist appropriation of the affordances associated to the 'information revolution' made possible the integration of corporate capitalism in a global network that gave a material dimension to the idea of a 'global market'.

This interpretation is compatible with the interpretations based on the same theoretical grounds of Third Cinema theory. Jonathan Beller, for example, coined the notion of "cinematic mode of production" to describe how the internet participate to the logic of corporate capitalism and the importance of cinema for twenty-first century capitalism. In this notion,

Cinema and its succeeding (if still simultaneous), formations particularly television, video, computers, and the internet, are deterritorialized factories in which spectators work, that is, in which we perform value-productive labor. With the rise of the internet grows the recognition of the value-productive dimension of sensual labor in the visual register. Perception is increasingly bound to production. (Beller 2006, pp. 1–3)

As other social processes, however, also technological development contains elements of ambivalence reflecting dialectical relationships, for example, between technology and its usage. As I will argue in a moment, the critical theory of technology offers useful conceptual tools to capture this ambivalence and ultimately to foster a re-appropriation of new technologies more in line with the subversive ambitions of local cinema.

Before that, however, I would like here to stress the idea that Neoliberalism is the ideological matrix that feeds the processes of globalization and digitalization. In relation to cinema, Neoliberalism is what Pierre Bourdieu described as a "programme for the methodical destruction of collectives" (Bourdieu 1998). The revival of national cinema can be interpreted as a response of national 'collectives': the 'imagined communities' famously described by Benedict Anderson (Anderson 1991 (1983)) that, for cinematic purposes, can rely on the appeal and intelligibility of established symbols, myths and ideologies.

In this perspective, local cinema is important because, on ideological grounds, it is the only, although eclectic and diverse alternative to the ideologies, realities and projects of global and national cinema. By claiming that the effects of globalization and digitalization are facing local cinema with formidable challenges I mean that *these processes establish objective constraints to the influence of ideological coordinates of the realities 'produced' by cinematic storytelling.* The nature of these constraints is relevant because it affects the competition for the control of the power of cinematic storytelling. In this competition, global and national cinema have distinctive advantages which is important to appreciate in order to better understand the grounds on which local cinema can become a more competitive alternative.

The cinema of globalization or 'global cinema' is influential because the digitalization of cultural and financial markets have on the one hand increased the amount of technology and capital available to global cinema and, on the other hand, increased the ubiquity or the marketability of the cinematic text produced within the apparatus of global cinema. In these conditions, global cinema/storytelling is successful and ideologically influential not primarily because its myths and realities are particularly appealing or convincing but because its texts are ubiquitous and profitable.

The influence of national cinema relies on the availability of national cinema apparatus, on the narrative appeal and intelligibility of symbols and myths with deep roots in institutional representations of national history and imaginary, on the relative proximity and easiness of access to transnational, regional or even 'global' cinematic infrastructure.

Compared to global and national cinema, the weaknesses of local cinema are perhaps more visible than its strengths. This form of cinematic storytelling cannot rely on an established apparatus; its narrative are often disruptive of established myths; it survives in relative isolation from large cinematic infrastructure; it is most vulnerable to the effects of 'market censorship' (see Rajala in this volume). In addition to these inherent weaknesses, local cinema suffer from the effects of global cinema on the visibility of local cinema among local audiences (see Lindblom in this volume). Iordanova aptly described these effects when she discussed "the awkward relationship with audiences – one that is marked by shortage of acceptance and appreciation" and "the low self-esteem and insecurities displayed by many small cinemas". She observed:

> We often see situations where wonderful films are made and released and yet not 'seen,' that do not manage to delight or leave a mark in the nation's discourse. Such situations are often blamed on the films themselves and filmmakers are often 'shamed' for failing to connect—whereas, strangely enough, no possible deficiencies of the country's public culture seem to be accepted. Thus, the position of the cinema in the public sphere of such countries is often one of a shy child who is trying to reach out to an emotionally unavailable parent. (Iordanova 2015, p. 261)

Albeit less visible than its weakness, the strengths of local cinema are nevertheless real and first among these is its resilience that Iordanova effectively pointed out:

> On the other hand, there are some national cinemas that swallow the bitter pill of insignificance. There are filmmakers who, courageously, reject the shame and opt to drop the uncomfortable silence and talk sincerely about difficult subject matters. (…) Not trying to please, it is a self-assured cinema that has managed to look a number of uncomfortable subject matters straight in the eye, and explore the abuse of the vulnerable, the calculated humanism, and the insatiable emotional void created by hurtful indifference. No need of big budgets or entertainment value here; it is a cinema that has taken a deep breath and has learned to speak in an even voice. (Iordanova 2015, pp. 262–263)

Thus, the fundamental strength of local cinema, one that may compensate for its vulnerability when it comes to technology and capital, consists in being the form of storytelling of choice for the expressions of discontent about the myths, the ideologies and ultimately the realities that find expressions in global and national cinema. What keeps local cinema alive, in other words, is not the market or the appeal of any particular myth but the discontent and the desire to voice opposition to the realities associated with the self-regulating market, nation-alism and globalization. Its resiliency, as Iordanova and others have pointed out, does not depends on branding, merchandise or national identity but on the sub-versive affordances associated with its narratives, the digitalization of cinematic apparatus and, perhaps most important of all, the interpellation of its public as participants rather than consumers.

Thus, the processes of globalization and digitalization challenge local cinema on ideological, cultural and economic grounds. On economic grounds, local cinema is an industry that cannot compete with global cinema. Globalization and digitalization are processes closely associated with the evolution of cor-porate capitalism in the last half a century and the possibilities to exploit their affordances are greater for national cinema than for local cinema. As national cinema relies on public funding, the challenge here is to find a funding model between the extremes of the 'self-regulating market' and state-controlled sub-sidy. In this challenge, however, local cinema has the relative advantage of being a form of storytelling that is the least dependent on capital and technology. On cultural grounds, the main challenge for local cinema is to resist the cultural vio-lence of the selective effacement of difference associated with both the neoliberal and nationalist programmes, to preserve alternative forms of imaginaries and ultimately to defend the autonomy of art from the logic of commercial profit-ability but also from the mortal embrace of nationalism. The survival of local cinema is important to avoid the market-driven extinction of alternatives to the cultural logic of late capitalism and of its populist reaction.

On ideological grounds, the myths of globalization and digitalization combine in support of an ideology with imperial ambitions, undermining the credibility and visibility of culture-specific myths and the cultures associated to them. The fundamental challenge for local cinema is to counter the influence of the neo-liberal programme, its globalist ambitions and ultimately the credibility of the self-regulating market utopia but also the credibility and socio-political influ-ence of the myths of the nation revitalized by the effort to resist the enforcement of this utopia.

Towards a critical political economy of local cinema

If cinema is a form of immersive storytelling depending on capital and tech-nology to perform fundamental functions of sense-making and reality-building, a critical approach that could support the functions of local cinema needs to be conceptually equipped to address issues associated with capital, technology and meaning, as these combine in the cinematic construction of reality. Within the critical tradition, there are at least three conceptual 'toolboxes' that can serve this purpose: the critical political economy of media and communication, the critical theory of technology and the critical theory of cinema.

For Janet Wasko, Graham Murdock, and Helena Sousa the critical political economy of media and communication is an approach that has at least four fundamental features:

> Firstly, it is holistic. Rather than treating "the economy" as a specialist and bounded domain, it focuses on the relations between economic practices and social and political organization. Secondly, it is historical. Rather than concentrating solely or primarily on immediate events, it insists that a full understanding of contemporary shifts must be grounded in an analysis of transformations, shifts, and contradictions that unfold over long loops of time. Thirdly, in contrast to economics that severed its historic links with moral philosophy in an effort to present itself as an objective science, critical political economy continues to be centrally concerned with the relations between the organization of culture and communications and the constitution of the good society grounded in social justice and democratic practice. Fourthly, critical analysis places its practitioners under an obligation to follow the logic of their analysis through into practical action for change. (Wasko / Murdock / Sousa 2011, p. 2)

For Jonathan Hardy, the critical political economy of media and communication is "a tradition that is concerned with how communication arrangements relates to goals of social justice and emancipation" (Hardy 2014, p. 3). Since "the goods produced by the media industries are at once economic and cultural", this tradition looks at "the interplay between the symbolic and economic dimensions of the production of meaning". Based on the idea that "different ways of organising and financing communications have implications for the range and nature of media content, and the ways in which this is consumed and used", the analyses in this tradition focus "on the unequal distribution of power and are critical of arrangements whereby such inequalities are sustained and reproduced" (Hardy 2014, pp. 6–7). The critical political economy of media and communication is relevant for cinema since, like cinema, also the media industry "affects the production and circulation of meaning, and connects to the distribution of symbolic and material resources that enable people to understand, communicate and act in the world" (Hardy 2014, p. 9)

The second useful 'toolbox' is the critical theory of technology. Originally formulated by North American philosopher Andrew Feenberg, this theory establishes a conceptual standpoint to emancipate technological development from the effects of capitalist ideology. In this tradition, the social role of technology is neither neutral (like in the theories of technological determinism and instrumentalism) nor reflecting some intrinsic values or biases that inevitably

supports certain end-means systems or ideological representations of the social
order (like in technological substantivism). Rather, the social role of technology
is mediated by social structures. In practice, this means that the same technology
can be used to serve different social purposes and participate to different 'means-
ends systems' (Feenberg 1991, 2002, 2009), thus opening up possibilities of resistance. This approach is useful for interpretative and normative purposes: to
interpret the ambivalent role of digitalization in support of local cinema and to
suggest forms of technological 'democratization' and re-appropriation serving
the ambitions of those seeking to support local cinema through alternative uses
of digital technologies (as e.g., Bergillos, Lesson, Grundström, Gaustad, Gran
and Torp in this volume).

Finally, the critical theory of cinema is a label describing the contributions
that seek to pick up and re-actualize the intellectual and cultural mission of
Third Cinema by re-deploying the normative concerns and the dialectic method
of Critical Theory to the social functions of contemporary cinema. Inspiring
these efforts is the acknowledgment that cinema performs fundamental ideological functions, coupled with the awareness that Marxism and Critical Theory
have important limits that undermine their normative ambitions.

If as, Beller argued, "...cinema is, in the twentieth century, the emerging paradigm for the total reorganization of society and (therefore) of the subject" (Beller
2006, p. 13), the narrow focus on economics that, according to Anna Coopers
characterises Marxists approaches in film studies, is utterly insufficient. As she
argued, "the discipline of film studies needs to significantly expand its understanding of neoliberalism as well as methodological approaches to its study in
relation to cinema" (Cooper 2019, p. 266).

For Fabio Vighi the limits of critical approaches to cinema are due to the
fact that the founding fathers of Critical Theory (namely Max Horkheimer and
Theodore Adorno) did not formulated a theory of cinema of adequate complexity to the challenge. For Vighi,

> Adorno's assertion of an unbridgeable divide between critically effective art (essen-
> tially, modernist art) and industrially produced, debilitating entertainment does not
> capture in its entirety the complex, ambiguous and fundamentally contradictory nature
> of cultural production under capitalism (…). While dissecting the cultural logic of
> capitalism, Adorno and Horkheimer omitted to articulate a rigorous analysis of those
> cultural products, such as Hollywood films, that they regularly dismissed ad 'infantile
> […] regression manufactured on an industrial scale' (Adorno 2001, p. 178). (Vighi 2012,
> pp. 3–4)

Intuitively enough, these intellectual limits may reflect the fact that, when
Horkheimer and Adorno published the first edition of The Dialectics of the

Enlightenment, in 1944, cinema was a rather different institution. On the other hand, the efforts to reformulate a more 'productive' critical theory of cinema starting from a critique of Adorno's attitude towards film, may neglect the fact that "In the sixties, Adorno's observations on cinema undergo a sea change as a consequence of his discovery of the work of Godard and the New German Cinema" (Brenez 2007, p. 76). These considerations aside, there should be little doubts about the convenience of a critical theory of cinema more capable of engaging the complexities associated with the influence of Neoliberalism. The efforts in this direction focus on at least two issues: a problematization of the relationship between cinema and ideology, and the (re)deployment of the dialectical method.

Earlier on, I have mentioned the important contribution of Žižek to the role of ideology in the social construction of reality, and its application to cinema studies in Rushton and other authors that have studied the social functions of cinema in the tradition of contemporary film theory. Brice Nixon argued for the relevance of the dialectic method as a distinctive feature of the critical tradition that can be usefully (re)applied to the political economy of culture (Nixon 2012) and to the political economy of communication (Nixon 2016). In relation to cinema, Wayne argued that this method is key to reach a deeper understanding of the relation between First, Second and Third cinema. In fact, he argued, "each cinema also has relations of dialogue, interchange and transformation between them as each works over and on the same cultural/political material (e.g., anti-colonial struggle), but pulls and shapes the material into different, often radically different, meanings and possibilities". (Wayne 2001, p. 13). In relation to the analysis of film, Vighi advocated

> Making use of Critical Theory's key methodological tool, namely dialectics… to show how capital's drive to churn out cultural commodities can be fruitfully hijacked by theory and made to reveal the profoundly contradictory and potentially liberating tendencies nestled at the core of the cultural commodity itself. (Vighi 2012, p. 4)

What Vighi and other seem to suggest, in other words, is that 'theory' (or presumably a critical theory of cinema) can subvert the relationship between the cinematic text and its audience because this relationship is dialectical and, roughly put, people can resist its oppressive effects by theoretically informed (mis)interpretations of these texts.

The problematization of cinematic reality in relation to its ideological dimension and the (re)deployment of dialectical method to the relationships between the cinematic texts and their interpretation, point to hermeneutics (and especially critical hermeneutics) as the key practice to understand and support the role of local cinema. In practical terms, this means that, among other storytelling functions, local cinema may indeed represent the alternative point of view for the critical interpretation of global and national cinema: the influence of their texts, their ideologies and myths, and the implications associated to their imaginaries, etc. Performing this (critical) hermeneutic function, local cinema thus become a form of immersive meta-storytelling, revealing what remains implicit in the forms of storytelling more dependent on capital and technology, on the myths relating to globalization and digitalization, and on to the ideologies supporting the neoliberal programme and the populistic response to it.

The contributions in this volume

The chapters in this collection are divided in two parts. The chapters in the first part, *Local Cinema and Digitization: Distribution and Exhibition*, suggests that new technologies can be used in support of the communitarian functions of local cinema: in construing the users of cinematic texts as participating subjects in the social construction of reality, rather than mere consumers or targets of ideological interpellation.

The chapters by **Ignacio Bergillos** and **Benjamin Lesson** describe experiences of adaptive responses to the challenges of digitalization that are compatible with the dialectic approach to the relation between global and local cinema within the new logics of cultural consumption generated by digital devices. In *The political economy of participatory community cinemas: CineCiutat as a standpoint of resistance*, **Bergillos** describes 'CineCiutat' as an experience of resistance against the influence and policies of mainstream film industry, based on citizens involvement and participation. In *Elements of a critical political economy of local cinema in Digital Era: Lo-bal process and double aesthetic of cinema in French film exhibitors*, **Lesson** discusses the response of French exhibitors to the challenges of global cinema in relations to measures that redefine the aesthetics of cinema. In the chapter, *Film distribution in Finland: Gatekeepers of local cinema*, **Heidi Grundström** applies the approach of critical political economy of the media to assess the impact of digitalization on a small market with few dominant distributors. Her analysis provides empirical grounds to the argument that digitalization does not 'revolutionise' distribution. Rather, the effects associated with the distribution of Hollywood films produce objective constraints to the commercial viability and ultimately sustainability of Finnish cinema. In *Digitizing Local Cinema: Lessons on Diversity from Norway*, **Terje Gaustad, Anne-Britt Gran and Øyvind Torp**, argue that the impact of digital technology on cinema is ambivalent and does not automatically supports the visibility of local cinema. Based on empirical data, the authors argue that while film repertoire and consumption in local Norwegian cinemas has turned culturally more diverse, the largest part of local supply and demand is increasingly concentrated around most popular or 'Hollywood' titles. In the chapter *The political economy of the Khaleeji cinema: Historical developments of Arab Gulf film industries*, **Abdulrahman Alghannam** discusses the development of transnational cinema, or 'Khaleeji cinema', in the Gulf region, especially between 2004 and 2017. In this process, economic and financial considerations combined with cultural and political challenges. Inspiring the process, was the desire of resisting the influence of Western culture but also the ambition to establish a cultural identity reflecting the cultural, ethnic, religious and linguistic diversity in the region.

The chapters in the second part of this collection, *Local Cinemas and Globalization: Struggles, Survival, and Sustainability*, problematize the responses to globalization through a reflection on content and the cultural purposes of local cinema.

In *Production of Main Melody Film in Post-Socialist China: A Deconstruction of Wolf Warrior 2*, **Xiaofei Han**, analyses the production of the Chinese blockbuster *Wolf Warrior 2* and applies the approach of 'critical transculturalism' to showcase how Chinese national cinema – in its process of rapid marketization and financialization since 1990s – managed to combine commercialization with ideological significance. In *In the land of Finnish Swedish cinema: A look into the political economy of local cinema in Finland*, **Daniel Lindblom** argues that the hegemony of global cinema present local or minority cinema with the twofold challenge of avoiding 'invisibility', but also avoiding extinction by 'dilution' in the mortal embrace with national cinema. In *ART AGAINST THE ODDS: The Struggles, Survival and Success of New Zealand Local Cinema*, **Natàlia Ferrer-Roca** focuses on the features and implications of the ambivalent position of New Zealand cinema, between the local and the global, the nature of the challenges and the processes that generated successful responses. In *Market Censorship and Finnish Cinema*, **Anne Lill Rajala** analyses the effects of 'market censorship' in Finnish cinema industry and argues this notion is useful to understand how the cultural hegemony of the 'self-regulating market' utopia supports a fundamental source of ideological constraints that limit the freedom of expression and the visibility of local cinema. In the last chapter, *Sustainability as a Framework of Analysis and a Guide for Policy-making: The Film Industry in Wellington, New Zealand*, **Argelia Muñoz Larroa** discusses 'sustainability' as an influential concept in the political economy of culture and a tool for the formulation of local responses to the cultural challenge of globalization. The author reports on the case of Wellington Film District to map five main constraints and suggests solutions to support the sustainability of local cinema.

On a final note, I hope the reflections and information contained in this collection will help the reader to appreciate the importance of local cinema and the challenges of globalization and digitalization. Of course, these challenges are many, quite formidable and stretching well beyond the debate about the future of cinema. Nevertheless, as the formulation of effective responses to these challenges, as well as the mere possibility of imagining the future, depends on storytelling, the case for local cinema is a case for cultural and ideological pluralism. In this spirit, the contributions to the political economy of cinema in this volume participate to an ongoing and much broader struggle to preserve the possibility of pluralism and diversity in the social construction of the future.

References

Allen, Richard. *Projecting Illusion: Film Spectatorship and the Impression of Reality*. Cambridge: Cambridge University Press, 1995.

Althusser, Louis. *On Ideology*. London: Verso, 2008 (1971).

Anderson, Benedict. *Imagined Communities. Reflections on the Origins and Spread of Nationalism*. 2nd ed. London: Verso, 1991 (1983).

Bacon, Henry. "Introduction to the Study of Transnational Small Nation Cinema." In *Finnish Cinema: A Transnational Enterprise*, edited by Henry Bacon, London: Palgrave Macmillan, 2016, pp. 1–19.

Barthel-Bouchier, Diane. "It's a Mad, Mad, Mad, Mad (Men) World": National and Corporate Strategies in the Global Audiovisual Market." In *Art and the Challenge of Markets: Volume 1. National Cultural Politics and the Challenges of Marketization and Globalization*, edited by D. Alexander Victoria, Samuli Hägg, Simo Häyrynen and Erkki Sevänen, 305–24. Cham, Switzerland: Palgrave Macmillan, 2018.

Barthes, Roland. *Mythologies*. Translated by Annette Lavers. London: Vintage, 2000 (1957). Original edition, Paris 1957.

Bazin, Andrè. *What is Cinema*. Essays selected and translated by Hugh Gray. Berkeley: University of California Press, 1967.

Beller, Jonathan. *The Cinematic Mode of Production. Attention Economy and the Society of the Spectacle*. Lebanon, NH: University Press of New England, 2006.

Beniger, James R. *The Control Revolution: Technological and Economic Origins of the Information Society*. Cambridge, MA: Harvard University Press, 1986.

Bourdieu, Pierre. "The Essence of Neoliberalism." *Le Monde diplomatique*, December, 1998.

Brenez, Nicole. "T.W. Adorno. Cinema in Spite of itself – But Cinema All the Same." *Cultural Studies Review* 13, no. 1 (2007): 70–88.

Bruner, A. D. "The Narrative Construction of Reality." *Critical Enquiry* 18, no. 1 (1991): 1–21.

Carey, James W. *Communication as Culture. Essays on Media and Society.* Boston: Unwin Hyman, 1988.

Casetti, Francesco. *Theories of Cinema, 1945–1995. Or title, Teorie del cinema, 1945–1990.* Austin: University of Texas Press, 1999.

Cooper, Anna. "Neoliberal Theory and Film Studies." *New Review of Film and Television Studies* 17, no. 3 (2019): 265–77.

Curran, James, Natalie Fenton, and Des Freedman. *Misunderstanding the Internet.* London/New York: Routledge, 2012.

Deleuze, Gilles. "On The Time-Image." In *Negotiations: 1972–1990*, edited by Gilles. Translated by Martin Joughin Deleuze, 57–61. New York: Columbia University Press, 1995.

Ezra, Elizabeth, and Terry Rowden. "General Introduction: What is Transnational Cinema?" In *Transnational Cinema, The Film Reader*, edited by Elizabeth Ezra and Terry Rowden, 1–12. London/New York: Routledge, 2006.

Falkowska, Janina, and Lenuta Giukin. "Introduction." In *Small Cinema in Global Market: Genres, Identities, Narratives*, edited by Lenuta Giukin, David Desser, and Janina Falkowska, vii–xxiv. Lanham: Lexington Books, 2015.

Feenberg, Andrew. *Critical Theory of Technology.* New York: Oxford University Press, 1991.

Feenberg, Andrew. "Critical Theory of Technology." In *A Companion to the Philosophy of Technology*, edited by J. K. B. Olsen, S. A. Pedersen and V. F. Hendricks, 146–53. London: Blackwell, 2009.

Feenberg, Andrew. *Transforming Technology: A Critical Theory Revisited.* New York: Oxford University Press, 2002.

Getino, Octavio, and Fernando Solanas. "Hacia un Tercer Cine [Toward a Third Cinema]." *Tricontinental* 14 (1969): 107–32.

Giddens, Anthony. *The Constitution of Society.* Cambridge: Polity, 1984.

Goffman, Erving. *Frame Analysis. An Essay on the Organization of Experience.* New York: Harper & Row, 1974.

Gottschall, Jonathan. *The Storytelling Animal: How Stories Make Us Human.* Boston: Houghton Mifflin, 2012.

Guneratne, Anthony R. "Introduction. Rethinking Third Cinema." In
    Rethinking Third Cinema, edited by Sumita S., Wimal Dissanayake
    Chakravarty and Anthony R. Guneratne, 1–28. London/New York:
    Routledge, 2003.

Hardy, Jonathan. *Critical Political Economy of the Media*. Oxon:
    Routledge, 2014.

Hjort, Mette. *Small Nation, Global Cinema: The New Danish Cinema*.
    Minneapolis: University of Minnesota Press, 2005.

Hjort, Mette, and DuncanPetrie. "Introduction." In *The Cinema of Small
    Nations*, edited by Mette Hjort and Duncan Petrie, 1–19. Edinburgh:
    Edinburgh University Press, 2007.

Iordanova, Dina. "Afterword: Unseen Cinema: Notes on Small Cinema and
    the Transnational." In *Small Cinemas in Global Markets: Genres, Identities,
    Narratives*, edited by Janina Flakowska, Lenuta Giukin and David Desser,
    259–69. Lanham: Lexington, 2015.

Iordanova, Dina. "Introduction." In *Cinema At the Periphery*, edited by Belen
    Vidal, David Martin-Jones and Dina Iordanova, 1–19. Detroit: Wayne State
    University Press, 2010.

Magerstädt, Sylvie. *Philosophy, Myth and Epic Cinema: Beyond Mere Illusions*.
    Lanham: Barnes & Noble, 2015.

Marzano, Nicola. "Third Cinema Today." *Off Screen* 13, no. 6 (2009). Accessed
    July 30, 2019. https://offscreen.com/view/third_cinema_today.

McChesney, W. Robert. *Digital Disconnect: How Capitalism is Turning Internet
    against Democracy*. New York: New Press, 2013.

Mosco, Vincent. *The Digital Sublime. Myth, Power, and Cyberspace*. Cambridge:
    The MIT Press, 2004.

Nixon, Brice. "Critical Political Economy of Communication and the Problem
    of Method." In *Marx and the Political Economy of the Media*, edited by
    Christian Fuchs and Vincent Mosco, 260–83. Leiden: Brill, 2016.

Nixon, Brice. "Dialectical Method and the Critical Political Economy of
    Culture." *tripleC* 10, no. 2 (2012): 439–56.

Norton, Anne. *Reflection on Political Identity*. Baltimore: John Hopkins, 1988.

Pines, Jim, and Paul Willemen. *Questions of Third Cinema*. London: British
    Film Institute, 1991.

Polanyi, Karl. *The Great Transformation. The Political and Economic Origins of
    Our Time*. Boston: Beacon Press, 2001 (1944).

Radović, Milja. *Transnational Cinema and Ideology: Representing Religion,
    Identity and Cultural Myths*. New York: Routledge, 2014.

Rawle, Steven. *Transnational Cinema: An Introduction*. New York: Palgrave, 2018.

Rushton, Richard. *The Reality of Film: Theories of Filmic Reality*. Manchester: Manchester University Press, 2010.

Schiller, Daniel. *Digital Capitalism: Networking the Global Market System*. Cambridge, MA: MIT Press, 1999.

Schiller, I. Herbert. "Whose New International Economic and Information Order?" *Communication* 5, no. 4 (1980): 299–314.

Seibel, Alexandra, and Timothy Shary. *Youth Culture in Global Cinema*. Austin: University of Texas Press, 2007.

Singer, Irving. *Cinematic Mythmaking – Philosophy in Film*. Cambridge: MIT Press, 2010.

Stam, Robert. *Film Theory: An Introduction*. Malden, MA: Blackwell, 2000.

Vighi, Fabio. *Critical Theory and Film: Rethinking Ideology through Film Noir*. New York: Continuum, 2012.

Wasko, Janet, Graham Murdock, and Helena Sousa. "Introduction: The Political Economy of Communications: Core Concerns and Issues." In *The Handbook of Political Economy of Communications*, edited by Janet Wasko, Graham Murdock and Helena Sousa, 1–10. West Sussex: Blackwell, 2011.

Wayne, Mike. *Political Film: The Dialectics of Third Cinema*. London/Sterling: Pluto Press, 2001.

Winkler, M. Martin. *Classical Myth & Culture in the Cinema*. Oxford: Oxford University Press, 2001.

Part 1   Local Cinema and
Digitization: Distribution and Exhibition

Ignacio Bergillos

The political economy of participatory community cinemas: CineCiutat as a standpoint of resistance

Abstract In line with recent research from political economy of communication that has dealt with alternatives to dominant corporations and power structures, this chapter approaches resistance in local cinema and presents the case study of CineCiutat in Mallorca, Spain. It illustrates the role of community theatres in local cinema. As exhibitors of independent art-house films, as headquarters of film festivals or as promoters of local talent, but also as sites for meaningful participation and opposition to the commercial logics of the media industries. Through observation, document review and interviews with the management team, volunteers and members of the community, this text explains the early success of this unexpected project. The pioneering initiative of CineCiutat represents an alternative to the established norms and practices of film exhibitors. The challenges and opportunities set by digitalization raise contradictions and ambivalences of an industry in transition. This case study introduces some of the tensions and participatory initiatives that shape the practices of the community of volunteers and professionals that manage the cinema and advances some issues for the future of this participatory theatre, a key agent of local cinema in Mallorca.

Keywords: participation, film industry, distribution, exhibition, community cinema, CineCiutat

Introduction

Community theatres are key for the development of local cinema. They offer diverse and plural programming, as well as support for local filmmakers and audiences. At the same time, as exhibitors, they are one of the most challenged agents in the film industry. In recent years, the digitalization of screens and distribution processes has forced cinemas to undertake important investments in technology, resources and equipment (Macnab et al. 2016). As a consequence, many have had to end their activities or adapt to a new context, which is shaped by digital distribution, a declining number of cinemagoers and increasing competition from new agents in the industry. Others, however, have found alternative ways of achieving their aims as exhibitors and as supporters of local cinema (Arnal and Salson 2017). These sites of resistance face a contradictory situation in which they have to follow the logics of a powerful industry while, at the same time, they are run and managed following alternative or participatory models where decision-making processes are shared with their communities.

This chapter has two objectives. First, from the perspective of political economy of communication, it frames community cinemas as alternative media and presents the unexamined case of CineCiutat as a site of resistance. Created in 2012, CineCiutat is a pioneering initiative in Spain. Supported by citizens from Mallorca, its participatory management model represents an alternative to the hegemonic system of film distribution and exhibition (Arnau Roselló 2016). Today, around a thousand citizen sustain a project that is directed by the decisions that arise from a horizontal, participatory structure. The success of the model has proven itself sustainable through an active involvement of the citizenship and the collaboration of the workers and management team. Members of the association elect the board of the cinema and have their say through self-managed working groups. This, of course, does not come without obstacles. Thus, a second objective of this research is to observe its efforts to build alternatives to the dominant commercial system in terms of funding, audience engagement or access to resources. The case study will point out the ambivalent and contradictory relationship between the cinema and the mainstream industry, as well as the tensions that arise with other agents, traditional and new, and the opportunities for collaboration that they are also developing.

Local, independent, participatory and community cinemas

Film programming and screening outside or in the margins of the global mainstream industry has been conceptualized under different – often overlapping – categories of film exhibition: independent, community, alternative, participatory, etc. All of them share a similar understanding of cinema as culture and defend its role in society, but they also come up against a common precarious context. They fulfil public service and they are committed to their contribution to local cinema. Through art-house film exhibition, audience development, event organization and alternative content, they position themselves against a more 'commercial' or 'mainstream' model, where big conglomerates and global companies compete in increasingly concentrated markets. However, there are nuances that differentiate these concepts at a theoretical level.

The broadest category would be 'independent' film exhibition, which takes place in a variety of venues, under different situations of ownership, where theatres develop their activities following both for-profit and not-for-profit, commercial and sub-commercial management models (Aveyard 2014, 2016, pp. 140–149). Europa Cinemas, the first film theatre network focusing on

European films, points out that "one of the critical differences between independent cinemas and some of the bigger commercial chains is that they are
based in, and belong to, their own communities" (Europa Cinemas 2017, p. 9).
Independent cinemas define themselves as different from commercial cinemas
and recognize a relationship with their own communities. However, their
activities as exhibitors are very much entangled with a consolidated industry.
Like many producers and distributors, independent exhibitors work under
conditions that are interrelated with the logics set by Hollywood (Holmlund and
Wyatt 2005; Wasko 2003). On the other hand, the relationship with its communities and their *belonging* can be analysed in terms of ownership or as part
of a wider social and cultural context. Within the first approach, small companies and family businesses run these small- and medium-sized cinemas that
are oriented towards serving local audiences. These independent theatres are
privately owned but committed to serving the community. Within the second
interpretation, there are *community cinemas* which screen films for regions and
neighbourhoods that usually have limited access (or no access at all) to movies.
These theatres are run and financed by public institutions, NGOs or community
associations. In the UK, for instance, the British Film Institute understands community cinemas as those which are volunteer-based non-profit organizations
that screen films to specific neighbourhoods or regions. Within that description,
film societies, cinema clubs and screenings in public venues are different kinds of
community cinemas. As summarized by Randall (2016, pp. 44–45), Becky Innes
and Jim Barrett identified five types of these venues: volunteer-run community
cinemas or films societies, mobile and rural cinema network venues, mixed-use
venues, and others, like education film clubs. The Community Screen Forum in
the UK argues that they "create social value by bringing local people together
in areas of the country where arts and cultural provision may otherwise be limited" and that "this social purpose overrides the profit motive of commercial
cinema operators, driving everything from the choice of film programme and
scheduling, to decisions around marketing, admission charges and the staging
of events" (Community Screen Forum 2017, p. 1). In the United States, a similar
concept is *community-supported cinema*. In this case, cinemas work as a place
of reunion and aim to be more than a theatre. They become sites for education
or filmmaking and a place to chat, exchange ideas and consolidate a closer relationship between film culture and the local community. However, within this
kind of theatres, there is a variety of management models and rules of audience
engagement. Some of them, although oriented towards the community, tend to
run these cinemas in a vertical model. Others embrace more participatory and
horizontal models of management and decision-making processes.

At the same time, community cinemas, if understood as community media, defend cultural expressions that reinforce local identity and often resist as social and political standpoints in contexts that marginalize them and make them invisible (Downing 2001; Gumucio 2014). Looking at the concept from that angle, community cinemas are a response to the needs of a certain community, which at the same time is organized and empowered through meaningful decision-making processes. Similar to the idea of citizen media or participatory media, they promote popular education and the exchange of ideas that potentially create situations of social change (Rodríguez 2001; Tufte and Mefalopulos 2009). There is a threefold nature of community media: a service to the community, a link to civil society and an alternative to mainstream media (Carpentier et al. 2003). For Carpentier, Dahlgren and Pasquali, community media in the 1960s and 1970s where the first experiences following that goal:

> All around the world, a heterogeneous galaxy of 'independent', 'underground', 'alternative', 'community', 'citizens', 'participatory' and 'radical' media flourished, comprising radio stations, newspapers, fanzines, independent theatres, filmmakers, music labels and publishers, revolutionary libraries and bookshops and so on. What these communicational practices shared was access by the community and participation of the community (and its constituent subgroups). (Carpentier et al. 2013, p. 291)

In that sense, participation is a key component of these initiatives and serves as a catalyst in these alternative, grassroots media that look after the needs of citizens (McQuail 2005). Independent cinemas might not be participatory, but most probably a community cinema will encourage some kind of meaningful participatory practice. Generally speaking, participatory communication supports the dialogue between media professionals and citizens and promotes social and cultural values. It stimulates the development of communities through strategies based on a balanced relationship between those involved. Central to the definition of participation is the concept of power. There are different participatory intensities and forms, from minimalist to maximalist (Carpentier 2011, 2016), depending on the structure of the organization and the decision-making processes it supports. In that sense, community media are equivalent to alternative media, since both of them are supported by meaningful and goal-driven processes of participation. As Carpentier underlines, "community and alternative media provide ordinary people with media settings where the more maximalist forms of participation can thrive [...], although not without facing a multitude of problems" (Carpentier 2015, p. 22).

Alternative media is "understood as a potential for a critical discourse, challenging neoliberalism" (Andersson 2012, p. 752). This means that it is not only a matter of participatory processes or interactive relationship between professionals and users, but also an engaged commitment to a critical approach that confronts the unequal dynamics of the industry and the neoliberal logics that govern media in general. But, can we conceptualize community cinemas as alternative media? What nuances do we have to consider in the context of the film industry?

Community cinemas as alternative media

Broadly interpreted, alternative media offer diverse content to audiences, who are regarded as collaborators rather than clients. They facilitate engagement with communities, they are independent from economic interests and they are oriented towards participatory processes and social change (Hackett 2018). If we follow Fuchs and Sandoval (Fuchs and Sandoval 2015), there are subjective and objective conceptualizations of alternative media. Subjective approaches focus on their (horizontal) structure and their decision-making processes that facilitate participation of citizen and communities. On the other hand, objective approaches are interested in contents and argue that alternative media help the circulation of critical discourses and worldviews that oppose dominant viewpoints and mass media. For Fuchs and Sandoval, the ideal model of alternative media combines subjective and objective approaches and involves critical publics that engage in media through a management model that promotes critical content and debates. This ideal, however, is difficult to achieve, since alternative media operate under social and economic conditions shaped by capitalism. The commercial structure of media can act as a form of economic censorship.

> Given that alternative media exist within capitalist society, a society based on fundamental inequalities, it is therefore not just important to study alternative media practices and structures, but to relate such studies to a critical political-economic analysis of alternative media and corporate media. (Fuchs and Sandoval 2015, p. 168)

If we frame community cinemas as alternative media, we will face this contradiction: while their self-organized activities and management gives them more independence from dominant agents of the industry, at the same time they need, as exhibitors, to follow industrial logics in order to be able to screen films and alternative contents, both independent and/or art-house. As James (Holmlund and Wyatt 2005) points out, the relationship between mainstream and alternative cinemas and subcultures has historically adapted itself to different contexts, but has been always determined by interdependence. We should avoid an 'either/or' explanation for the relationship between alternative and mainstream media: it is contradictory, contested, hybrid and convergent (Kenix 2011; Rauch 2016). Also, there is not only one dimension of alternative media but rather more than one meaning of it (Fuchs and Sandoval 2015). Again, a key word for understanding their contradictory situation is power. While within community cinemas power tends to be equal and horizontal, there are huge imbalances that affect exhibitors' relationship with distributors and with other industrial agents. In many markets, Hollywood majors have a big influence in cinema programming and exhibition (Wasko 2003). Through strategic mechanisms such as blind bidding or block booking, they take advantage of their powerful position in the negotiations of film distribution. As a consequence, community cinemas have limited access to key resources and promotion. However, their participatory models engage users in a critical approach to cinema-going and the film industry. Their engagement feeds their volunteer base and the commitment of the staff. But, as Fuchs and Sandoval (2015) call attention to, "the history of alternative media is a history of precarious voluntary work" (p. 168) and "self-exploited labour, the consequence of a political economy that limits the possibilities for civil society because hearing alternative voices is a matter of money and political resources that afford visibility." (p. 173). Under the lens of political economy of communication, we can approach the power relationships that operate in independent film exhibition and the challenges for community cinemas by analysing the tensions involving funding, distribution and sustainability. In order to do that, let's introduce the case of CineCiutat: an independent, community and participatory cinema in the Spanish island of Mallorca.

Brief history of CineCiutat: A story of participatory resistance

Although CineCiutat is the first case of a new community cinema in recent years in Spain, we can find other precedents worldwide that represent an alternative – at a local level – to the hegemonic model of film distribution. For example, U.S. community supported cinemas can be found in many states. Some like FilmScene in Iowa or The Loft Cinema in Arizona have been recently created, but many others like Cinemapolis in New York accumulate decades of experience. The first projects like Images Cinema in Massachusetts can be dated back to the first decades of the twentieth century. Similarly, associative and art-house cinemas as well as grassroots film clubs across Europe have provided film watching experiences to different local communities. Forsher (2003) has analysed how cinemas have fostered the creation and growth of a sense of community in cities and how they have become a central element of urban living and socialization. Some of these initiatives arise from a citizenship that defends cultural projects that enrich the community experience. This is the case of Plaza Cinema in Liverpool, which has survived thanks to the contributions and efforts of its members and volunteers since 1995. In other cases, such as CineCiutat, community cinemas were born in response to a business decision to finish film exhibition.

Back in 2012, the only film theatre in Mallorca that regularly screened art-house cinema and films in their original language was Cines Renoir, a four-screen cinema owned by Alta Films, an independent Spanish company with integrated production, distribution and exhibition activities. During those years, the economic crisis in Spain affected many areas, including the cultural industries. Cinemas had to intensively invest in order to adapt their screens to the digital age, a move forced by the big players in the industry, especially major production and distribution companies. Whereas in other countries different financing options helped to move forward the digital conversion of cinemas, in Spain there were enormous difficulties to access financial help or public subsidies. In the last ten years, Spain has lost a third of its art-house cinemas. Alta Films closed many of its Renoir cinemas in Spain, including the one in Palma, and kept only a few in bigger cities like Madrid or Barcelona.

Few days after Alta Films closed the cinema, a group of citizens, encouraged under the slogan *Salvem els Renoir* [Let's save the Renoir] began the reinvention of this particular cinematic space. Some of them were worried that film programming in original language would not be offered on the island. Others were passionate film lovers who appreciated film as culture and art-house film-making. There were many who fought to keep a cinema in the city center and next to the popular neighbourhood of Blanquerna. All of them wanted to resist against the decision of closing the cinema and raised their concerns. After spontaneous demonstrations in front of the theatre, they started to collaborate in the organization of formal meetings that only two weeks later led to the creation of Xarxa Cinema (catalan for Network Cinema), a non-profit organisation that represents the core of the initiative and officially managed the reopening of Cine Renoir. Alta Films, moved by the spontaneous reaction and the good faith of the association, donated the seats, screens and 35 mm projectors.

In less than a year, more than 1,300 citizens signed up as members of Xarxa Cinema and, through an annual contribution of 100 euros, helped to consolidate a model that is directed by the decisions that arise from a horizontal, participatory structure. The success of the project proved itself sustainable through an active involvement of the citizenship. Members of the association elected the board of Xarxa Cinema and had their say through nine commissions that managed different aspects of the cinema: Participation, Sustainability, Programming,

CineFilms, Communication, Translation, Educational Activities and New Technologies. A small group of paid staff coordinated and ran most of the basic daily activities and encouraged a close connection between the community and the organization. The direct relationship of the citizens with the nuclear group that manages CineCiutat constitutes what Carpentier (2011) categorizes as a maximalist participatory practice. The activities of CineCiutat, in terms of Carpentier (2011, p. 229), "often render their participatory backstages visible and offer a discursification of their material participatory practices." Interestingly, the community that eventually saved the Renoir chose a name that highlights the participatory nature of the organization. Xarxa Cinema identifies the association with its aim of generating physical and virtual spaces for participation and collaboration. On the other hand, the renaming of the cinema from Renoir into CineCiutat, strengthened its linkage to the city while paying tribute to film history (Cinecittà film studios in Rome) and local culture (Ciutat is the name given traditionally to Palma de Mallorca by people from the rest of the island). These brands, Xarxa Cinema and CineCiutat, summarize the philosophy of both the association and the cinema. The creation of a networked and participatory project linked with the local community and with other similar initiatives elsewhere.

In a short period of time, CineCiutat became a reference of quality cinema in Palma de Mallorca through the promotion of diversity and pluralism in film programming. Since its first days it has screened classic films, short films by local directors, workshops for kids and schools, film contests and meet and greets with directors, actors and producers. As an acknowledgment of its activity and the contribution to the local community, CineCiutat received in 2014 the Gold Medal of the City of Palma. As the first recent case of citizen-managed cinema in Spain, CineCiutat became a reference in the whole country. Soon, other cinemas with similar characteristics were created in Madrid, Zaragoza and Santiago. All of them contacted Xarxa Cinema in order to follow their steps. After these collaborations Xarxa Cinema put forward the idea of creating the first network of art-house cinemas in Spain: CineArte. At an international level, CineCiutat became a member of Europa Cinemas and engaged in different initiatives with European cinemas.

Today, CineCiutat is still open and presents a year by year increase in visitors, events and educational activities. However, it still faces challenges at internal and external levels. On one hand, tensions within the community and commissions arose, staff members who retired or left were difficult to replace, and the total number of volunteers fell noticeably. At the same time, on the other hand, new local competitors appeared and old ones started to program movies in original language as well. Also, while small and independent distributors were happy to collaborate with the cinema, others were unwilling or reluctant if not openly against building any collaboration with the community cinema.

How are these developments concerning and affecting the strategies and activities of the community cinema? How is CineCiutat navigating the tensions between its participatory model and its role as film exhibitor? What problems arise as a consequence of the power imbalances in place and/or the self-organization of the management model?

The political economy of CineCiutat

The extraordinary story of CineCiutat illustrates an unlikely possibility. Its existence is a manifestation of the resilience of local cinema. Even in front of the challenges posed by digitalization and the powerful agents of the industry, this cinema has been capable of building an alternative to the commercial logics that threatened its viability. Although its future is uncertain, the survival of the project guarantees that control is not only in the hands of the established institutions and global giants, but also in the actions and discourses of the citizen. At the same time, CineCiutat gives continuity to a hitherto emblematic space for cinematography in Palma de Mallorca. It is rather a disassembled and unstable space that is required to continually rethink itself in order to be in a constant conversation with its community. From the perspective of contemporary political economy, we can consider CineCiutat as an example of one of its current research trends. Attending to Mosco (2009, p. 113), "the emphasis on resistance is increasingly generalized in research on the contemporary political economy, marking a shift in the central standpoint from a focus on capital, dominant corporations, and elites to alternatives that draw from feminist and labor research." The participatory management and financing of the cinema integrates users within the structure that manages every aspect of the theatre, from the ticket office to film programming and promotion. The main objective of the organization is to maintain diversity and pluralism in the decision-making process through their close relationship with the community. Their concern is to adapt the cinema to the preferences of the community and to consolidate their participatory model. However, this can lead to a dependence on voluntary work that benefits both the cinema (since it reduces costs and saves time to the staff) and capital (it serves as unpaid labour for the normal functioning of the industry). "Focusing on worker self-organization captures an enormous range of activities and problems that are simply not addressed in traditional research that concentrates on how capital exploits workers. Both are important, but it is time to restore the balance by describing the active agency of communication workers." (Mosco 2009, p. 119)

In the case of CineCiutat, the activities developed by workers and volunteers are interrelated and interdependent. They collaborate, help each other and coordinate their efforts with specific objectives. Moreover, part of the staff are also members of the association and are engaged as volunteers. Many dedicate more hours to the cinema that what they are paid for. And while their motivations are related to the well-being of the community and the continuity of the project, these activities generate commodities and unrewarded benefits to the whole industry.

Since 2018 CineCiutat is implementing a new method of managing the association; one "that advocates for a new model of business that overcomes the limitations of the conventional business model." (Robledo 2016, p. 84) The nature of this ideal, based on a three-dimensional theory of management, is integral, humanistic, post-conventional and socially responsible (Robledo 2014, 2016). Under this new logic, any member of the staff or the association can create self-managed circles with specific objectives. These 'circles' work as a similar agent as the 'literacy circles' by Paulo Freire: they eliminate hierarchies, they acknowledge the dialectical relationship between those involved and they are oriented towards action (Freire 1970). The aim of this initiative is to empower all the members of the community and to offer a more flexible way to participate. At the same time, any associate of Xarxa Cinema can join the meetings of the board and directly participate in the strategic decisions of the cinema. This openness and transparency seek to integrate the community at different levels and to take every opinion into account.

At the same time, Cineciutat aims to acknowledge the experience of going to the movies by rediscovering the ritual of watching films and by experiencing innovative forms of cinema-going. Javier Pachón, president of the board of CineCiutat, wants the users of CineCiutat to have the opportunity to be part of an experience that shows that the hegemonic model of film distribution and exhibition is not the only possibility to enjoy cinema. He rephrases Gaiman when talking about one of the main values of the film theatre: "In a world where Google can bring you back 100.000 answers, a librarian –or in this case CineCiutat– can bring you back the right one." CineCiutat has experimented with a number of innovative projects for film screening and they are willing to collaborate in activities such as Youfeelm.com or Screen. ly. These are online platforms that organize screenings based on the desires of the community. This *theatre on demand* model gives audiences the opportunity to access the cinema and organize private screenings or shared events. The synergies that CineCiutat as an exhibitor establishes with these projects give the audience quality film culture experiences while avoiding conflict with distribution companies that usually would not take risks with these experimental initiatives.

In fact, as Javier Pachón reveals, one of the key strategies behind the creation of CineArte, the Spanish association of independent art-house cinemas, was to help these venues with their programming efforts and ease the process of negotiation with distribution companies. One of the biggest challenges for CineCiutat is to reach agreements with big agents for the distribution of independent, art-house or author films. In order to avoid this situation, an organization *à la* Independent Cinema Office, which supports cinemas in the UK and offers programming services at different levels, would help small community cinemas to get access to a wider range of films. In Spain, the traditional exhibitors association is FECE, led by big chains like Cinesa or Yelmo. CineArte appears as a result of the motivation of independent cinemas to strengthen their position in front of bigger chains and lobby for appropriate public policies. CineArte, however, is failing to carry out its strategies successfully. On the one hand, Javier Pachón points to the limited resources of the cinemas. They are all small structures with precarious contexts. Their staff members cannot devote much time or effort to new projects, since they are all struggling with their daily commitments. This is why most of the independent cinemas showed interest but could not build a regular collaboration. Pachón bemoans the slow evolution of CineArte, especially in comparison to other countries, like Croatia, where the association of art-house cinemas has been a success.

On top of the pressure from the industry, CineCiutat had to face little help from public institutions. In many countries the digitalization process was solved rather quickly thanks to public mediation and subsidies. In Spain, state support was inefficient and, at a regional level, institutions disregarded this matter. CineCiutat tried to convince local governments through a proposal that was inspired by the Dutch model, where banks financed the digitalization of the screens with the endorsement of public institutions. The basic need CineCiutat had was not to be left alone in front of banks or other financing agents in a moment of crisis. In that period financial institutions did not have any interest in supporting not-for-profit business models or community projects. Again, the community took a step forward and collaboratively financed the necessary digital projectors. The digitalization of the screens was gradually implemented. First, one DCP projector was installed and complemented with BluRay screenings in other rooms. In a second stage, other two screens were enabled for DCP screening. The new distribution model was agreed upon the application of the virtual print fee (VPF) that distributors had to pay in order to balance out the costs of digitalization. Accordingly, the distribution company had to pay each week an amount of money for each digital screening. Soon, independent distribution companies wanted to avoid this fee by distributing the films only after enough weeks passed so that they could save the total amount or part of the fee. For Pachón, independent film distribution and exhibition should share the costs of digitalization through a VPF that focuses on the number of cinemagoers, instead of focusing on screened weeks. The commercial logics applied during the first years of digital distribution affected diversity programming, release plans and the experience of cinema-going as a whole.

In line with the contradictory and ambivalent nature of the cultural industries, the consequences of digitalization at CineCiutat were at the same time promising and discouraging. Digital media, not only screening technologies, allow new possibilities to the cinema. Javier Pachón expects CineCiutat to become a place where anything can happen: from online live-Q&A, gaming sessions or screening rooms that can be adapted to any activity. A key word in this sense is eventification. Through experiences related to film exhibition and the cinema as a place, CineCiutat tries to engage the community and build new audiences. Since its opening, it has served as main venue for most of the local film festivals, but also for contests for young filmmakers, and other forums related to environmental sustainability, classic film clubs, university screenings and many cultural and social events. CineCiutat gives local audiences access to diverse programming and events while serving as a site of get-together and cultural expression. Also, digital technologies introduce opportunities for automated theatre management and automatization. In the short term it saves costs, but the management team of CineCiutat prefers to plan long-term strategies. The reduction of costs related to these operational processes is reinvested in marketing or communication efforts. This means that the staff can access training and reorient their obligations towards new competences: curation, communication and or public relations; all intended to develop new initiatives in relationship to the community.

On the other hand, digitalization has emphasized some tensions between distribution companies and local cinemas. While distributors are still oriented to economic benefit, through the maximization of viewers per copy, community cinemas claim that this mindset punishes their model. Distributors are influenced by sales agents, who will close agreements only with those companies that can reach high rates in low number of distributed copies. For many independent exhibitors like CineCiutat, this is a short-term perspective that does not consider the contribution to local communities that community or arthouse exhibition can have and that could potentially lead to a stable model in the long term.

These tensions also appeared during another initiative by the community of CineCiutat: the 'solidary seat'. In order to facilitate access to films for people who are in disadvantage or cannot afford the price of a ticket, any member can anonymously invite another person. Different associations helped to reach the invitations to dozens of people who took advantage of this initiative. These tickets, however, were identified by distributors as regular entrances to the cinema. That means that distribution companies got their agreed percentage of the price independently from the 'solidary' nature of the ticket. The way distributors and sales agents consider entrance tickets have been, since the first days of the project, an important issue for the cinema. The fact that, from their perspective, CineCiutat operates just as another exhibitor means that their agreements are based on established industrial rules that do not acknowledge the particularity of the project. Thus, the initial intention of Xarxa Cinema to give away one ticket per month to each member of the community had to be cancelled, since distributors would demand a higher price for their revenue share. These conflicts won't disappear, as CineCiutat is determined to struggle in the interest of its community and resist against the constant pressures from other agents of the industry.

Conclusions

Political economy of communication deals with issues related to power and the complex, ambivalent and often contradictory relationships between agents in the industry. It aims attention at the contexts where media and communication struggle to develop balanced opportunities for the production and distribution of texts. Mosco underlines that political economy research "has also expanded its commitment to the history of communication, especially the history of resistance to dominant powers in industry and government. In doing so, it has uncovered the unexamined stories of efforts to build alternatives to the dominant commercial system that fed into wider oppositional movements" (Mosco 2009, p. 125). This chapter has presented CineCiutat and its characteristics as independent exhibitor, as community cinema and, eventually, as alternative media. Its history shows how it constitutes a site of resistance to the dominant logic of the film industry. Commercial imperatives make it difficult for alternatives to compete or challenge the unequal and dominant nature of mainstream film exhibition. Different forms of resistance have appeared around the world, but the big players' domination has continued uninterrupted (Wasko 2011). It remains to be seen how invited spaces for maximalist participation (Carpentier 2011), where power is shared by engaged communities, will influence local cinema.

It seems, however, that the relationship between the alternative and the mainstream is rather interdependent than oppositional (Rauch 2016). In Spain, CineCiutat represents an example of the success of citizen participation and a powerful reverse to dominant trends and discourses in the film industry. It is noteworthy that it was created during the backwash of the economic crisis in Spain, as a spontaneous reaction of citizen against the decision to dissolve and close an independent cinema. Although voluntarism defined the first period of the project, CineCiutat is trying to adapt its participatory management model to the requirements of a competitive market and a demanding audience while reflecting on the working conditions and the acknowledgment of voluntary labour. Following Mosco, "while it is important to understand how corporate power, new technology and conservative governments are changing labour, it is equally important to determine what labour is doing about this." (Mosco 2015, p. 45) The three-dimensional management model that the cinema is implementing tries to overcome the tensions that arise in a self-organized, voluntary intensive, working context.

The future of CineCiutat depends on its ability to use its participatory model to readjust the power imbalances that describes the film industry. Digital distribution has brought new challenges, but at the same time it gives local cinema the opportunity for thematic specialization and to invest in community engagement, eventification, diverse programming and alternative content that can help to educate and build new audiences (Heredero Díaz et al. 2018). CineCiutat strives to remain a space permanently open to the community while succeeding as an alternative space for engagement, communication and local development. How private and public interests will intervene in this participatory space will be a key issue in the future stability of local cinema.

References

Andersson, Linus. "There Is No Alternative: The Critical Potential of Alternative Media for Challenging Neoliberal Discourse". triplec 10(2), 2012, pp. 752–764.

Arnal, Mikael, and SalsonAgnès. The Emerging Practices of Cinema Exhibition in Europe. Paris: CNC, 2017. Retrieved 28.1.2019, from www.tourdescinemas.com.

Arnau Roselló, Robert. "Independent Cooperatives between Film Exhibition and Cultural Management: Citizen Cinema at the Industry's Periphery". Obets Revista de Ciencias Sociales 11, no. 2 (2016): 419–39.

Aveyard, Karina. "Film Consumption in the 21st Century: Engaging with Non-theatrical Viewing". *Media International Australia* 160, no. 1 (2016): 140–49.

Aveyard, Karina. *The Lure of the Big Screen: Cinema in Rural Australia and the United Kingdom*. Bristol/Chicago: Intellect Books, 2014.

Carpentier, Nico. "Beyond the Ladder of Participation: An Analytical Toolkit for the Critical Analysis of Participatory Media Processes". *Javnost – The Public* 23, no. 1 (2016): 70–88.

Carpentier, Nico. "Differentiating between Access, Interaction and Participation". *Conjunctions: Transdisciplinary Journal of Cultural Participation* 2, no. 2 (2015): 9–28.

Carpentier, Nico. *Media and Participation*. Bristol: Intellect, 2011.

Carpentier, Nico, Peter Dahlgren, and Francesca Pasquali. "Waves of Media Democratization: A Brief History of Contemporary Participatory Practices in the Media Sphere". *Convergence: The International Journal of Research into New Media Technologies* 19, no. 3 (2013): 287–94.

Carpentier, Nico, Rico Lie, and Jan Servaes. "Community Media – Muting the Democratic Media Discourse?". *Continuum: Journal of Media & Cultural Studies* 17, no. 1 (2003): 51–68.

Community Screen Forum. *Fact sheet 2: Community Exhibition & Social Value*, 2017. Retrieved 28.1.2019, from https://www.uea.ac.uk/documents/12814720/0/CSF+Fact+Sheet+2+low+res.pdf

Downing, John D. et al. *Radical Media: Rebellious Communication and Social Movements*. London: Sage, 2001.

Europa Cinemas. "Strategic Investments in the Future of Film. An Extensive Survey of the Europa Cinemas Network". *Network Review* 30 (2017). Retrieved 28.1.2019, from https://www.europa-cinemas.org/en/publications

Forsher, James. *The Community of Cinema: How Cinema and Spectacle Transformed the American Downtown*. Westport: Praeger, 2003.

Freire, Paulo. *Pedagogy of the Oppressed*. London: Penguin, 1970.

Fuchs, Christian, and Marisol Sandoval. "The Political Economy of Capitalist and Alternative Social Media". In *The Routledge Companion to Alternative and Community Media*, edited by Chris Atton, pp. 165–75. London: Routledge, 2015.

Gumucio, Alfonso. *Cine Comunitario en América Latina y el Caribe*. Bogotá: Fundación Friedrich Ebert, 2014.

Hackett, Robert. A. "Planetary Emergency and Sustainable Democracy: What Can Media and Communication Scholars Do?". *The Political Economy of Communication* 6, no. 1 (2018): 98–106.

Heredero Díaz, Olga, and Francisco J. Reyes Sánchez. "The New Models of Cinematographic Exhibition in Spain: Between Cooperativism and Self-management". *Index Comunicación* 8, no. 1 (2018): 57–79.

Holmlund, Chris, and Justin Wyatt. *Contemporary American Independent Film. From the Margins to the Mainstream*. London: Routledge, 2005.

James, David E. "Alternative Cinemas". In *Contemporary American Independent Film. From the Margins to the Mainstream*, edited by Chris Holmlund and Justin Wyatt, 50–58. London: Routledge, 2005.

Kenix, Linda J. *Alternative and Mainstream Media: The Converging Spectrum*. Bloomsbury London: Academic, 2011.

Macnab, Geoffrey et al. "Ways of Seeing. The Changing Shape of Cinema Distribution". *Sight & Sound* 26, no. 8 (2016): 38–48.

McQuail, Denis. *McQuail's Mass Communication Theory*. London: Sage, 2005.

Mosco, Vincent. "The Political Economy of Communication: A Living Tradition". In *Power, media, culture. A Critical View from the Political Economy of Communication*, edited by Luis A. Albornoz, 35–60. London: Palgrave, 2015.

Mosco, Vincent. *The Political Economy of Communication*. 2nd ed. London: Sage, 2009.

Rauch, Jennifer. "Are There Still Alternatives? Relationships between Alternative Media and Mainstream Media in a Converged Environment". *Sociology Compass* 10, no. 9 (2016): 756–67.

Randall, Amanda. "Keep it in the Community". *Sight & Sound* 26, no. 8 (2016): 44–45.

Robledo, Marco A. "3D Management: An integral Business Theory". *Integral Leadership Review* 8, no. 31 (2016): 72–85.

Robledo, Marco A. "Building an Integral Metatheory of Management". *European Management Journal* 32, no. 4 (2014): 535–46.

Rodríguez, Clemencia. *Fissures in the Mediascape. An International Study of Citizen´s Media*. Creskill: Hampton Press, 2001.

Tufte, Thomas, and Paolo Mefalopulos. *Participatory Communication. A Practical Guide*. Washington, DC: World Bank, 2009.

Wasko, Janet. "The End of Hollywood: Exaggeration or Reality?". In *The handbook of political economy of communications*, edited by Janet Wasko, Graham Murdoch, and Helena Sousa, 307–30. West Sussex: Wiley-Blackwell, 2011.

Wasko, Janet. *How Hollywood Works*. London: Sage, 2003.

Benjamin Lesson

Elements of a critical political economy of local cinema in Digital Era: Lo-bal process and double aesthetic of cinema in French film exhibitors

Abstract With the entry of new information and communication technologies (NICTs) and digital devices in film broadcasting, the fundamental tension is now less between mainstream and alternative film exhibitors than it is between the field of film exhibition and the new broadcasting platforms. In this chapter, I argue that the new broadcasting platforms offer a radical development of the Glocal logic: they offer a set of content, more or less adapted to a global market, with targeting strategies that allow them to adapt their proposals to the particular taste of the audience. In addition to this, the facilities offered by new technologies tend to change consumption patterns, making obsolete usual film exhibition practices. However, in response, film exhibitors focus their strategies on highlighting the singularity of the cinema apparatus. Multiplexes offer high-quality and new sensorial experiences; local cinemas focus on collective experience, as if a cinema is a kind of *agora*. Starting with some examples of French-speaking countries film exhibitor's strategies, this chapter aims to define a new concept of cultural mediation in the era of digitalization and globalization: the "lo-bal". The "lobalization" starts with local specificities, proposes particular ritualizations and aims, ultimately, to open up the local culture to global culture. In other words, this is the contrary of "glocalization": it starts with specificities and aims to commonness. We must notice that this process is experimental, because it implies a new shape of offer, a revision of the economic models. What seems really interesting is that it shows us that the socialization processes are counterparts of multiplicity of choices. In a way, the spectator's freedom of choice is not only in the film, but also in the context in which the spectator wants to experience the film. Finally, I will argue that these strategies imply a review of what define the aesthetics of cinema. This would not be limited to the aesthetics of films, but also imply the aesthetic of reception: the framework around film experience (ritualization, socialization, etc.). In the concluding section of this chapter, I will re-read the crises of the film exhibition in relation to the aesthetic of cinema.

Keywords: Local cinema, film exhibition, film market, political economy, ICTs, aesthetic of cinema

Introduction

My argument in this chapter is in line with Bergillos' chapter in this volume and proposes a widening of the problem he handled. In his chapter, Bergillos shows the tensions between the mainstream logic and the (multiple) alternative logics inside the network of film exhibitors. The main point of his chapter was to focus on one example of alternative logic. In this chapter I will also analyse examples of alternative logics (here, the case of exhibitors from French-speaking countries), but I will widen the focus and look at the impact of New Information and Communication Technologies (NICTs) in the field of film exhibition. These technologies do not only modify the logic of film productions: they offer new broadcasts and tend to have an effect on the consumption patterns and on the aesthetic experience.

Thus, in addition to the important problem posed by Bergillos (opposition between mainstream and alternative logics), this chapter discusses the appearance of a third supply of audio-visual content and a new form of film consumption.

In this perspective, the fundamental tension is less between mainstream and alternative exhibitors than it is between the film exhibition field and the new broadcasting platforms. In this chapter, I will argue that the new broadcasting platforms are ultimately designed to facilitate film consumption: access to content is easier and the viewer is increasingly considered as a kind of expert. The logic of the new broadcasting platforms is inspired by notions of value and offer associated with the 'glocal' logic: they offer a set of content, more or less adapted to a global market, and they have targeting strategies that allow them to adapt their proposals to the particular taste of the audience – targeting which is more and more accurate because digital devices make possible to profile, from the consumption made, the tastes in a home. Film exhibitors, be they mainstream or alternative, cannot offer such flexibility.

This state of affairs makes the analysis of the practices of alternative exhibitors even more interesting, because their business models are flexible enough to adapt to this situation. The examples I will discuss in a moment are interesting because they describe the adaptive efforts of alternative film exhibitors, but also because they offer theoretical insights in the political economy of culture and on the definition of the aesthetics of cinema.

The core aspect in the strategy of alternative film exhibitors is to value the theatrical experience, that is to say the collective spectatorial practice. The mainstream exhibitors also value the theatrical experience by offering more comfortable and more efficient reception apparatus (the multiplex). The notable difference between alternatives' and mainstreams' logics is that the former focus on the collective experience, on the idea of sharing experience, while the latter are in an intermediate position, essentially proposing a better quality of reception than home consumption. In other words, in the case of alternative cinemas, the spectator experience would be a kind of micro *agora*, organized around the interest shared by all the social actors involved (e.g., alternative film exhibitor and his audience) for a certain glance on the world that the cinema proposes.

From this starting point, alternative film exhibitors can proceed by progressively expanding the type of content, the forms of aesthetic experiences, the forms of sociabilities (that is to say the forms of social relationships) etc. We can call this kind of process "lo-bal": "lo-bal" logic is based on the specificities of a local market (a local audience) which is gradually opened up with an expansion of content and/or a multiplicity of practices resulting from a more global market. In other words, these exhibitors offer a certain spectatorial identity which allows, in a second step, to confront a multiplicity of content and forms of experience. The political gesture of these exhibitors consists in developing a human-scale entry into an increasingly globalized and complex market.

This case is interesting in three ways. First, from the analysis of the operating sector point of view, the entry of new actors leads to a radical change in the logic of film consumption: henceforth, film theatre is no more than a way of access to films, which appears less convenient than new broadcasts. Second, from the point of view of the political economy of local film exhibition, this new paradigm contains a number of problems, especially for the spectator. The "lobalization" appears to be a significant response. Finally, the logic of the offers proposed by these alternative exhibitors leads to a massive redefinition of the aesthetics of cinema: it would be double, composed of the aesthetics of the film as well as an "aesthetic of the reception". At the end of this chapter I will re-interpret the crises (in the plural) of film exhibition to argue for the importance of the "aesthetics of the reception" in the critical political economy of local cinema.

The values inside contemporary film markets

In the digital age, film exhibitors have to deal with new devices, new broadcasting platforms (with their specific offer) and new consumers' behaviours, which, therefore, change the practices and values in the film market. The massive use of the smartphone (more than three billion users in the world) suggests that the screen of this device is becoming the main screen of cinema; what this implies is that to the usual "no parking, no business" is now added "no smartphone, no business".[1] Smartphones are not only bringing a new audio-visual

---

1   Jean-Marie Dura, *La salle de cinema de demain*, CNC Report, 2016.

culture (with the increase in the number of smartphone users, YouTube has more and more views, which indicates a greater consumption of videos on the Internet through mobile devices), but also represents a notable information source for their users. As such, we can note new intermediaries and, thus, new logics of valuation of movies in society[2]: the role of prescriber, traditionally devolved to professional critics, is becoming more and more performed in a peer-to-peer logic. In this peer-to-peer logic, spectators consider the exhibitors' programming work not flexible enough, compared to the offers available on the Internet.[3]

One of the consequences of facilitating access to content and progressive disinterest in traditional prescribers is that the choice to watch a film in a cinema tends to appear as a kind of "investment". The price of this investment is not only monetary (even if the ticket price appears expensive compared to the cost to watch a film through the Internet), but also temporal (the travelling time to the cinema theatre appearing as lost time).[4] The contents circulation facility, increased by digital devices, lead spectators to consider films as "informative goods"; film experience inside a film theatre is only an increase in value, a possible (but not compulsory) added value in film experience. It leads to high competition between cinema and other broadcasting places – especially subscription video-on-demand (SVOD).[5] This peer-to-peer logic means a paradigmatic change in the approach of the contemporary spectator.

Indeed, numerous sociologists noticed a reorganization of Pierre Bourdieu's principle of "distinction" (that is the expression of a desire for social recognition through cultural consumptions): one rather tries to distinguish ourselves by taste eclectism than through social recognition of the

---

2   In this paper "valuation" means recognition of social values (of a film, of spectators, etc.).

3   Benjamin Lesson, "Singularités cinéphiliques," in *Economie de la cinéphilie contemporaine*, Cahiers de champs visuels N°14/15.

4   Tilman Rotberg, GFK: "Young, busy and so many choices – How can we make cinemas more attractive for young audience", *UNIC Cinema days*, 21 October 2015.

5   Gilles Le Blanc, "Innovations numériques, distribution et différenciation: le cas de la projection numérique dans le cinéma", *Entreprises et Histoire* 2, no. 43 (2006): 82–92. In ten years, in the USA, the annual attendance per capita, passed from 5.5 to 3.8 entries per year, despites great successes. During this time, Netflix, Amazon Instant Videos, etc., seduced more and more users, and substitute themselves for the other film release ways. L&F Capital Management, *The compelling argument for buying shares of regal entertainment group*, retrieved from https://seekingalpha.com/article/3982750-compelling-argument-buying-shares-regal-entertainment-group

contents. Sociologists called that "omnivorous tendency".[6] So, cinema is confronted with a double trend which complicates the demand:

> [S]tand together [in this demand] specialized interests and wider (as well as more super-ficial) interests. (…) if we can be, at the same time, serious and superficial, each behaviour depending on context, the various components of a cultural directory (collective one as well as individual one) seem to be able to occur differently in social setting: on one hand, mainstream art forms can serve as a common denominator, and so they can supply the base of a daily sociability ; on the other hand, minority practices can supply mutual identification rites with their specific codes which are shared by narrower communities (whose status is, nevertheless, not the same that common status). So, phenomena of "distinction" can well remain in a confined way (including in popular environment). What would characterize the "omnivority" would be the capacity to play these various communications registers by updating them, according to the situations.[7]

Thus, film exhibitors must, on one hand, highlight fringe demands (recognition of individual specificities), and, on the other hand, maintain a kind of mainstream demand (which show collective benchmarks). It is in its entirety that the film market embraces all this apparent paradoxical demand. The film market is made up of three main streams of film offerings, each of which enhances the film and its consumption in a particular way: the SVOD, the Multiplex and local cinemas.

The SVOD way mainly considers films as "experience goods". In this approach, broadcasting is mainly a question of offering multiple contents and a question of facilitating the spectator access to these contents (in particular, to broadcast them through multiple devices). In this value chain (when a content is exploited through different "windows"), *cinema is a supply-led market where exhibitors are the gatekeepers for curating entry into the theatrical retail environment.*[8] This way, the value of films and film consumptions is supported by new a way of consumption brought about by the "Active Audience":

> Active Audience refers to the emergence of a new group of technology-savvy consumers who primarily consume media product via the Internet. [Bloore] identifies active audience consumers as fulfilling two key value-related functions: The first is purchasing the

---

6   Guy Bellavance, Myrtille Valex, and Laure de Verdalle, "Distinction, omnivorisme et dissonance: la sociologie du gout entre démarche quantitative et qualitative", *Sociologie de l'Art* 2 (2006), L'Harmattan. My translation. I kept the French word 'distinction' in my translation because the authors refer to Bourdieu's concept.

7   Ibid. 141.

8   Keith Kehoe, "The Impact of Digital Technology on the Distribution Value Chain Model of Independent Feature Films in the UK", *International Journal on Media Management* 17, no. 2 (2015): 93–108.

product and allowing financial value to return down the chain (customer consumption); the second is that the long-term 'library' value and reputation of the film is highly
influenced by the response of both the general audience in driving word-of-mouth
through social networks and as critical voices.[9]

Film exhibitors can't offer such a wide spectrum of content. It is not the ease of
access, but the singularity of the access modalities that becomes interesting here:
the fact of watching a film in a site which gives, to the fact to watch a film, a certain value and a certain collective meaning. This strategy relies on some "experience economy" principles, especially on the fact that *consumers will pay premium
for authentic personal experiences, such as live concerts and sporting events*[10]. In
other words, this strategy takes note of consumer's propensity to accept "to
invest" in a experience whose "added value", consists in the event nature of the
content watching.

The event nature of the content watching offered by the multiplex consists in
a high-quality experience of (mainly) mainstream films: the Apparatus is highly
comfortable, with high-quality images and new sound technologies which create
a new sensoriality. In this way, the multiplex add to the "experience good" (the
film) a high quality "experience service" (the context).

This strategy is successful because, sometimes, it appears that their spectators
seem to focus more on going to the cinema than movie-going. As Emmanuel
Ethis noticed, 35% of accompanied spectators (with one person or more) go to
the multiplex still not knowing what they are going to watch – as if the interest
was more to go to the cinema than to watch a particular film, although this investment is costly in travel time and in money. When Ethis interviewed these unde-
cided spectators, he discovered that they considered the quality of the Apparatus
and the spectacular organization of the place as assurances of a good investment
for an event experience.[11]

In their own ways, the local cinemas and art film theatres also offers something more than just watching a content: they focus on collective experience and
the film theatres appear as a kind of *agora*. They propose a correlation between
a specific programming and a spectatorial practice: sometimes it is according
to the tastes of their audience that the film exhibitors develop their programming (especially in case of local film theatres); sometimes a special practice is
generated according to the specialized programming (specific rituals, especially

---

9   Ibid.
10 Ibid.
11 Emmanuel Ethis, "La caisse de cinéma: quand il faut décider", *Communication et
    Langage* 125, 3e trimestre (2000).

in the case of art film theatres). This correlation between valuing public tastes and inventing new practices is also having some success. As Michaël Bourgatte argued, if spectators "attribute some value to the film objects without any institutional consideration",[12] there is, nevertheless, a strong link between the cinema theatre and the value that the spectator puts on the film. In other words, there is a micro institutional effect in the valuation of the film and of the experience, especially for the art film theatres.

In short, NICTs not only offer new forms of access to films, but they also create a new logic of consumption, which is paradoxical because it demands the availability of mainstream as well as specific contents. It also demands the recognition of particular practices while ensuring the practices of a common culture. This paradoxical demand can be satisfied by the broad spectrum of supply in the film market. Digital devices provide access to content; film theatres offer added value. In multiplex, this added value is the *total show* where the experience of the content is enhanced by the Apparatus; in local cinemas, this added value is in revealing the collective values shared by the audience. In other words, digital devices offer easy access to the contents, multiplex offer enhanced experience of the contents, and local cinemas offer collective significance to the experience.

The strategies of some French-speaking countries exhibitors: The *lo-bal* process

The omnivorous consumption could appear as a double bind: it seems impossible to satisfy both a need for collective benchmarks and, at the same time, to recognize individual specificities. But, we must remember that the work of film exhibitors has two dimensions: film programming and rites. As each dimension of exhibitors' work can satisfy one of the requests, the combination of these two dimensions can resolve the apparent double bind. Moreover, each film exhibitor can create a specific way to combine these two dimensions, thus offering a singular way to satisfy the double request.

We will see a strong tendency of programming and ritualization, which considers the double demand in its own way: The "lo-bal" process.[13] The "lo-bal"

---

12 Bourgatte, Michael, and Vincent Thabourey (dir.), *Le cinema à l'heure du numérique. Pratiques et publics*, p.186. Paris: MKF, 2012.

13 Benjamin Lesson, La Torpille Numérique. Problématiques métier de l'exploitation cinématographique à l'heure des multiplexes et des offres multi-supports (doctoral thesis), 13 December 2011, Université Lyon 2, retrieved from http://theses.univ-lyon2. fr/documents/lyon2/2011/lesson_b#p=0&a=top

process is a strategy that concentrates on the particular demand of its public, and participates in local cultural production as well as local cultural animation. It is because of this that we qualify this positioning "lo-bal" opposite to the "glocal". If "glocal" is the strategy of an international brand in which standard products are adapted to the specificities of local markets, "lo-bal" starts with local market specificities and opens them up toward a more global logic. Another way of understanding (or interpreting) this "lo-bal" concept is in terms of a "global" construed from a very local point of view, as if this local market could be a small window we can open to the world.

The use of the digital devices allowed some establishments to considerably revise their offer, but also their role as *agora* and influencers. I will describe three main aspects of the "lo-bal" process with some examples. (We must notice that this process is experimental, because it implies a new shape of offer, a revision of the economic models.)

First main aspect: a new editorial approach. A film exhibitor is an intermediary, a creator of "meetings" between audience and content; the programming work not only consists in the choice of films, but also in the articulation of these with other contents.

For instance, *Les 400 coups* in Angers, systematically programs, in the daily last sessions, a short film before the main film.

The flexibility of digital devices also allows to offer a window to small productions, local works, and even amateur works. For instance, *Nova* in Brussels, organizes "open screen" session, that is program composed by short films, without thematic constraint (the only constraint is the format). After the sessions, audience discuss and evaluate the films. The editorial work did not limit itself to the enriched film programming, but also opened towards other forms, as if cinema-addiction was a starting point to develop an aesthete culture. *Nova* in Brussels, proposes collective listening sessions, where, in the twilight, the audience can listen radio programs, documentaries and sound creations.[14]

Other establishments paid attention to videogames. *Quai 10* in Brussels even integrated a videogames room within the establishment. The idea is not only to attract a wider public, but also to extend the cultural mission of film exhibitors:

---

14 Mikael Arnal, and Agnès Salson, *Les pratiques émergentes de l'exploitation cinématographique en Europe*, 2016, retrieved from http://tourdescinemas.com/wp-content/uploads/Les-pratiques-émergentes-de-l-exploitation-cinématographique-ARNAL-SALSON.pdf (translated by me)

A game is a cultural and artistic creation. Inside entertainment industries, the videogame industry is the most important one and I want to show that there are good and bad videogames inside of thousands of available ones, as the films in the world of cinema. We do not tell to users what is 'correct', we want to attract young people in all their diversity and this is the same mission as we want to make with the cinema.[15]

The target audience is the same as the one which goes to this cinema in the framework of school sessions. The establishment shows the same values in videogame session and school session: collaborative works and social problems to be studied (racism, sexism, etc.).

Last but not least, the programming work does not limit itself into the framework of the concrete establishment. A part of the possible audience is lost because of more or less practical and logistical reasons (elderly, young parents, etc.). Some film exhibitors try to keep in touch with this audience by using video-on-demand (VOD) devices on their websites. For instance, *La Toile* is a French company which manages this device for film exhibitors from various countries in Europe, and *Le Lux* in Caen has its own VOD service called *NetfLux*, in parallel of a rental service inside the establishment and film sessions. The price is the same as the ticket price, allowing access during 48 hours. The content can be a movie presently offered in film sessions (day and date), as well as selected films which are no more programmed in sessions (VOD), as films planned to be especially broadcasted through this window (*e* cinema). The question is not to compete with other VOD or SVOD devices, but of building and strengthening the link between the establishment and its (potential) public; it is also a question of widening the offer and of deepening a theme.

The second main aspect is the organization of space inside the establishment and its position taken in a geographical context. In response to the digital culture, which create offsite links without logic of proximity, film theatres ensure to make concrete, to make manifest, the aesthetic experience in the public space and to offer a continuity between this singular experience and usual urban experience. In other words, by creating a concrete space in synergy with the public space, they make manifest the continuum between aesthetic experience and social experience. To conceive cinema as *agora* means to recognize the bridges between these two experiences and to create a framework where they can meet. Here, the meeting is done in terms of appropriation: appropriation of art inside public space and appropriation of some public spaces under the pretext of art.

---

15 http://www.quai10.be/projets-pedagogiques/gaming/. My translation

That's why some cinema theatres are located at traffic junctions in their area. New architectural strategies are not limited to utilitarian dimensions, but also aim to be a passage in the city, bringing a playful dimension and a possibility of appropriation of the space by its users (who are not only spectators). The key words, the main ideas, are conviviality (by the users) and user-friendliness (by the cinema theatre). Moreover, this political strategy can be profitable: more and more local cinemas have their own bars, restaurants, bookstores, etc.

Thierry Decuypère (architect of V+ agency, which participated to the reconstruction of the former National Bank of Belgium into a new cinema – *Quai 10*) gives us an example of the new consideration of the function and the place inside the public space of the film theatre:

> Our role as architects is to transform a building, a space where films are shown, into an identifiable location in the city that occupies a firm place in people's minds above and beyond its basic function. This idea has been developing over the past 20 years. Through different programming measures and ways of making the public feel welcome, cinemas may become more than locations for film consumption. The Sauvenière cinema, for example, has become a place where people meet without necessarily going to see a film. The cinema is like an extension of public space. In itself, the inside of the theatre is an unrewarding architectural object because it's an opaque box. This constraint has shifted the focus to the areas around the theatres, so as to interact with the environment. The current project in Charleroi is even more ambitious in terms of interaction with the public space. In this industrial city, the new cinema is part of the larger context of a general restoration of the downtown area and the refurbishing of the docks. One part of the building will be the film theatre, and the other part will be dedicated to connected spaces such as a bar, an art gallery, residences for artists, offices... In addition, to maintain contact with public space, a passage has been opened up right through the building.[16]

Architecture is not the only way to connect and enjoy the public space: some film exhibitors have a partnership policy and organize "off the wall" screenings. For instance, *Le Lux* in Caen, organize screenings in the University and outdoor screenings. The principle consists in discovering a place, as the same time as (re) discovering a film. This gesture is not only aesthetic, but also political: this is an appropriation, which become significant because it has collective meanings.

The third main aspect is about new communication strategies. In the same way as the market leaders, local cinemas learnt to exploit digital devices and their practices to develop communication strategies more coherent with the current

---

16 Thierry Decuypère' speech, during Europa Cinema symposium, 21–24 November 2013, Athens.

peer-to-peer tendencies. Because these cinemas do not have to develop a large-scale strategy, they have more flexibility and they can more easily have a characteristic communication, which not only consists of bringing information to the public (price rates, programming, etc), but also in creating and in extending the sociability generated by the local cinema.

One of the most obvious examples is *Les 400 coups* in Angers which offers, on its website, some audio contents (presentations of the films, debates, etc.). So, the events and the policy of programming benefits from an additional visibility. This practice is already rather common in the UK and we can suppose that it will be even more in use in the near future. The film experience does not limit itself to the time of the screening, but also involves particular debates about the films[17]; here, the local cinemas provide the time and space for these discussions. In a way, this strategy tends to make the film theatre more "approachable", its policy appears more personal and less institutional. The personification of the film exhibitor creates trust because it makes obvious the intermediary and his (or her) logic. Thus a better closeness with the public is developed, the latter can identify itself (or not) with the film exhibitor and his/her logic.

Besides, film exhibitors offer a variation of the social networks' peer-to-peer logic. Many film theatres show public rates. Some other film theatres delegate to some spectators a function of intermediary between the cinema and a public fringe. For instance, *Le Méliès* with its young audience:

> We try to perceive the film theatre through the films we programme and then as a particular experience such as one might have at home with one's friends, the auditorium acting as a living room. Here are three of the initiatives we have put in place. With Get on the bus we invite our filmgoers to come on a trip to the National Cinema Museum in Turin. The first event took place in October 2013 and there were approximately 50 of us on the bus. This also allowed the film theatre's team to talk to our filmgoers, to get to know them better, and to forge new links. Skype me if you can offers a monthly discussion, via Skype, with a foreign filmmaker. It is very relaxed. For example, we talked to William Friedkin in his kitchen; discussion is particularly spontaneous. Film-loving ambassadors: We are running a competition to recruit two students aged between 15 and 18. They shall become ambassadors for the film theatre in their schools. Every month they have to choose their favourite film and justify their choice with a short

---

17 Benjamin Lesson, "La règle et le sentiment: deux formes de spectation à travers l'exemple de Stnaley Cavell et de Jean Louis Schéfer", *Raison Présente*, 187 (2013).
    One of the main contributions of Stanley Cavell's *The World Viewed* consists exactly in showing the importance of the discussion in the general experience we have of a film.

written text that we subsequently print on flyers. In this way, young filmgoers can identify with the opinions of their peers, whom they perceive more positively.[18]

The local film theatre is not only a simple place of aesthetic experience, but also
a kind of network, a place of sociability, of exchange and of expression. Local
film theatres testify that the discussions about films are as essential as the film
experience as such.

Thus, at a time when cinematic forms are sufficiently established to be broadcasted in multiple ways, film theatres have focused on the importance of the
Apparatus in the experience spectators can make of these forms. The multiplexes
are spaces where the experience is enhanced; local cinemas disseminates a political, because collectively shared, dimension to this experience. The contemporary spectator is, therefore, confronted with a wide spectrum of content, but also
with a wide spectrum of experiences.

The strategy of local cinemas is not only interesting as a trick in a very competitive context; it also leads us to carefully review what define the aesthetics of
cinema. This would not be limited to the aesthetics of films (otherwise, the new
broadcasts would capture the entire market). There would be another dimension
that local film theatres and multiplexes highlight: the *aesthetics of reception*. In
the same way that cineastes exploit a cinematographic grammar to produce significant forms, Apparatus create a framework that models, modifies and gives
meanings to the confrontation to these significant forms. Multiplex enhances the
sensory dimension of this aesthetic of reception, while local cinema reinforces its
(collective) significance. In other words, besides the aesthetic of moving pictures
there is the aesthetic of the show.

To conclude this chapter, I argue for the importance of this double side of aesthetic of cinema (the aesthetic of film and the aesthetic of the show) through a
short review of the history of film exhibitor crises in France.

The history of film exhibition crisis: A problem of disconnection inside the double side of the aesthetic of Cinema

From the appearance of sound films to the crisis of the 1980s, the function of
film exhibition was mainly to exhibit films, as if the only matter that counted
was to watch a film. Thus, there was a disconnection inside the double aesthetic
of cinema: the aesthetic of film was the main aesthetic taken in to consideration.
Film theatres had to adapt themselves to new film technologies and to the entries

---

18 Sylvain Pichon, film exhibitor of Le Méliès, symposium Europa Cinema, 21–24
    novembre 2013, Athens.

of new broadcasts. However, if we consider film exhibition practices, from early cinema to nowadays, we discover the importance of the Apparatus, which was essential in early cinema and which becomes important again today. In other words, the aesthetic of cinema has always had two sides: the moving picture and the actual show. Throughout the twentieth century, this fact has been regularly ignored by film exhibitors and this ignorance is at the origins of these crises. Here, I propose to sketch a history of film exhibition crises that challenges the usual ideas of the causes of these crises.

Tom Gunning and André Gaudreault argued that early cinema was essentially elaborated for exhibitionist confrontation (more than a narrative dimension).[19] In other words, to watch a film and to experience its spectacularity was more significant than the actual story of the film. That is why they called early cinema "cinema of attractions": a show composed of autonomous units and edited for the purpose of given emotional effects in the spectator rather than for purpose of narrative effects. (Indeed, the first avant-garde aesthetic was a radicalization of this logic). This way to create and to show films still exists, nowadays, inside the film experience, but it is shadowed by the massive consideration we put on the film aesthetic and on the diegetic process.

We can find two combined explanations of this radical change of focus from spectacularity to narration of Cinema valuation. (1) The evolution of the aesthetics of film, where some creators worked and refined the narrative process, particularly through the montage (for instance, David Griffith's Work) and put the basis of later film aesthetics which focus on diegetic and narration. (2) The imposition of film rental (instead of film sale) by Charles Pathé (who was the most important film producer on the beginning of the twentieth century). In this way, film exhibitors could no more manipulate footages and create new contents from different films and each film became an autonomous object. Narrative aesthetic became more and more important, visual effects became a matter of style, and effects became matter of avant-garde.

We must keep in mind the importance of this paradigmatic change, because it has changed the valuation of film experience and the social status of cinema. Through the autonomy of the film, cinema became recognized as an art which progressively implies new practices. One of these practices consisted, for example, in the respect of the principle of session (like in theatre) which started with short films and ended at the end of the main film. Before this practice was applied,

---

19 Gunning Tom, «Le Cinéma d'attraction : le film des premiers temps, son spectateur et l'avant-garde», *1895*, 50 [2006], retrieved from : http://journals.openedition. org/1895/1242

people could enter and exit the film theatre at any time (which was not the case previously, where we entered and went out at any time). The introduction of this practice implied that the public behaviour had to follow the scheduling of the projection and therefore the formal logic of the film. It generated a legitimizing social speech about cinema and new spectatorial attitudes which are comparable to those of the theatre.

The value of cinema consumption changed: from mass experience to, nowadays, film experience, the spectator has been more and more considered as competent, connoisseur, etc.[20] (That is why, in academic research, we can easily find aesthetic of film studies, sociology of spectator studies, etc.)

A second crisis occurred with sound films (1927). Film exhibitors had to invest to improve the equipment of their establishments. In France, it took four years to improve more than a quarter of the national cinema theatres with the adequate technology. However, during that time, numerous theatres had to close because they couldn't afford it. The lesson to be learned from the effects of this crisis was that the theatres have to adapt themselves to technical requirements of films if they want to continue to attract people. As if innovation (and attractivity) could only come from the films (which require more and more technics). However, the crises which appeared in the second half of the twentieth century led to problematize more specifically the function of film exhibition.

A new important crisis occurred during the 1960s. The market for cinema exhibition declined because of a double modification of the demand. First, more and more homes were equipped with television sets, and spectators were getting more and more interested in the exclusivities and novelties. Second, the strong economic development, joined by an increase of purchasing power, offered spectators the possibility of diversifying their cultural consumption, increasing the competition between cinema and other forms of entertainment. This double modification of the demand deeply changed the organization of the market. We can characterize the 1960s and the 1970s period as a concentration policy period and the market became oligopolistic.[21] Film theaters which belonged to groups

---

20 This is exactly the starting problem discussed by Stanley Cavell: because of the institutionalization of the film session, which involves a start and an end of the session, the status and the pleasure have changed from pleasure of "poaching" to a more classical (theatrical) posture. In the first case, we "steal" a view on the World with "companions"; in the other case, we all contemplate a single object and we aim to distinguish ourselves through our singular points of view. Stanley Cavell, *The World Viewed: Reflections on the Ontology of Film* (New York: Viking Press, 1971).

21 It means that a low number of companies possessed a wide market share, whereas the larger number of film theaters were divided from restricted parts.

(like Pathé, which is producer and exhibitor) benefited from being in an integrated sector which allowed them to easily have exclusive films to offer to their audience. The way to survive was to be able to offer novelties and exclusivities on regular basis. Obviously, local film theatres couldn't adapt themselves to this requirement of novelty and tended to close; the only solution they had was to integrate in an independent federation.

During the 1970s, there was a concentration of screens in reduced number of exhibitors: a new kind of film theatre appeared – the *complexes* – which are multiscreen. Their economic principles are similar to supermarket economy: extension of the offer to the customers, where novelties create an attraction and substantial savings, because management fixed costs are not proportional among screens. These places were not really comfortable nor beautiful, but the assumption here was that the main value of movie-going was the film. So these film theatres focused on increasing the number of films, and thus, the consumptions of film.

This kind of offer, which concentrated all the value on access to a multiplication of content at the expense of comfort and of the beauty of the place, led to the 1980s' crisis, when spectators went less and less to the film theatre. The weak quality of the installations was severely challenged by home entertainment devices (video recorder, high-quality TV) and by the quality of TV programming (for instance, Canal + showed some novelties). Moreover, in France, the government started to think about a timetable of film broadcasting (that is a legislating distinction of different broadcasts – cinema, toll TV channels, free TV channels, etc.).

A posteriori, we understand that the problem did not appear because of television and other new broadcasts (as we thought then) but because the low quality of film theaters affected detrimentally the practice of movie-going. This crisis showed that the film is not the only point of interest of movie-going, that the quantity of contents is not the only value of an establishment and that the quality of the film theatre matters.

Pathé Group found a way to seduce spectators: the *multiplex*. This kind of film theatre is a big *complex*, with high-quality equipment, great comfort and spectacular architecture. Additionally, these kind of theatres offer other activities besides movie-going: we can find restaurants, sometimes bookshops, and sales of DVD etc. This innovation was successful and increased the number of tickets sold in France.

The *Multiplex* appears as a first step in the recognition of the importance of the aesthetic of reception. The cinematographic experience have meaning in a particular context, which is the cinema theatre. The multiplex exploits a number of significant elements which frame the film experience: these elements are architectural, as well as ritual, or associated with the rites generated by the interactions insides the establishments, the establishments' speeches about film and film current events, as secondary consumptions.

The aesthetic of reception always existed. The early period of cinema had its "palaces" (luxury establishments). The post-war crisis encountered by film exhibitors testify the need to recognize the importance of this aesthetic and, thus, to know its codes and its logics. Nowadays, each film exhibitor is characterized according to the way s/he deals with and exploit this double aesthetic. Every way of showing this double aesthetic implies a specific valuation of cinema, a specific valuation of movie-going, which can seduce a particular audience.

By its programming and its architecture, for example, the multiplex supports the entertaining and distracting aspects of cinema. Movie-going is going to a *heterotopy*, an "other space",[22] distinguished from public and ordinary spaces. Movie-going firstly means going to a *show* leaving to the spectators the possibility to also consider Cinema as art. In the opposite logic, local cinemas and «Art et Essai» (Art film) theatres focus their offer and their speech on an existential logic: cinema is considered there as a "window opened to the World"[23] and these film theatres lean on regular customers and the particular sociabilities which take place there. In this case, movie-going means primarily going to contemplate an art work, leaving to the spectators the possibility to also consider cinema as entertainment. Globally speaking, and with the exception of rural and isolated areas, spectators benefit from a wide offer of films and a wide offer of spectatorial habits. Movie-going not only means going to a movie, but also to have a particular habit.

Conclusion: Some epistemological considerations about studying lo-bal process strategies

Nowadays, film exhibitors do not only exhibit film: they make cinema concrete and significant inside the public space. The novelty of their practices consists in finding, in a new way, the attractive and surprising character of the early cinema: multiplexes are attractive because of the sensoriality they offer; local cinemas create surprise with unpredictable reception of the audience.

---

22 Michel Foucault, "Des espaces autres", *Le corps utopique* suivi de *Les heterotopies* (Paris: Editions Lignes, 2009).

23 André Bazin, *Qu'est-ce que le cinema?* (Paris: Cerf, 1976, My translation).

Film market and the wide spectrum of broadcast appears as a kind of "archipelago" in which the spectator can "navigate" and find some benefits there. In this idea, we can distinguish three main logics: (1) The one which mainly values content experience (VOD and SVOD); (2) the one which consists in insisting on the extraordinary character of the film experience in a cinema, by offering high-quality devices, spectacular architecture, etc.; and (3) the "lo-bal" process, which tries to conciliate aesthetic of film and aesthetic of reception through a whole work on experience, sociability and, globally, the framework around film experience. Each logic does not necessarily excludes the others. For instance, some local cinemas use some video-on-demand devices and, actually, *Amazon* is investing on film exhibition. In other words, these three logics participate together in an "ecosystem" of supply which answers the public demand which tends to be "omnivorous".

In this context, the specificity of local cinemas (and their contributions inside the public space) consists in emphasising the collective character of the film experience. The programming takes care of the specific taste of the local audience. But there are also specific rites and offers which sometimes exceed the simple frame of cinema, and pay attention to the (concrete and symbolic) inscription of the film experience in the public space. Additionally the transition to digital technology did not transform, but rather toughened and/or enriched the offer the film exhibitor.

However, the examples we studied are still a minority of cases. It remains to be seen in the coming years if their offers will be followed by more exhibitors. And it will be interesting to compare their results with those of the film theatres that preferred to stick to a more conventional logic.

It should be noted that we are still only in a phase of transition where the developers experiment the possible uses of the digital technologies. Partnerships are in the course of elaboration between VODs, distributors and developers, thus these practices are not institutionalized yet. Also, the opening towards contents other than film is going to pose questions of copyrights.

Finally, because we are talking about political economy, it will be interesting to pay attention to the possible evolution of the (French) political support to these film theatres. Will France still support film theatres because of the specific films they program or will France also support film theatres which contribute to the social and cultural life of a locality? In this chapter, I offered an early account of an emerging cultural logic (in film exhibition). The answers to these questions will be significant for the evolution of cultural dynamics.

References

Arnal, Mikael, and Agnès Salson, *Les pratiques émergentes de l'exploitation cinématographique en Europe*, 2016. Retrieved from http://tourdescinemas. com/wp-content/uploads/Les-pratiques-émergentes-de-l-exploitation-cinématographique-ARNAL-SALSON.pdf

Bazin, André. *Qu'est-ce que le cinema?*. Paris: Cerf, 1976

Bellavance, Guy, Myrtille Valex, and Laure de Verdalle. "Distinction, omnivorisme et dissonance: la sociologie du gout entre demarche quantitative et qualitative", *Sociologie de l'Art*, OPuS 9&10 (2006/2), L'Harmattan, pp. 125-143.

Benjamin, Walter. *The Work of Art in the Age of Mechanical Reproduction* (1939 version). London: Fontana, 1968.

Bourgatte, Michael, and Vincent Thabourey (dir.). *Le cinema à l'heure du numérique. Pratiques et publics*. Paris: MKF, 2012.

Cavell, Stanley. *The World Viewed: Reflections on the Ontology of Film*. New York: Viking Press, 1971.

Dura, Jean-Marie. *La salle de cinema de demain*, CNC Report, 2016.

Ethis, Emmanuel. "La caisse de cinema: quand il faut decider", *Communication et Langage*, 125, 3e trimestre (2000). Paris : Armand Colin, pp. 44-55

Foucault, Michel. "Des espaces autres." In *Le corps utopique* suivi de *Les heterotopies*. Paris: Editions Lignes, 2009.

Gunning, Tom. "Le Cinéma d'attraction : le film des premiers temps, son spectateur et l'avant-garde", *1895*, 50 [2006]. Retrieved from http://journals. openedition.org/1895/1242

Kehoe, Keith: "The Impact of Digital Technology on the Distribution Value Chain Model of Independent Feature Films in the UK", *International Journal on Media Management* 17, no. 2 (2015–), pp. 93–108.

L&F Capital Management. *The compelling argument for buying shares of regal entertainment group*. Retrieved from https://seekingalpha.com/article/3982750-compelling-argument-buying-shares-regal-entertainment-group. Last accessed on September 10, 2018

Le Blanc, Gilles. "Innovations numériques, distribution et differrenciation: le cas de la projection numérique dans le cinema", *Entreprises et Histoire* 2, no. 43 (2006). Paris : ESKA (123 p.), pp. 82–92

Lesson, Benjamin. "Singularités cinéphiliques." In *Economie de la cinéphilie contemporaine*, Cahiers de champs visuels N°14/15., Paris : L'Harmattan (186 p.), pp. 31–60

Lesson, Benjamin. "La Torpille Numérique. Problématiques métier de l'exploitation cinématographique à l'heure des multiplexes et des offres multi-supports" (doctoral thesis), 13 December 2011, Université Lyon 2. Retrieved from http://theses.univ-lyon2.fr/documents/lyon2/2011/ lesson_b#p=0&a=top Last accessed on 10 January, 2011

Lesson, Benjamin. "La règle et le sentiment: deux formes de spectation à travers l'exemple de Stanley Cavell et de Jean-Louis Schéfer", *Raison Présente* 187 (2013). Paris: Union rationaliste (133 p.), pp. 65–74

Heidi Grundström

Film distribution in Finland: Gatekeepers of local cinema

Abstract This chapter aims at providing an overview of how the distribution of feature length fiction films is structured in Finland. Furthermore, the powerful gatekeeping function of distribution companies for local cinema is analysed based on material collected through expert interviews, industry analysis and media reports. Through the theoretical framework provided by critical political economy of the media, this chapter hopes to offer some insights and interesting openings for further research. The initial findings introduced in this chapter highlight the importance of the distribution agreement, not only for the dissemination of the final product, but also at the pre-production stages of the film as well as the financing. The first part of this chapter introduces the central characteristics of feature film distribution through discussing how global and local distribution systems are intertwined to one other. In the second part, the structure of Finnish film distribution is discussed in relation to production, release strategies, windowing and box office revenues. The third part introduces recent examples of alternative distribution methods employed by Finnish production companies. Finally, these descriptive accounts of the system are followed by the discussion of how the division of distribution resources in Finland impacts local cinema.

Keywords: Film distribution, critical political economy of the media, digitalisation, local cinema, film production

Introduction

In recent years, film distribution has become a central topic in industry discussions and academic research. The rising interest in researching film distribution is largely due to the changes brought by digitalisation and multiplication of online delivery platforms. However, the power of film distribution and distributors within the film industry is often overlooked. In public discourse film distributors are understood as middlemen, wholesalers and marketers of films whose main task, put it simply, is to deliver the film from the hands of the producers to the hands of the exhibitors and finally to the attention of the audiences. There is essentially nothing false about understanding the distributors role as a wholesaler, a type of an intermediary along the film industry value chain connecting feature film producers with the audiences. This is a valid description, but when looking at the role of the distributor with a wider focus and considering the significance of the distributor in the lifecycle of films, this description seems too partial. As Wasko (2003, p. 84) describes it, "most industries have wholesalers…their role is almost always more narrowly defined than in the film industry." Describing the distributor as a wholesaler easily leads to misunderstandings of the role of film distributors, because the power distributors have in the film industry is considerably more far-reaching than that. As Lobato (2007, p. 115) has fittingly summarised, "distribution determines who gets to watch films, under what circumstances and why." The question of how extensive the role of the distributor is, usually depends on what point of the film production the distribution deal is agreed on (Crisp 2015, p. 17). In a recent report of digital distribution in the UK Smits et al. (2018, p. 1) have described film distributors as "performing a powerful gate-keeping function between the structures of production and consumption." Descriptions like these regarding the influential position of the distributors make it rather alarming that film distribution has received limited academic attention until recently. Although, this might to some extent be explained by the lack of access to sources that would enlighten the ins and outs of distribution business which are well guarded due to trade secrets. In this chapter, it is precisely this "powerful gatekeeping function" that will be addressed through exploring film distribution in Finland and what implications the current organization of distribution resources might have for local cinema.

To shed light on these questions, this chapter delves into an analysis based on research and media reports, documents and statistics. Furthermore, the background knowledge regarding distribution in Finland has been acquired through interviews with professionals working in the Finnish film industry as well as through personal observations collected at industry events. It should be noted that as the film industry in Finland is relatively small, the background information received from practitioners is treated in a manner that will carefully protect their anonymity. The chapter is split into four parts. The first part introduces the central characteristics of feature film distribution through discussing how global and local distribution systems are intertwined to one other. In the second part, the structure of Finnish film distribution is discussed in relation to production, release strategies, windowing and box office revenues. The third part introduces recent examples of alternative distribution methods employed by Finnish production companies. Finally, these descriptive accounts of the system are followed by the discussion of how the division of distribution resources in Finland impacts local cinema. To limit the scope of this chapter, the topic of film distribution will be analysed here in terms of feature length fiction films, thus leaving out documentaries as well as short films. Another limitation is that the topic will be considered with an emphasis on theatrical distribution, although other modes of distribution are inevitably linked to the question at hand.

The study of film distribution

According to Crisp (2015, p. 18), previous studies on film distribution have concentrated mainly on two aspects: the distribution deal and film marketing. Before moving any further on the subject of distribution, it is necessary to briefly comment on the existing literature. Rather than offering an exhaustive review, this is intended as an indicative sample of relevant approaches to the topic. It should be noted that studies of film distribution are often hidden within more general studies about the film industry (ibid.). As mentioned earlier, it's only recently that film distribution research has begun to gain a more central position within the academia and to large part this is due to technological developments that have made it possible to employ other types of distribution strategies that have the potential (at least in theory) to breakdown some of the barriers of the traditional distribution model. For instance, Smits (2017) has analysed the involvement of gatekeepers with online distribution and introduced the practices of 'self-distribution' and 'direct distribution' through case studies as the alternative models for organizing distribution. Another important and recent analysis that is useful for illustrating a more thorough account of the current structure of film distribution is the work by Crisp (2015). In her work, Crisp analyses the varying modes of distribution: formal distribution, independent distribution, disruptive innovators and informal distribution and calls attention to the blurred lines between them. A further point made by Crisp (ibid., p. 20) is that there is a lack of research into why certain films get distribution deals and others don't. However, a recent study by Munoz and Ferrer-Roca (2017) has approached this topic through investigating the relationship between producers and distributors in New Zealand by shedding light on how the local film producers struggle to get distribution deals. Indeed, the findings of Munoz and Ferrer-Roca share a resemblance with how film distribution is organized in Finland, where the leading distribution companies are subsidiaries of large international companies.

This chapter will approach the topic of film distribution through the theoretical framework of critical political economy of the media (Hardy, 2014). This means that the attention of the analysis is placed on the unequal distribution of power. Furthermore, it means critically analysing structures that reproduce and sustain such inequalities (ibid.: 6). In relation to cultural products such as film, critical political economy has tended to examining three core themes: production, content and audiences (ibid., pp. 10–14). As distribution is the function that connects these themes together, studying the topic through the framework of critical political economy means this chapter employs three key steps from the framework described by Hardy (ibid., p. 9) for researching media or in this case the local cinema: 1) studying how film distribution works through examining ownership, finance and support mechanisms 2) studying the organisation of film distribution in relation to film production by focusing on the creative autonomy of the producers and 3) the relationship between film distribution and the broader structure of society. Previous studies that have addressed film distribution from a political economy standpoint include, for example, works by Wasko (2003) and Miller et al. (2005) which both concentrate on Hollywood systems and their power that extends globally across film markets. In this chapter, the aim is to make some initial comparisons between the Hollywood distribution system and its much smaller Finnish equivalent. Having said that, being limited in scope, this chapter is a preliminary outline rather than an in-depth analysis of the topic. If anything, the descriptive accounts produced here will function as an indicator for further research needs in relation to film distribution structures in Finland.

From global to local distribution

Although the aim of this chapter is to analyse film distribution in Finland, it makes sense to begin by briefly commenting on Hollywood studios' distribution practices and how the impact of these practices has a global reach. Globally film distribution is ruled by the six biggest Hollywood studios (often referred to as "the majors") and their dominance is no exception in Europe. Looking at the market shares from 2017, US films had a 66.2% market share in EU countries (European Audiovisual Observatory, 2018) and a 59.4% market share in Finland (The Finnish Film Foundation , 2018). As Crisp (2015, pp. 31–32) has outlined, it is the structure of Hollywood distribution system that enables their powerful position on both domestic and foreign markets. First of all, Hollywood studios are part of large multinational media conglomerates which means they are financially secure and can afford risk taking beyond the capabilities of smaller companies. The structure the major Hollywood studios have created for film production through their own distribution arms, means that they have control over their films from pre-production to exhibition. In this way they can make deals that ensure their investment is returned regardless of box office success (ibid.).

Market share of admissions from all films in Finland (%)

Distribution company	2017	2016	2015	2014	2013
SF Studios Oy	30,4 %	30,0 %	30,0 %	37,0 %	29,6 %
The Walt Disney Company Nordic	24,0 %	25,0 %	18,0 %	16,0 %	20,9 %
Nordisk Film Oy	20,2 %	20,0 %	26,0 %	26,0 %	19,7 %
Finnkino Oy	16,9 %	15,0 %	20,0 %	11,0 %	14,4 %
Others	8,4 %	10,0 %	5,0 %	10,0 %	15,4 %

Fig. 1· Market share of cinema admissions from all films in Finland 2013–2014. SF Studios Oy was known as SF Film until 2015. Nordisk Film was known as Nordisk Film Theatrical Distribution until 2013 (The Finnish Film Foundation 2014, 2015, 2016, 2017a, 2018).

In Finland, there are currently 24 distribution companies listed on the website of the Finnish Film Foundation (The Finnish Film Foundation 2018). With a closer investigation 16 out of these 24 companies seem to primarily concentrate on feature film distribution. Whereas others have more narrow focuses relating to specialised film distribution, for example, distributing films to schools or only distributing short films. There are also three national television channels included on the list, one teleoperator that has a video-on-demand (VOD) platform and one media house that operates an online video platform. From these 24 distribution companies listed on the Finnish Film Foundation's website there is a clear divide between the leading companies and the rest in terms of cinema admission market shares (Fig. 1). Leading companies: SF Studios, The Walt Disney Company Nordic, Nordisk Film and Finnkino have kept their positions rather steady over the past five years with only slight variation between themselves.

The distribution practices of the Hollywood majors form the basis for the leading film distribution companies in Finland. Each major is represented by one of the largest distribution companies in Finland (Fig. 2). However, the distribution agreements are subject to change and shifts happen often. According to the Finnish film industry professionals this has very little to do with the distribution companies in Finland, but the changes happen as part of international deals made between the parent companies. The reason for this is that the global marketplace for distribution rights has been organised into different distribution territories and Finland belongs to the Scandinavian distribution territory alongside other Nordic countries (Smits 2016, p. 31).

Tracing the ownerships of the four leading distribution companies in Finland swiftly leads to international parent companies. First of all, Nordisk Film's parent company Egmont Group is a Danish media corporation and SF Studios is a part

Conglomerate	Hollywood studio (the majors)	Distributed in Finland by
Fox Entertainment Group	20th Centrury Fox	Nordisk Film Oy
Sony Pictures	Columbia Pictures	The Walt Disney Company Nordic
Viacom	Paramount Pictures	Finnkino Oy
NBCUniversal	Universal Pictures	Finnkino Oy
Walt Disney Studios	Walt Disney Pictures	The Walt Disney Company Nordic
WarnerMedia	Warner Bros. Pictures	SF Studios

Fig. 2: Hollywood studios and which distribution companies in Finland distribute their films. Situation as in autumn 2018.

of Bonnier Group, a Swedish media company. Whereas, the recent changes in the ownership arrangements of Finnkino lead further overseas. Finnkino, which is also the largest cinema company in Finland, was sold in early 2017 to AMC Theaters. AMC Theaters is based in the US, however it belongs to the media conglomerate Wanda Group which in turn is a Chinese company. The Walt Disney Company Nordic is a subsidiary of Walt Disney Studios Home Entertainment Ab which is owned by the Walt Disney Company based in the US.

Zooming in on the local distribution business, it makes sense to shift the focus to domestic feature length films. Looking at the market shares in terms of cinema admissions of domestic films, the same four companies can be seen leading the statistics (Fig. 3). However, there are a few smaller locally owned distribution companies that get mentioned in the Finnish Film Foundation's yearly *Facts and Figures* reports (The Finnish Film Foundation 2015; 2016; 2017a; 2018). For example, B-Plan Distribution, a Helsinki based company which was founded in 2013, has held a little over 2% market share in three consecutive years since 2015.

In her analysis, Crisp (2015, pp. 23–24) suggests that the metaphor of 'hour glass effect' (see also Deuze 2007, p. 211) could be applied to the Hollywood model of film distribution. Meaning that while there are several film production companies and films being produced, there is a small number of film distributors who are in the middle of the hourglass and control the distribution of films to audiences at the bottom. The same metaphor is suitable for how the distribution of domestic films in Finland is organized. For example, in 2017 twenty feature length fiction films were produced in Finland (excluding international co-productions) and out of these twenty films, ten were distributed by Nordisk Film. The rest were divided between companies that each distributed between one to three films. Similar patterns apply to previous years, in 2016 there were twenty-three feature length fiction films produced in Finland (excluding

Distribution company	2017	2016	2015	2014
B-Plan	2,9 %	4,0 %	2,0 %	n/a
Finnkino	5,2 %	n/a	n/a	n/a
Future Film	n/a	5,0 %	n/a	n/a
Isla Sales	n/a	n/a	n/a	1,0 %
Kuusan Kino	n/a	4,0 %	n/a	n/a
Nordisk Film	44,4 %	57,0 %	78,0 %	68,0 %
Others	2,1 %	1,0 %	1,0 %	2,0 %
Pirkanmaan elokuvakeskus	n/a	n/a	n/a	1,0 %
SF Studios	45,4 %	2,0 %	7,0 %	12,0 %
Snapper Films Distribution	n/a	n/a	n/a	3,0 %
The Walt Disney Company Nordic	n/a	27,0 %	12,0 %	13,0 %

Fig. 3: Market share of admission from domestic films released in Finland. (The Finnish Film Foundation 2015, 2016, 2017a, 2018).

international co-productions) and nine out of the twenty-three films were distributed by Nordisk Film. In 2015, eleven films out of the total twenty-one that were produced were distributed by Nordisk Film. This hour glass effect also has implications for the production of feature length films as will be explained in the next section.

Distribution deals

As outlined by Wasko (2003, p. 61), "one of the most important arrangements in the life of a film is the distribution deal or agreement." Crisp (2015, pp. 24–25) has introduced main types of distribution deals that are usually done in Hollywood, these are the PFD (production, financing and distribution) agreement and a 'negative pick-up'. The PFD agreement means that the distribution deal is made early at the script stage, whereas the 'negative pick-up' refers to making a distribution deal after the production of a film. Of course, there may also be other types of deals and each deal is always case specific. In a PFD agreement, the distribution deal makes up a part of the production's costs. In order to illustrate the case of distribution deals for domestic films in Finland, it is necessary to first look at the financing structure of domestic feature film production. A significant proportion of films' production budgets are covered by the production support allocated by the Finnish Film Foundation. The foundation is supervised by the Ministry of Education and Culture and the funds directed to the foundation come from the national lottery funds. According to the Finnish Film Foundation's statistics from 2017, on average 37.8% of the production budgets of feature length fiction premieres were covered by production funding received from the agency. The production companies' average was 21.5%, television channels' 14.3% and 8.6% came from the distribution companies. The remaining 17.8% came from several other financing sources both national and international. In order to receive production support from the Finnish Film Foundation the production companies must apply for it before a production is completed. In the Finnish Film Foundation's support guidelines, it is stated that:

> It is a condition of granting production support that the film is guaranteed professional commercial distribution reaching an appropriate, optimally broad audience and visibility for the film in cinemas, on television, on digital discs, or through other forms of public exhibition and distribution. (The Finnish Film Foundation 2017b, p. 12)

Thus, meaning that in order to receive production support, the production company will need to have secured a distribution deal for the film. In practice this means having a distribution deal with an established distribution company including a 'minimum guarantee' advance payment. The application for production support is required to have a marketing and distribution plan as an appendix that provides detailed information of the distribution strategies and marketing plan. It also needs to have the signatures from both the producer and the distribution company's representative. Therefore, while the earlier mentioned percentage that distribution companies covered on average on the budgets of feature length film productions might seem insignificant, the real value of a distribution deal in the typical financing structure of Finnish feature films is central. Without the distribution deal, it would be difficult to receive production support which in turn is a major part of the budget on most domestic film productions. Hence why, in Finnish film productions the deals for domestic distribution are made at early stages of production and this in turn emphasises the central role of the distribution companies for Finnish films. Not only are the distributors gatekeepers in terms of controlling the distribution of films to audiences, but their gatekeeping function begins already when a production is at the idea development or script stage. This makes the 'hour glass effect' metaphor seem like an insufficient way of describing the structure of film distribution in Finland.

Moving away from the 'hour glass effect' metaphor, one way of looking at the distributors' gatekeeping role is to investigate the process as a horizontal structure. In this horizontally spread image of a film's lifecycle the distributor is in the middle and it is easier to grasp how distributors' influence extends to both directions (Fig. 4). According to Wasko (2003, p. 61), Hollywood distribution deals are "influenced by power and clout" and furthermore "depend on when and

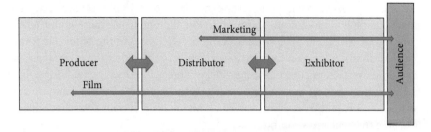

Fig. 4: Distribution as a horizontal structure.

how a film commodity becomes associated with one of the major distributors." In Finland, the financing structure of films and the fact that distribution deals are made in advance of productions, usually means that the distribution company pay an advance for the producer. There is no set amount for this 'minimum guarantee' advance, instead the amount varies from production to production. The advance payment then covers some of the production's budget. In any case, it is only an advance payment which the distributor receives back when the film is released and has generated some income.

In terms of Hollywood production, it seems that the distributor also has tremendous power before and during the production when a distribution deal is made at early stages (Crisp 2015, pp. 17–18). The marketing strategy of the film is considered early on and may impact decisions regarding script and title changes, casting decision, final edits and financing of the film (Wasko 2003, p. 60). This is something that is often overlooked. Film titles are usually connected to a particular director, leading actor or in rare cases a well-known producer, but hardly ever to distributors, even though distributors may have more creative control over the film than most people could imagine (Crisp 2015, p. 18). While it should be kept in mind that the film industry in Finland shouldn't be directly compared to the one in Hollywood, this provides an interesting topic for investigation also for domestic film productions. There is very little information available on this topic from previous research. However, the subject has been touched upon in relation to casting decisions from a production point of view by Virtanen (2012, pp. 53–56). In the interviews collected for Virtanen's work (ibid.), the distribution professionals briefly describe how they might suggest suitable actors for the film, however they emphasize that it is more important to have an interesting director and a producer with a good 'track record' in producing feature length fiction films. The interviews conducted with the film industry professionals for the purpose of this chapter revealed that there are varying opinions as to what extent the distributors have impact on the decisions made during pre-production and production. On one hand, there is an understanding that each are professionals in their own area. On the other hand, the optimal situation is when the distributor can get involved at the early stages of idea development. Furthermore, a producer noted that when negotiating a distribution deal, a savvy producer will sense if the distributor is not content with certain aspects of the production package and make room for changes in order to secure the deal. These opinions echo what emerges in the interviews collected by Virtanen (ibid.), that in order to make a distribution deal there needs to be mutual understanding between the producer and the distributor regarding the potential target audience of the film.

Release strategies, windows and box office revenues

If in one respect the distributor functions as the gatekeeper towards the production in terms of distribution deals and financing, in another respect her gatekeeping role involves the selling and marketing of the films. As this chapter focuses on theatrical releases, this means analysing the relationship between the distributor and the exhibitor as well as, to at least some extent, audiences in the case of marketing. As mentioned earlier on, the recent interest within the academia to study film distribution is due to the potential impacts digitalisation could have on disrupting the existing structures of it. Certainly, recent technological developments have changed the landscape of distribution in many respects. Indeed, taking the digitalisation of cinemas as an example, it has become possible to have a film premiere in several places simultaneously as expensive film copies and the logistics tied to that particular format are now a thing of the past. In Finland, the digitalisation of cinemas was subsidised by public funding allocated by the Finnish Film Foundation and had a significant effect for cinemas especially in smaller towns and rural locations. According to public discourse on the topic, smaller cinemas were rescued by the shift to digital technology. As for the technological developments disrupting the existing distribution models, the most enthusiastic accounts have described the possible impacts as revolutionary. However, such a description is an exaggeration of the changes to date. For example, Crisp (2015, p. 22) has pointed out that while the media landscape is always undergoing some shifts, there are plenty of those "who wish to protect their interests by enabling the continuation of the status quo." Therefore, while changes have taken place in distributing films to theatres in Finland, the changes have been subtle and haven't had a big impact on the overall structure of theatrical distribution.

Kolehmainen et al. (2013, p. 6) studied how digitalisation of film in theatre release affected the Finnish film industry's practices and profitability. This study was conducted quite early on after the digitalisation of cinemas had been completed with the help of public funding. In their early remarks on the impact of digitalisation on business practices, they noted that while producers, distributors and exhibitors all have their own domain, some mixing up of functions had started to happen. As an example they put forward that digitalisation made it easier for the producers to distribute their own films. Now some years on, such mixing up of roles is still scarce if barely visible. The biggest feature length fiction films produced in Finland are still distributed to cinemas by the "traditional" distribution companies. Another issue linked to the digitalisation of distribution is the question of release windows, meaning the time between a film is exhibited in a cinema and before it is released in other formats or today more commonly on another platform. Distributors and cinemas in Finland have held on to a conventional four-month theatrical release window, before the film can be released in other formats or platforms. There have been some exceptions that have broken the traditional boundaries and tried out alternative strategies regarding the theatrical windows. One recent example that received a considerable amount of publicity was *Teit meistä kauniin* (2016). The film was released on Elisa Viihde VOD platform a month after its theatrical release. This then lead to the film being kicked out of several cinemas as soon as the news of its VOD release went public. However, there were a few individual cinemas that kept screening the film.

Just like distribution deals, release strategies are case specific and vary depending on the film. According to a Finnish distribution professional, some films are better released first on fewer screens and then moving on to wider distribution depending on the film's performance. Exhibition schedules are made only for the following week and based on how well the film has performed the previous week or weekend. This could be seen as one of the downsides of digitalisation, there's an excess of films on offer and they can be moved around quickly. Another downside of this excess is that smaller cinemas don't necessarily have the capacity to screen as many films as their larger competitors because their 'prime time' is limited to one or two slots in the evening. In the case of domestic feature length films there seems to be some room for negotiation in regards to release strategies among the industry professionals. For example, if there are several domestic productions coming out around the same time, distributors have been known to negotiate to some extent a longer gap between the releases. This inevitably benefits the exhibitors as well due to them getting a steadier flow of domestic releases. Such an arrangement is however not always possible and certainly doesn't apply to international films as they are released in the same schedule around the world.

The distributors make their income out of the box office revenues of each film that they distribute. How the revenues are shared between the distributor, exhibitor and producer are divided is confidential information and there is no way of knowing what percentage each partner gets. However, the estimate is that the exhibitors keep approximately half of the box office revenues which leaves the other half to be divided between the distributor and the producer based on the shares agreed in the distribution deal. There has also been a recent widely publicised disagreement in Finland regarding the issue of how the box office revenues should be divided. This happened in 2017, between the largest distributor of Finnish feature length films, Nordisk Film and the leading cinema theatre chain Finnkino. The disagreement began as Finnkino demanded a larger cut from the box office revenues than before, this lead to Finnkino announcing that they won't be exhibiting the Finnish comedy *Yösyöttö* (2016) in their theaters. Despite of the disagreement lasting for a few months the film was able to reach an audience that was possibly bigger than what it would have been without the publicity the disagreement brought it. As Finnkino is the leading cinema chain in Finland, it meant that the distributor lost several screens from the original release strategy due to the disagreement. However, alternative options were widely publicised and the film got extra screenings in many other theaters. On top of this it was shown at pop up cinemas and auditoriums to make up for the initial loss of screens. Approximately two months after the public disagreement between the distributor and the exhibition company, it was announced that they had reached an agreement and the film in question was going to be shown in Finnkino's cinemas after all. The film went on to have over 200 000 admissions which can be considered as a box office success in the domestic market.

Moving away from the formal distribution

Even though the majority of domestic feature length fiction films are distributed by the larger traditional distribution companies, there are some examples of alternative ways of distributing films in Finland that have been pursued by some production companies. 'Direct distribution' is a distribution model which acknowledges the expertise of the distribution gatekeepers, while leaving the control of the distribution rights to the producer. The way it works is that the production company will not sign a deal with a distribution company, but instead hire a distribution consultant to sell and market the film (Smits 2017, pp. 124–125).

Such a model, or variations of it, have been used by some Finnish production companies. However, in terms of acquiring production support from the Finnish Film Foundation for a production planned to be distributed through direct distribution, it inevitably means that the production company needs to be able to show that they have sufficient capital to make up for the advance payment that a traditional distribution company would normally contribute to the production budget.

Continuing from the previous example of *Teit meistä kauniin* (2016) film's production company Optipari Oy distributes their films employing a strategy close to what could be defined as 'direct distribution' which enables the production company to exercise control over distribution rights. They do most of the work that a traditional distribution company would do such as marketing and communications, billing of theatres, exhibition rights, DVD rights and the logistics of delivering the film to the company that provides the service system for digitally distributing the films into theatres. However, they also purchase a service from Kuusan Kino distribution company who then takes care of distributing the digital exhibition links to the theatres, booking of screens as well as reporting the admission figures. There are at least two other Finnish companies that have alternative arrangements for distributing films, one through their own distribution brand and the other through a subsidiary. MRP Matila Röhr Productions Oy have their own brand MRP Distribution, but it should be noted that the majority of their own productions are still distributed through the larger and more traditional distribution companies. Production company BUFO on the other hand have a subsidiary under the name of B-Plan Distribution. B-Plan distributes films produced by BUFO, but they also take on films from other production companies both foreign and domestic. Their company description outlines that their aim is to 'further streamline the steps in between production, selling and distribution'.

Analysing distribution

As argued in the previous sections, the role of the film distributor entails much more than mere selling, marketing and distributing the film copies to exhibitors. The idea that film distributors are in fact gatekeepers is a fitting description of their function within the film industry. The Finnish model of funding feature length fiction films requires distributors to get involved already before a production is greenlighted. Not only is the minimum guarantee that the distributors pay to the production companies a crucial part of a production's budget, but a solid distribution plan and agreement are important pieces in the puzzle of applying for production support allocated by the Finnish Film Foundation. Therefore, acquiring a distribution deal could be seen as the key step for producing local films. This indicates that distributors have a dual role in terms of power within this system, through their financial contribution and through guaranteeing professional distribution of the film. According to Munoz and Ferrer-Roca (2017), local producers in New Zealand find it difficult to acquire distribution deals as the larger distribution companies aren't interested in small scale local productions and concentrate on big budget Hollywood films. On the other hand, they found that smaller 'independent' distributors were not able to take on local films as their livelihood depended on importing foreign titles. In New Zealand, the market share of admissions for local productions was only 2% in 2017 (European Audiovisal Observatory 2018, p. 49), whereas in Finland the market share of admissions for domestic films in the same year was 27.4% (The Finnish Film Foundation 2018, p. 17). Out of this rather shallow comparison, it could be concluded that in Finland it is worth the distributors' effort to make distribution deals with local producers. However, as outlined earlier, in recent years one distribution company Nordisk Film have distributed more domestic films than any other distribution company. In terms of critical enquiry, this could be seen as a problematic setting where power is concentrated to the hands of the few larger distribution companies. However, smaller distribution companies don't have the financial resources to take on as many local productions, at the same time. Thus, this would mean that if the larger distribution companies would cease financing local productions, a smaller number of domestic films would be produced. This might then lead to the same problem as producers currently have in New Zealand, where the efforts of most distributors would be directed to foreign titles.

Digitalisation has brought with it technological developments that have eased the logistics of film distribution. In the early stages of digital distribution these developments were often described as 'revolutionary'. However, a revolution would mean significant power shifts and renewal of prevailing structures. Looking at how film distribution has developed in these past few years, the developments have been less revolutionary and more adapting the already existing structures to digital working environments. Having said that, now that physical film copies are a thing of the past, the exhibitors even in small town cinemas are able to premiere the films at the same with larger cities. Power shifts, on the other hand, have been from non-existent to subtle. In theory, digitalisation could mean that the producers could leave the middleman out and distribute the films themselves.

However, while some alternative arrangements have been seen in terms of how producers organise their distribution, the majority of Finnish feature length films are still distributed by traditional distribution companies and traditional release strategies. Alternative release strategies include direct distribution which means buying the expertise and services of distribution professionals for film distribution while not entering a traditional distribution agreement and managing the distribution rights in-house. Direct distribution is not to be confused with self distribution which is an alternative strategy that has so far been popular only among up and coming filmmakers where the film is usually uploaded online (for free) in the hopes of reaching a wide audience (Smits 2017, p. 125). Through case studies, Smits (2017) has pointed out that alternative distribution models aren't widely used as they require so much attention and effort from the side of the production company. The idea of managing the production, marketing and distribution strategies at the same time might be one of the reasons producers do not find the alternative distribution models attractive. In the case of producing feature length fiction films, an alternative distribution model inevitably also means that the production company would have to have sufficient financing to make up for the part that a distributor usually pays in advances.

Although only scratching the surface of analysing film distribution in Finland, the rather descriptive account produced in this chapter indicates several important opportunities for further research. First of all, as the distribution deal is a crucial step in a film's lifecycle, we need studies concentrating on analysing why certain films get distribution deals when others don't. Additionally, as there are only a handful of distributors that control the market in Finland, it would be an important contribution to this field to research the power relations in decision making when it comes to distribution deals. Who is it that decides which films are picked for distribution at the early stages of pre-production and on what basis are these decisions made? As for alternative distribution strategies, an in-depth analysis of the current cases would shed light on what works and what doesn't in terms of these alternative models on the Finnish market. Perhaps alternative models of distribution could be more widely exploited and thus provide the producers with more freedom in terms of their productions. In summary, Hollywood dominates film distribution globally and Finland is no exception to that. Local cinema, however successful Finnish films are on the domestic market, is dominated by the distribution of Hollywood films through subsidiaries of large international companies.

References

Crisp, V. *Film Distribution in the Digital Age: Pirates and Professionals.* Palgrave Basingstoke: Macmillan, 2015. Available at EBSCOhost (Accessed 9 October 2018).

Deuze, M. *Media Work.* Cambridge: Polity, 2007.

European Audiovisual Observatory. *Focus 2018: World Film Market Trends.* Cannes: Marche du Film, 2018.

Hardy, J. *Critical Political Economy of the Media: An Introduction.* Abingdon: Routledge, 2014.

Kolehmainen, K., J. Jaalivaara, A. Talvitie, A. Viertola, and M. Westman. *Digitalisoitumisen vaikutus elokuva-alan kannattavuuteen ja toimintatapoihin elokuvateatterijakelussa Suomessa.* 2013. Available at: http://ses.fi/fileadmin/dokumentit/Digitalisoitumisen_vaikutus_elokuva-alan_kannattavuuteen_ja_toimintatapoihin_elokuvateatteri-jakelussa_Suomessa.pdf. (Accessed: 9 October 2018).

Lobato, R. Subcinema: "Theorizing Marginal Film Distribution". *Limina: A Journal of Historical and Cultural Studies* 13 (2007): 113–20.

Miller, T., N. Govil, J. McMurria, R. Maxwell, and T. Wang, *Global Hollywood 2.* London: British Film Institute, 2005.

Munoz, A., and N. Ferrer-Roca. "Film Distribution in New Zealand: Industrial Organization, Power Relations and Market Failure". *Media Industries* 4, no. 2 (2017): 1–21.

Smits, R. "Gatekeeping and Networking Arrangements: Dutch Distributors in the Film Distribution Business". *Poetics* 58 (2016): 29–42.

Smits, R. "Film Distribution: A Changing Business". In *DVD, Blu-Ray and Beyond: Navigating Formats and Platforms within Media Consumption,* edited by J. Wroot and A. Willis. Palgrave Macmillan: Cham 2017. Available at: ProQuest Ebook Central (Accessed: 5 October 2018).

Smits, R., A. Higson, H.D. Jones, J. Mateer, B. D'Ippolito. "Distributing Films Online. Workshop report". *Journal of British Cinema and Television* 15, no. 2 (2018): 291–9.

The Finnish Film Foundation. *Fact and Figures 2013.* Helsinki: The Finnish Film Foundation, 2014. Available at: http://ses.fi/fileadmin/dokumentit/Elokuvavuosi_2013.pdf (Accessed: 5 October 2018).

The Finnish Film Foundation. *Fact and Figures 2014.* Helsinki: The Finnish Film Foundation, 2015. Available at: http://ses.fi/fileadmin/dokumentit/Elokuvavuosi_2014_Facts_Figures.pdf (Accessed: 5 October 2018).

The Finnish Film Foundation. *Fact and Figures 2015*. Helsinki: The Finnish Film Foundation, 2016. Available at: http://ses.fi/fileadmin/dokumentit/ Elokuvavuosi_2015_Facts_Figures.pdf (Accessed: 5 October 2018).

The Finnish Film Foundation. *Fact and Figures 2016*. Helsinki: The Finnish Film Foundation, 2017a. Available at: http://ses.fi/fileadmin/dokumentit/ Elokuvavuosi_2016_Facts_Figures.pdf (Accessed: 5 October 2018).

The Finnish Film Foundation. *Support Guidelines 1 January 2017*. Helsinki: The Finnish Film Foundation, 2017b. Available at: http://ses.fi/fileadmin/ dokumentlt/FFF_Support_Guidelines.pdf (Accessed: 5 October 2018).

The Finnish Film Foundation. *Fact and Figures 2017*. Helsinki: The Finnish Film Foundation, 2018. Available at: http://ses.fi/fileadmin/dokumentit/ Elokuvavuosi_Facts_Figures_2017.pdf (Accessed: 5 October 2018).

Virtanen, J. *Roolitusprosessi tuotannollisesta näkökulmasta* (Master's theses). Helsinki: Aalto University, 2012.

Wasko, J. *How Hollywood Works*. London: SAGE, 2003. Available at: EBSCOhost (Accessed: 5 October 2018).

Terje Gaustad, Anne-Britt Gran, and Øyvind Torp

Digitizing local cinema:
Lessons on diversity from Norway

Abstract Digitization contains a promise of limitlessness, and the digitization of local cinemas is typically associated with intentions and expectations of greater repertory diversity. Yet, in the case of local cinemas, the promise of limitlessness encounters not only the physical constrains of single or few screens, which is typical of many local cinemas, but also the constraining influences of market forces. In theory, the self-regulated market can both increase and reduce diversity. Chris Anderson's "Long Tail"-theory predicts that, with digital technology, local cinema film supply and consumption will be spread over a greater number of titles. However, Anita Elberse's "Blockbuster"-theory predicts the opposite effect, that digitized local cinemas would increasingly focus on few, popular titles to maximize attendance. This chapter studies the repertory effects of digitizing Norwegian local cinemas. Within a period from 2009 to 2012, all local cinemas were equipped with digital projection technology, making Norway the first country in the world to fully digitize its cinemas. Yet, due to a virtual print fee introduced to finance the conversion, parts of the "analogue" business model stayed in force until 2016, when the fee was retracted. By studying local cinema repertory and attendance in 2008, 2013 and 2017 we can thus draw a picture of how digital technology affected local cinema in Norway. As to the effects of globalization and digitalization on cultural homogenization our results are ambivalent: We find elements of long-tail effects in the form of a greater number of culturally diverse titles offered to local patrons, but also blockbuster effects as local supply and demand remains concentrated around popular titles.

Keywords: Local cinemas, digitization, diversity, blockbuster effect, long-tail effect

Introduction

Digitization contains a promise of limitlessness, and is intuitively associated more with developments in home video than in local cinemas. Where it is easy to relate the endless shelf space and flexible viewing experience of video-on-demand streaming services with digital limitlessness, listings of your typical single-screen local cinema reveals that even digitized cinemas are limited in terms of screening capacity and times. Yet, digitization may affect local cinemas in a number of ways. First, digital projection and operation offer operators greater programming flexibility. Switching films between screenings used to imply unloading and loading heavy and cumbersome film roles, but with digital technology it can be done at the push of a button and programmed in advance. Second, digital distribution offers operators greater and easier access to a variety of titles as the shipping of expensive and heavy film rolls is replaced by transfer of digital files. Also, digital technology offers better sound and picture quality, especially for many local cinemas that previously had to wait for film rolls first playing in bigger, urban cinemas and thus being worn and torn on arrival in local cinemas. Eliminating such delays furthermore allows local cinemas to offer more relevant titles as there is no scarcity of digital copies. In these and other ways digitization has considerable impact on local cinemas, introducing elements of digital limitlessness to the limited physical world.

Digitization of local cinemas matters not only for the cinema and wider film businesses, but as cinema is a cultural event, it matters also for cultural policy. Cinemas offer public arenas in which audiences enjoy, in an activity of intense and relatively sustained attention, the performance of a particular film. In local cinemas, where some of the audience may be acquainted with each other, the cinema belongs to the community while the film typically comes from outside. The cinema admission provides two distinct but combined things: the possibility of viewing a film and the cinema as an anticipated experience. Anticipation of a pleasurable performance, the performance of a particular film and the performance of cinema itself, is what prompts the exchange of money and access (Ellis 1982) (see also Lesson in this volume). Combined market studies suggests that there are four major factors determining whether people decide to go and see a film: (a) the quality of the film itself; (b) the location of the cinema; (c) the starting time of the screening; and (d) the overall quality of the cinema (Finney and Triana 2015). The latter three is directly related to the local cinema, while the first is film-related and indirectly related to the cinema through its repertoire choices. A local cinema's impact on theatrical film consumption in its community can therefore hardly be overstated, particularly for communities where the distance to cinemas in neighboring communities preclude them as viable or attractive alternatives. How digitization affects local cinemas influences an important part of local cultural offerings and consumption and is therefore a matter of cultural policy on both local and national levels.

In this chapter we show how the digitization of Norwegian local cinemas and distribution influenced local cinema and attendance, producing greater repertoire diversity while at the same time preserving a market firmly concentrated around the most popular films. The Norwegian experience offers unique lessons on the effects of digitization because: (a) all local cinemas were more or less concurrently digitized within a relatively short period, and (b) a central database operated by the cinema owners' association offers detailed data on both film supply and sales throughout the period, allowing us to accurately track changes in repertoire, screenings and attendance. The rest of the chapter is organized as follows: In the next section we review the literature on digitization-effects, before we describe the process of digitizing Norwegian local cinemas. Then follows a section on empirical methods and data. The following three sections provide descriptions and discussions of findings, and the final section conclusions.

Diversity or concentration?

Competing theories suggest that digitization may create greater diversity or greater concentration in content markets such as film markets. According to the long-tail theory (Anderson 2006) digitization causes shifts in markets away from few hit products towards many niche products. On the supply side, physical limitations are greatly reduced or eliminated, and suppliers may furthermore use digital technology to tailor their offerings to market demands (Brynjolfsson, Hu, and Smith 2006, 2010). In cinema markets such supply side effects include lower costs of distributing films to cinemas and lower costs for cinemas to switch films between screenings. On the demand side, digital technology contributes to reducing consumers' search costs, making it easier to find content that suits their particular preferences (Brynjolfsson, Hu, and Simester 2011).

According to long-tail theory, when the costs of both supplying and consuming niche products drop, it creates incentives for retailers, in our case local cinemas, to increase the diversity in their offerings. Content providers, such as film producers and distributors, will have similar incentives to provide products targeting narrower segments of the markets. Two arguments from consumer behavior theory support the long-tail theory: first, greater diversity will enable consumers to find products that better fit their preferences (Kahn 1998), and, second, consumers value greater variety in itself (Kahn 1995). So according to this, a cinemagoer will value a diverse offering not only because more movies are likely to match her taste and preferences, but also because she will value the variety in itself.

When blockbuster-theory suggests that digitization has the opposite effect on diversity, with increased consumption of the most popular titles at the expense of the less popular, it is primarily due to different consumer behavior assumptions (Elberse 2008, 2013). If consumers face a great variety, making a choice may become overwhelming, confusing and frustrating, an effect coined by Gourville and Soman (2005) as *overchoice*. From this perspective, great diversity in the supply of a product or service is not necessarily of positive value for consumers.

The blockbuster-theory is also based on empirical research showing that consumers tend to floc towards the most popular titles, no matter how diverse the supply. Rosen (1981) refers to this as the superstar effect, which he explains as follows: first, a lesser talent will always be a poor substitute for a better talent, so why should anyone listen to the world's second best tenor if they could listen to the best. Second, as new technology brings the marginal cost of distribution down towards zero, products with broad appeal will benefit more from scale economies than those with narrower appeal.

In their discussion of *winner-takes-all* markets Frank and Cook (1995) also argue that superstars may appear out of consumer behavior. Due to their social nature, people often wish to view the same films as others, and this creates positive network-effects making popular titles dominant.

In sum, theory tells us that digitization may lead to more diversity in the form of a broader supply better serving and satisfying different niches among audience tastes, and it may lead to less diversity with consumption concentrating around the most popular titles. Which of these effects that materialize and dominate will to a large degree depend on consumer behavior and preferences among the cinema-going audience. The blockbuster effect may dominate when tastes are homogenous, while long-tail effect is likely to be stronger the better a diverse offering satisfies audience preferences.

Digitizing Local Cinemas in Norway

When the last Norwegian cinema switched from analogue to digital projection in 2012, Norway was the first country in the world to reach 100 percent digital cinema penetration (Film and Kino 2012b). A coordinated roll-out that involved all Norwegian cinemas started only three years earlier, and four years later the removal of a temporary fee for digital bookings, used to finance the roll-out, marked the conclusion of the digitization process.

A political decision was made by the Norwegian Ministry of Culture in 2007 to support digitization of cinemas with public funding. The primary cultural policy objective was not related to cinema repertoire, but to securing a future for local cinemas. People should have access to cinema no matter if they live in urban or rural communities also after the introduction of digital cinema (Norwegian Ministry of Culture 2007). One feared that, without public support, local cinemas would not be able to carry the necessary, but substantial, investments into digital equipment. And that, if so, digitization would only benefit larger urban cinemas while local cinemas would run out of business with outdated analogue equipment. Yet, even if regional policy may have dominated the decision-making, repertoire concerns were also voiced. The government emphasized that cinemas should not only participate, but they should retain control over repertoire choices. The cinema owners' association, Film and Kino, which were delegated the responsibility for implementing and coordinating the digitization process, added as specific objectives that digitization should secure also the distribution of films appealing to narrow and niche audiences and local cinemas' access to films concurrent with their national premiers (Film and Kino 2012a). As such, policy objectives were related to both safeguarding a digital transition of local cinema and to repertoire diversity.

The total cost of digitizing cinemas was split three ways between the government, which contributed about 30 percent, the cinema owners, also carrying about 30 percent, and the film distributors who contributed 40 percent (Film and Kino 2012a). Distributors carried the largest share as they would also benefit from the biggest savings by abandoning the production and shipping of expensive and heavy film rolls in favor of digital copies, Digital Cinema Packages (DCP), which were first sent on small external hard disks and later online. Their contribution was organized, as it has been in many countries, though payments of a fee per booking of a film, known as a Virtual Print Fee (VPF). It was charged for the first 90 bookings of a film, which on a Norwegian scale represents a very wide release. However, this encouraged distributors to saturate releases of popular films as cinemas beyond the first 90 could be added at no cost. For films targeting narrower audience segments, the VPF represented a challenge since distributors sometimes would decline requests made by local cinemas if they estimated revenues below the VPF cost. To compensate reduce the frequency of such declines a booking support system was established and operated by Film & Kino from 2010 to 2013. Despite the cost of VPF, distributors realized substantial savings from digital distribution, and by mid-2016 the VPF was abolished as their total VPF-payments had covered their share of the digitization costs.

Empirical Method and Data

In this study local cinemas are defined as cinemas located in rural municipalities, according to Statistic Norway's Classification of centrality (Statistics Norway 2018). The classification is made by two sub-indexes based upon inhabitants' travel time to workplaces and service functions, and is operationalized on a 6-point scale. We define the three least central codes on this scale as the rural municipalities, and it is within these municipalities the local cinemas are being located. Urban neighborhood cinemas are thus excluded, even though they may be defined as local cinemas.

By examining film supply and ticket sales in local cinemas during three periods, each of one full calendar year, throughout the digitization process we can assess how cinema offerings and audience attendance change with each step of cinema digitization. We use data for 2008, which was the last year before the digitization process roll-out, for 2013, which was the first year all cinemas operated with digital equipment, and for 2017, which was the first year of operation with both digital technology and economy (without VPF).

We use a comprehensive database of daily screenings and ticket sales per film title and cinema obtained from the cinema owners' association, Film & Kino, that tracks all cinema screenings and ticket sales in Norway. All distributors and cinemas continuously feed the central database with data on films, screenings and attendance, and it is recorded per cinema, enabling us to identify and subtract local cinema data. It thus provides complete sales and screening data of all films released on any Norwegian local cinema and allows us to avoid working with samples within each of the three years studied.

To assess diversity, we divide films in three categories by origin: national films, which generally are considered valuable contributions to national and local culture and identity; American films, which in general are seen as representing 'global cinema'; and other foreign films, which generally are seen to represent cultural diversity as a supplement to national films and American entertainment cinema. These are broad categories based on the nationality of the (main) production company, and films are not coded for other dimensions of cultural diversity. Yet, given the global dominance of American entertainment cinema (Waterman 2005), the categories provide a relevant measure for diversity in many countries outside the USA.

To further assess changes in diversity and concentration of film supply and consumption we study the distribution of film screenings and ticket sales among all titles released each year, following a method applied by Murphy (1984) and others (Elberse 2008; Kumar, Smith, and Telang 2014; Vogel 2015) to create Lorenz curves showing the skewness in both market access and attendance. Since increases in screenings or sales for popular titles can reflect either a blockbuster effect or a surge affecting the whole market, we use market shares rather than absolute screening and attendance numbers to control for this potential bias. It allows us to study changes in distribution of relative market access and sales between popular and niche films by comparing Lorenz curves for each year.

Quantitative data on films, screenings and attendance is supplemented with qualitative data from a workshop with representatives from Film & Kino including cinema owners and operators, where digitization and diversity were discussed partly based on a presentation of preliminary quantitative findings.

Local cinema supply and demand

The physical infrastructure of local cinema remained stable throughout period in which Norwegian cinemas were digitized in terms of screens on offer. The total count of local cinemas was 138 in 2008 and 137 in 2017. Most of these, about three out of four, are single-screen cinemas, while the rest are multiplexes with two or three screens. None has four or more.

Yet, local cinemas offered significantly more cinema-going opportunities as they were digitized. The total number of screenings increased by 41 percent from 2008 to 2017, from an average of 1.1 per day in 2008 to 1.5 in 2013, and to 1.6 per day in 2017. This may still seem low, but not all have daily screenings as they are also used for other purposes. Digital technology has thus allowed local cinemas to utilize their physical infrastructure better, offering local patrons more screenings within the confines of the existing buildings.

A major anticipated improvement of local cinema from digitization was the ability for local cinemas to access copies of films at the time of their national premiere and avoid the wait for prints, during which the general interest in the title would naturally decline. Right before cinemas were digitized in 2008, local cinemas in average had to wait for four weeks from the national premiere until they could launch their local premiere. By 2013 the average lag between national and local premiere had dropped to six days, and by 2017 further to four days. The average delays measured in 2013 and 2017 are mostly a natural result of single-screen cinemas not being able to show all national premieres on the same day, but having to prioritize so that some are first shown with one or a few days' delay. Hence, the lag caused by print access is eliminated, and this has much improved local cinemas ability to offer their patrons relevant titles.

As may be anticipated with the combination of more frequent screenings and more relevant titles, attendance figures for local cinemas were also up following the digitization. Local cinema attendance increased 18 percent from 2008 to 2017, while it dropped five percent on a national level (including urban cinemas) in the same period. Most of the local cinema increase came between 2008 and 2013, when attendance was up 15 percent.

Local cinema repertoire

The number of titles, or unique films, release in local cinemas also increased significantly when cinemas were digitized. However, the rise in number of titles only came in the second phase, when distributors' contractual cost related to releasing in additional cinemas, the VPF, was eliminated. From 2008 to 2013, the number of titles release in local cinemas was actually down four percent, but by 2017 it was up 41 percent. To achieve greater diversity in titles, it thus seems like digital technology alone is not sufficient if the reduction in marginal costs of distribution to additional cinemas is not realized.

The rise in the number of titles was driven by national and "other foreign" titles, up 88 and 78 percent respectively, while the number of American titles remained relatively flat, up five percent. Consequently, the American share of all titles released in local cinemas dropped from 52 percent in 2008 to 39 percent in 2017, while national films went from 16 to 22 percent and other foreign films from 31 to 40 percent.

Since the increase in the number of titles is almost identical with the increase in screenings, the average number screenings allocated each film shown in local cinemas remains the same after cinemas were digitized as it was before. There are, however, major changes among national, American and other foreign films. While the number of American titles has remained relatively stable, the number of screenings given each American film has increased by 33 percent. For national films, however, which saw the number of titles increase by 88 percent, the number of screenings given each title is down 35 percent. For other foreign films than the American it is up five percent. This means that American films has retained their share of local cinema screenings at 66 percent, despite the strong increase in the number of other foreign and national titles.

The strong increase in national and other foreign titles is not matched by an equal rise in attendance for these titles, so the average attendance per title is down. This effect is strongest for national titles, which in 2017 on average had 50 percent lower attendance than in 2008. Attendance per other foreign title was also down, but only by eight percent. American titles, however, increased their average attendance by 22 percent.

Distribution of Screenings and Attendance

The film business has long been considered a winner-takes-all business, where results do not gravitate towards an average, but where extreme outcomes in the form of strong gains and steep losses are common (see e.g., De Vany 2004). Such distribution of outcomes have also been identified in the Norwegian film industry (Gaustad 2009). A basis for these extreme outcomes is the concentration of sales around the most popular titles. This is the point of departure for both the long-tail and blockbuster theories, and it is more than three decades since Murphy (1984) showed that, in the North American market, ten percent of films generate 50 percent of ticket sales.

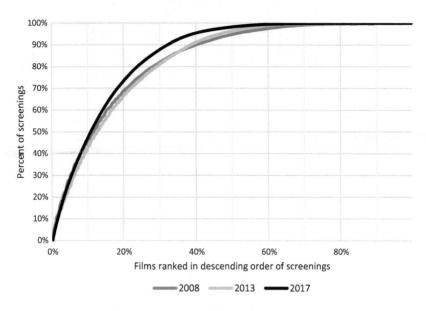

Fig. 1: Distribution of screenings among all films released in local cinemas each year.

As with other products, there is an interdependency between supply and demand (Elberse and Eliashberg 2003; Reibstein and Farris 1995). Cinema operators will choose films based on their own assessments of demand and other factors, and following the local premiere adjust screening schedules according to actual attendance. On the other hand, distributors' marketing investments will depend on screening commitments from the cinemas as they will not be willing to market films that are not made available to audiences. Due to this dynamic interdependency between supply and demand for specific titles, we examine changes in both the concentration of screenings and attendance.

The skewness of the allocation of screenings between films has increased with the digitization of local cinemas. The Lorenz curves in Fig. 1 below show that ten percent of films, those most extensively screened, take about 45–50 percent of the screening capacity, and that 50 percent of the films take more than 95 percent of the screenings. The 2017-curve shows the highest concentration, particularly in the 5–50 percent interval of films, indication that digitization is creating a blockbuster effect in the supply of films. However, the 2013-curve stays below the 2008-curve for the 35 percent most screened films, indicating a long-tail effect. Hence, the blockbuster effect seems primarily to be driven by an increase in the number of titles. When there is a slight dip in titles combined with more

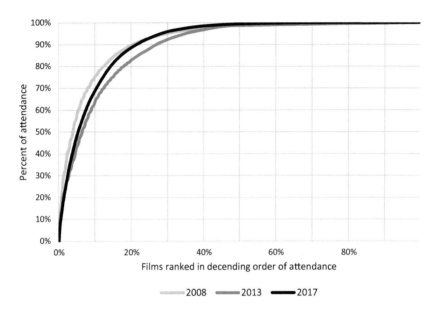

Fig. 2: Distribution of attendance among all films release in local cinemas each year.

screenings, between 2008 and 2013, the screenings become slightly more evenly distributed. The sharp rise in titles between 2013 and 2018 consists mostly of national and other foreign films with the effect that more of the American popular films ends up in the top percentiles of most screened films.

The skewness of attendance between films is stronger than for screenings, but has not increased with the digitization of local cinemas. The Lorenz curves in Fig. 2 below shows that ten percent of films, those with the highest attendance, take about 60–75 percent of total attendance, and that 50 percent of the films take about 99 percent of the attendance. Corresponding to the screening data, the 2013-curve stays under the 2008-curve, indicating a long-tail effect when there is a slight drop in the number of titles. When the number of titles rises in 2017 concentration increases, but not above the 2008-level for the 25 percent most seen films.

The rise of local cinema self-distributed films

With digitized distribution it has become easier for local cinema operators to license films from other sources than normal film distributors. This has triggered a rise of self-distribution among local cinemas, where the cinema operator licenses titles directly from producers or foreign distributors, arranges for delivery of the digital print, and markets the films to their patrons. The phenomena is similar to 'direct distribution', as described by Grundstöm in this volume, but represents a pull-version initiated by cinemas rather than the push-version initiated by producers. One cinema operator from a community with a substantial number of foreign workers told us that he has started importing films directly from their home countries, which he screens in original language versions in time slots when attendance from native patrons would typically be low. This enables him both to offer highly relevant titles for particular audience segments and to increase attendance in otherwise 'slow' timeslots.

In 2008, before local cinemas were digitized, self-distributed films counted less than ten percent of the titles distributed, and more than three out of four of these films were Norwegian. By 2017 the number of self-distributed films was more than tripled, with a 214 percent increase, representing about 20 percent of all titles. The increase was strongest for American and other foreign films. Consequently, the national share was reduced to 45 percent, with the rest quite evenly divided between American and other foreign films.

As these self-distributed films are typically only shown a few times in a single local cinema they are representing only marginal shares of the total screening capacity and audience, however they draw the highest average audience per screening. Attendance per screening is particularly high for national self-distributed films: In 2017 the average was 81, compared with an average of 25 for all films in regular distribution. One reason seems to be that they represent hyperlocal content such as documentaries about the local community or region and low-budget dramas from local filmmakers. The case of local cinemas' self-distributed films provides an illustration of how digitization in certain situations may enable films based on local storytelling traditions to outperform those designed to reach global and culturally unspecified audiences, and it is an example of how digitization does not only promote globalization, but also localization (Friedman 1990).

Conclusions

While our study does not fully support the main tenet of the critical theory of technology (see Stocchetti in this volume), it does not offer a clear-cut counter story either. Rather, it suggests that we may better understand the effects of digitization and globalization on local cinema as many heterogeneous stories creating a more ambiguous narrative.

In some important ways film repertoire and consumption in local Norwegian cinemas has turned more culturally diverse. With digitized projection and distribution, local cinemas make better use of their physical structure in the sense that they offer patrons substantially more screenings than they used to. They also offer more relevant titles and a greater diversity. Local cinemas no longer have to wait for available copies of the films they wish to show, and the number of unique films shown has increased as much as the number of screenings. Furthermore, the increase is primarily in titles typically associated with cultural diversity, those of national origin and from foreign countries other then the USA. Local patrons seem to appreciate these changes as admissions to local cinemas are up in a period where there has been an overall slight decline.

Yet both local supply and demand remains concentrated around popular titles. Each American film is given more screenings and draw larger local audiences than they used to, while the average admission to other films has declined. Niche titles draw niche audiences to limited screenings, some filling cinemas to record levels, but in total this newfangled diversity takes place in a very long but narrow tail of the demand curve, while popular films continue to serve popular tastes in the much wider head of the curve.

For local patrons of culture, digitization of cinemas may not offer limitlessness, but our findings suggest is has provided more experiences of pleasurable performance.

References

Anderson, Chris. *The Long Tail: Why the Future of Business Is Selling Less of More*. New York: Hyperion, 2006.

Brynjolfsson, Erik, Hu, Yu Jeffrey, and Duncan Simester. "Goodbye Pareto Principle, Hello Long Tail: The Effect of Search Costs on the Concentration of Product Sales." *Management Science* 57, no. 8 (2011): 1373–86.

Brynjolfsson, Erik, Hu, Yu Jeffrey, and Michael D. Smith. "From Niches to Riches: Anatomy of the Long Tail." *MIT Sloan Management Review* 47, no. 4, 67–71.

Brynjolfsson, Erik, Hu, Yu Jeffrey, and Michael D. Smith. "Long Tails Vs. Superstars: The Effect of Information Technology on Product Variety and Sales Concentration Patterns." *Information Systems Research* 21, no. 4 (2010): 736–47.

De Vany, Arthur. *Hollywood Economics: How Extreme Uncertainty Shapes the Film Industry*. London: Routledge, 2004.

Elberse, Anita. "Should You Invest in the Long Tail?" *Harvard Business Review* 86, no. 7–8 (2008): 88–96.

Elberse, Anita. *Blockbusters: Hit-Making, Risk-Taking, and the Big Business of Entertainment.* New York: Henry Holt, 2013.

Elberse, Anita, and Jehoshua Eliashberg. "Demand and Supply Dynamics of Sequentially Released Products in International Markets: The Case of Motion Pictures." *Marketing Science* 22, no. 4 (2003): 329–354.

Ellis, John. *Visible Fictions.* London: Routledge, 1982.

Film & Kino. *Ettårs evaluering av digitaliseringen av norske kinoer.* Oslo: Film & Kino, 2012a.

Film & Kino. *Høring av utkast til endringer i film – og videogramloven med forskrifter.* Oslo: Film & Kino, 2012b.

Finney, Angus, and Eugenio Triana. *The International Film Business: A Market Guide beyond Hollywood.* 2nd ed. New York: Routledge, 2015.

Frank, Robert H., & Philip J. Cook. *The Winner-Take-All Society.* New York: The Free Press, 1995.

Friedman, Jonathan. "Being in the World: Globalization and Localization." *Theory, Culture & Society* 7 (1990): 311–28.

Gaustad, Terje. "Sweetening the Deal: To What Extent Can Public Funding Attract Private Film Investors?" *Nordicom Review* 30, no. 2 (2009): 179–97.

Gourville, John T., and Dilip Soman. "Overchoice and Assortment Type: When and Why Variety Backfires." *Marketing Science* 24, no. 3 (2005): 382–95.

Grundström, Heidi. "Film Distribution in Finland: Gatekeepers of Local Cinema." In *Political Economy of Local Cinema in the Digital Age: A Critical Approach*, edited by A. Rajala, D. Lindblom, and Matteo Stocchetti. Bern, Switzerland: Peter Lang, 2020.

Kahn, Barbara E. "Consumer Variety-Seeking among Goods and Services." *Journal of Retailing and Consumer Services* 2, no. 3 (1995): 139–148.

Kahn, Barbara E. "Dynamic Relationships with Customers: High Variety Strategies." *Journal of the Academy of Marketing Science* 26, no. 1 (1998): 45–53.

Kumar, Anuj, Smith, Michael D., and Rahul Telang. "Information Discovery and the Long Tail of Motion Picture Content." *Mis Quarterly* 38, no. 4 (2014): 1057–78.

Lesson, B. "In Quest of the Commonness: The Lo-Bal Process as Strategy of French Speaking Countries Film Exhibitors." In *Political Economy of Local Cinema in the Digital Age: A Critical Approach*, edited by A. Rajala, D. Lindblom, and Matteo Stocchetti. Bern, Switzerland: Peter Lang, 2020.

Murphy, A.D. "Box Office." *Daily Variety* (1984, July 31).

Norwegian Ministry of Culture. *Veiviseren for det norske filmløftet. St.meld. nr. 22 (2006–2007)*. Oslo: Norwegian Ministry of Culture, 2007.

Reibstein, David J., and Paul W. Farris. "Market Share and Distribution: A Generalization, a Speculation, and Some Implications." *Marketing Science* 14, no. 3 (1995): G190–G202.

Rosen, Sherwin. "The Economics of Superstars." *The American Economic Review* 71, no. 5 (1981): 845–58.

Statistics Norway. Classification of centrality. (2018). Retrieved September 30, 2018, from https://www.ssb.no/en/klass/klassifikasjoner/128/om

Stocchetti, Matteo. "Critical Political Economy and Local Cinema: An Introduction." In *Political Economy of Local Cinema in the Digital Age: A Critical Approach*, edited by A. Rajala, D. Lindblom, and Matteo Stocchetti. Bern, Switzerland: Peter Lang, 2020.

Vogel, Harold L. *Entertainment Industry Economics: A Guide for Financial Analysis*. 9th ed. New York: Cambridge University Press, 2015.

Waterman, David. *Hollywood's Road to Riches*. Cambridge, MA: Harvard University Press, 2005.

Abdulrahman Alghannam

The political economy of Khaleeji cinema: Historical developments of Arab Gulf film industries

Abstract The chapter examines the local cinemas of six Arab Gulf States and how they struggle to maintain authenticity and recognition within the scholarship of national and transnational cinema. It highlights the lack of research about the Gulf region cinema and film industries in film studies and Arab cinema discourse. It introduces the term – Khaleeji – as a way for classification of the Gulf States' film industries that are based on shared and historical interests and struggles. The chapter traces the development of film and cinema from the 1930s to 2010s and the role of states and corporations on the transnational sphere of Gulf cinema and industry. The chapter argues for the need to examine the cinema of the Gulf States as one Khaleeji cinema, and looks at how the cinema as an industry has developed in the region, noting three essential stages that have been shaped by political-economic relations.

Keywords: Khaleeji cinema, Gulf Corporation Council, Film festivals, oil and cinema, United Arab Emirates, Qatar, Saudi Arabia, Kuwait, Bahrain, Oman, film industry, Gulf cinema

Introduction

The culture of the Gulf States and the broader MENA region (Middle East, North Africa, Afghanistan, and Pakistan) had a significant impact on the development of the cinema industries during the early days, as we shall see. The culture of the region must be considered as the result of a dynamic relation of power, formed along several axes. First, the relation between syncretic popular culture and elitist high culture. Second, between the different regional 'cultures' of various peoples and ethnic groups, religions, and languages. Third, between the indigenous culture as a whole and the influences that stem from other cultural environments. Even apparently 'authentic' movements like present-day fundamentalism or nationalism do not invalidate this model. Despite the parameters of Arabic language and Islam having, since national independence, been pushed increasingly into the foreground to serve as a starting point for cultural purification and preservation, the idea of a pure Arab-Muslim culture is a myth. Nationalism and Islamic fundamentalism, which may be considered movements of purification, are instead the product of modern mass culture and are shaped by mass movements and ideologies. The arrival of Western companies to exploit the riches of the oil in the region started the revolution 'exposing' the region to the socio-economic ways of the West, including the media.

The film medium was invented in the West at the end of the nineteenth century, a time in which significant parts of the Middle East and the Maghreb were already considered as British and French protectorates. Two decades later, through the Sykes-Picot agreement, the two superpowers had divided almost the whole Arab world between them. The result was a long-lasting political and economic dependency which, except in Egypt, considerably hampered the creation of national film industries and the development of Arab film culture. The Arab market was flooded by European products, essential areas of the economy were dominated by foreign investors, and native entrepreneurs were hardly able to survive.

Literature review

In the literature of film and cinema about the "Gulf", "Arabian Peninsula", there are at least two main misperceptions. First, the focus of the literature of Middle Eastern cinema(s) is on the study of the larger cinema industries such as the Egyptian, Iranian and Turkish industry. Even in the literature about Arab cinema, which focuses more on the theme, style and identity of Pan-Arabism than on its industrial configurations, the study of the cinema of the countries of the Arabian Peninsula has received little attention. Arab cinema scholarship commonly seeks to understand the cross-border activities and reception of art-house and mainstream films by paying close attention to Levant countries, such as Egypt, Iraq, Jordan, Lebanon, Palestine and Syria, as well as the Arab countries of Northern Africa, primarily Algeria, Morocco, Tunisia and Libya. The term 'Gulf cinema' or 'cinema of Gulf countries' is less examined in the literature of both Arab cinema and Middle Eastern cinema such as Viola Shafik (2007)'s *Arab Cinema: History and Cultural Identity*; Lina Khatib (2006)'s *Filming the Modern Middle East: Politics in the Cinemas of Hollywood and the Arab World*; Gönül Dönmez-Colin (2007)'s *The Cinema of North Africa and the Middle East*; Roy Armes (2015)'s *New Voices in Arab Cinema*; and Lura Marks (2015)'s *Hanan al-Cinema: Affections for the Moving Image*. These seminal works on Middle Eastern cinema and Arab cinema usually include the six Gulf countries, including countries such as Yemen and Iraq. In addition, these studies rarely examine the interconnection of cinematic practices, industry configuration and the transnational filmmaking and film consumption in the six Gulf countries.

The second problem in the bulk of academic discussion about the Gulf region cinema and film is the tendency to mix the notion of "Persian Gulf countries", which includes Iran, Iraq and Yemen – with the six Gulf countries members of the Gulf Corporation Council (GCC). To avoid this problem, in this study I propose to use William Beeman definition (2009) and to use the term Khaleeji or Khalijijs1 to indicate the six Gulf countries.[1]

In *For a Theory of Regional Cinemas: Middle Eastern, North African and Central Asian Cinemas*, Hamid Naficy (2008) highlights the rapid transformation in the role of the nation-state in the discussion on film and cinema of the 1990s as it emerges in the debates about National cinema, Third cinema, postcolonial cinema, world cinema and global cinema. Middle Eastern, North African and Central Asian countries are rarely included in these analysis. Naficy argues for a critical discourse of Regional Cinema that "discover and theorise the many contextual and textual similarities and shared features that run through both these societies and their artistic productions" (2008, p. 98). In fact, among the few works Naficy mentioned that attempt to situate the Middle Eastern, North African and Arab with concepts such as national cinema and postcolonial cinema, the six countries in Arabian Peninsula remained neglected case studies of these works in Regional Cinema.

Although few works frame the nascent state-level development and projects in the UAE and Qatar as part of the new Arab cinema,[2] applying the lenses of critical transnationalism to the Gulf States may provide an understanding of the transitional operations between the six countries that share a neglected history of cinema. Given the late development of local film and institutions in most of the Gulf States, this chapter aims to illustrate the historically tense relationship between state and cinema, including filmmaking and regulation, in most of the Gulf States since the last century.

The history of local cinema in the Gulf region is vital to our understanding of the development of contemporary film industries in the Gulf States. The analysis of political economists generally focus on the four components that are core to

---

1   Al-Khaleej (Arabic: الخليج) is an Arabic word which means Gulf. We will be using Khaleeji/Khalijis interchangeably to refer to people of the Arabian Peninsula, especially those associated with the Gulf Cooperation Council states.

2   Between 2006 and 2018, a number of researches examine the relationship between globalisation's effects and Gulf States' film and media developments and initiatives with its building of the modern Gulf State (Hudson 2017; Yunis 2011, Yunis 2015; Dickenson 2016; Leotta 2015; Iordanova 2014).

contemporary political economy research or "social change and history, social totality, moral philosophy, and Praxis" (Mosco 1996, p. 25). This research traces the historical process of capitalism and the growth and expansion of film and cinema enterprises and technologies, and the level of the state's intervention between the 1930s and the 2010s to show how these conditions affected the development of the development of the concept of Gulf cinema as transnational cinema.

What Khaleeji cinema means

As the cinema of Gulf state is seldom studied as part of the Middle East or Arab regional cinema, a transnational approach is vital to understand how transnational histories shaped national and regional cinemas. Gulf States' cinemas have seldom been regarded as part of the discourse of the Middle East or Arab regional cinema. In the next section, I endorse Hamid Naficy's call for a critical discourse of Regional cinema to "discover and theorise the many contextual similiarities and shared features that run through both these societies and their artistic productions" (Naficy 2008, 98), through a periodization that aims at pin point these similiarities and shared features across the Gulf countries. Before that, however, I would like to ground the analytical relevance of the concept of Khaleeji cinema on the anthropological approach of William Beeman (2009) and on Mette Hjort and Duncan Petrie notion of "small nation cinema".

Thus, my case rests on two notions. First, the geographical boundaries of the Gulf cinema and William Beeman's (2009) *Gulf Society: An Anthropological View of the Khalijis - Their Evolution and Way of Life*, where the term Khaliji is introduced "to make the case for these individuals as Gulf residents, independent of an exclusive Arab or Persian identity" and to scrutinize "the nature of the ethnic identity of the denizens of this region" (p. 147). Beeman (2009) continues:

> Communities become "imagined" when enough people believe they belong and develop symbols and institutions that unite them. The Gulf community is the opposite. It is an "unimagined community – a community in fact, but not in name and not in its social identification. The roots of its existence as a community are centuries-old and are now so commonplace that few of the people of the region bother to think about it. (p. 148)

Beeman (2009, p. 148) offers five candidates for scaling Khalijis, which include food, language, social customs and dress architecture. The chapter attempts to contextualize the cinema of the Khaliji and how it historically evolved the Gulf region as 'unimagined community'.

In *Locating Emirati Filmmaking within Globalising Media Ecologies*, Dale Hudson (2017) provides a profound understanding of the implication of globalisation on the filmmaking of the Emirate with reference to the 'Khaleeji' countries. Hudson (2017) argues that the emergence of the circuit of international film festivals and Khaleeji films "signal a different moment in the history of the Middle East, one that claims it is right to determine its articulation of modernity within the current flows and networks of globalisation". However, Hudson cautions that the Gulf States distinctive mode of "constructing, consolidating and contesting national identities" has to be carefully taken into account when examining the development of national and transnational filmmaking in the Gulf region. Hudson (2017, p. 184) explains that "critical self-representation by Gulf filmmakers that question *asala* and cosmopolitanism, thus, is important both at home and abroad as a corrective to misrepresentations and erasures". Hudson provides four critical factors that shape and construct the Emirati filmmaking today, and these can be applied to the regional Khaleeji filmmaking as well:

> (1) the relatively recent unification of distinct tribes and families into a single state in 1971; (2) historical marginalization of the Gulf emirates within Arab and Muslim cultures; (3) centuries-old cultural and economic ties to South Asia, Iran, and East Africa; and (4) cultural submersion by a majority expatriate population, including middle-class families and migrant 'bachelors' (men whose families are not permitted residency under their work visas) from South Asia that constitute a substantial percentage of the overall population, but also significant African, Arab, and Southeast Asian professionals and domestic workers. (Hudson 2017, p. 184)

The second element is the notion of "small nations cinema". Mette Hjort and Duncan Petrie (2007) delineate how globalization has had a significant influence on the nation-state, bringing about "aggressively transnational imperatives of finance capital, the deregulation of markets, the increasing geographical mobility of labour and the global penetration of communications networks facilitating business, information, entertainment and other forms of cultural exchange" (Hjort / Petrie 2007, p. 8). Mette Hjort and Duncan Petrie (2007) offer four criteria to think of small nation cinema: population, GDP, territory and history of rule by non-co-nationals. With small populations, small territories and a history of colonial rule, the cinema of Gulf States (and thus their filmmakers) face more significant challenges and difficulties than of other Arab states and filmmakers. The small cinema of Gulf filmmakers has been shaped by social, political-economic relations that resulted, deliberately and unintentionally, in various transnational alliances across the six Gulf countries. Hjort (2011, p. 1) explains that "the point of these measures is that they help us to be attuned to, and thus able to identify, the particular challenges that small nation film practitioners are likely to be grappling within any given case". In this way, the Gulf States' national model continues to offer a great understanding of Gulf cinema and filmmaking that is influenced by the politics of difference that emerge within such transnational flows.

Periodisation

The socio-political and economic developments of Gulf States remain the leading indicators for the periodization of cinema in the Gulf: the cinema before and after the introduction of foreign oil companies, the cinema after the State independence in the 1970s and the cinema following states' national diversification plans in the post-2000s. This research covers the three periods that shaped the development of film industries in the Gulf region by analysing the political-economic relations implied in its cinema.

(1) Khaleeji cinema and the rise of foreign oil companies

When cinema was invented, in the late 1890s, the Arabian region of the Gulf was a dynamic multicultural location for interregional trade and migration. In the early years of the 1900s, Gulf's dates and pearls were famous exports to markets in India, Europe and North America which contributed to flourishing Gulf merchant families and immigrant merchants (Bishara et al. 2016). This global demand for both commodities – before the collapse of the pearling economy in 1929 – introduced the Gulf region, with its intermixing of peoples and cultures, to the film medium. The presence of British and, in the early 1950s, American officials in the Gulf profoundly influenced the region's political-economic developments (Ulrichsen 2015, p. 7) but not cinema. The development of film exhibition and distribution in the Gulf States began to take shape in the 1940s under the control of foreign oil companies, few expatriate traders and local merchant families.

Film exhibition and distribution

Before the arrival of foreign oil companies in the Gulf countries, cinema had developed considerably with the movement of merchant families and expatriates from and to Asian countries, mostly India, through which the importation of

Indian films took shape (Al-Nouwairy 2011). Even though some points to the initial rejection of the idea of cinema by some religious groups, oil companies and individuals' efforts led to establishing the initial building blocks of cinema culture in their territories. At first, cinema came to the Gulf region through the efforts and dedication of locals and expatriates. The Mobile cinema started to take shape in the early 1920s in Bahrain and Kuwait, screening mostly Indian and Egyptian films. In Bahrain, Mahmoud al-Saati established in 1922 a small cottage located on the Bahraini seafront to screen films. The cinema theatre was equipped with cement floors to allow for as many people as possible, which at the time consisted of about thirty seats (Al-Nouwairy 2011). The location was carefully selected to attract the people waiting for the return of the dive ships (Sarhan 2005). In Kuwait, Izzat Jaafar brought the first film projector in 1936 and rented it for home usage for some of the wealthy people (Al-Nouwairy 2011).

In the 1930s, with the discovery of oil resources in the region, the Gulf States sought to attract foreign oil companies. Thus, the high financial returns of oil rents resulted in a period of economic boom. A few expatriate individuals and merchant families began to invest in the business of showing films in the major cities of the Gulf region. As Bahrain was the first Gulf country to discover and produce oil in 1931, its exhibition and distribution business began to flourish with the creation of the Bahrain Theatre in 1937.

Ali ibn Isa Al Khalifa, of the ruling family in Bahrain, established the Bahrain Theatre in 1937, consisting of two buildings, one for the summer and one for the winter. The summer building was an ample open space surrounded by four walls, one of which was used as a display, and in which wooden chairs were fixed to the ground. The winter building was roofed, but this did not prevent cold air and rainwater from entering the building. It is good to note that the availability of electricity, which was introduced in the region from the 1930s, was one of the leading factors that determined the site of construction in the region. Despite the unsatisfactory annual income in 1938, which did not exceed 154 rupees, or around £1.66, the Bahrain Theatre was able to influence the Bahraini and even Saudi Arabia exhibition scene (Manama story 2017). This was due to the fact that the owner of the Bahrain Theatre had a familial relationship with the Bahraini ruler.

By contrast, in the UAE, expatriate merchants had helped the development of cinema culture in Sharjah and Dubai. In 1961, there was a Harun cinema, which was created by a Pakistani businessman who embraced the idea of cinema and built it as an open-air cinema theatre, showing only Hindi films (Mousa 2011). Indian films were developing in popularity in the region due to the presence of the large segment of Indian and Pakistani communities in these countries. In 1966–1967, the cinema theatre was bought by the Mullahs, and movie shows continued until the late 1960s when they.

This period also saw foreign oil companies involved in the construction of film theatres and distribution of movies, mainly granting distribution rights of American and European films in their territories and screening for their employees – large Western expatriate communities and the few local workers (Al-Nouwairy 2011). In Bahrain, the Bahrain Oil Company built its first cinema, Al-Awali, in the late 1940s, which was only for Western (British-European) expatriates before it was opened to the public in early 1950s (Sarhan 2005). Most of the oil companies' new cinema constructions started with open areas surrounded by four walls in which wooden chairs were fixed. Also, with the advance of electricity, they reintroduced the mobile cinema project to reach rural communities in the 1950s. For instance, the Bahrain Oil Company reintroduced mobile cinema for educational films in the buildings of Bahraini clubs and public squares. The mobile cinema project was conducted under the supervision of the emergent Bahraini director, Khalifa Shaheen, who would become an influential figure in the Bahrain film production.

In Saudi Arabia, the California Arabian Oil Company (later renamed Aramco) was the first to introduce cinema theatres in the eastern part of Saudi Arabia, where it installed large screens in its residential compounds, in the eastern part of the kingdom during the 1940s, screening only American and European films (Ajel.SA 2017). In Saudi Arabia, within the residential complexes of foreign employees, public film screenings spread to four Saudi cities, namely Riyadh, Jeddah, Taif and Abha, until the number of theatres in Jeddah alone reached 30 screens (ibid.). Most of these initiatives were supported by some individual businessmen exhibiting mostly Egyptian films and Asian action films within the sports clubs and without the need for an official licence.

Film production

Oil companies, however, not only brought with them the cinema infrastructures (distribution and screening of US films) but they also influenced the landscape of film production, narratives and the styles of a few local films. Oil companies outsourced several American studios and producers to make films, mostly short documentaries and educational programmes about the region. Additionally, they also contributed to what could be characterized as the creation of a new generation of more liberally minded filmmakers who were sent to study film in Western countries.

By the time indigenous filmmakers started to appear in the region, oil companies had advanced film studios and equipment, such as 35 mm and 16 mm movie cameras. The Bahrain Oil Company, BAOC, and Saudi Arabia Oil Company (Aramco) had been active during the 1950s and 1960s in making films and facilitating international production in the region. There had been some Gulf individuals, some of which were sent by national oil companies, to study filmmaking abroad in countries with well-established film history. For instance, the Bahraini filmmaker Khalifa Shaheen was sent by BAOC to London Film School and graduated in 1965. The Kuwaiti filmmaker Khalid Sadiq, studied in India and returned in 1961, and the Saudi filmmaker Abdullah Al-Muhaisan studied at the London Film School and graduated in 1974. At the same time, some international productions were coming to the region by invitation through the oil companies and local rulers.

For instance, Khalifa Shaheen, who after his return to Bahrain, worked at the Bahraini oil company, and was able to facilitate the production of *Hamad and the Pirates* 1971, which was produced by Walt Disney and shot entirely in Bahrain in 1969. This 'knowledge transfer' should have influenced the landscape of development of the film industry at that period. However, as seen in many other commercial sectors and businesses, the transfer of knowledge has been slow to be taken up by nationals and, as a result, expatriates continued to be the mainstay of innovation in the region. As most of those people attempted to engage in the business of filmmaking upon their return to the region, the number of political-economic events – and the transfer of the ownership of most of the oil companies in the Gulf region from foreign to government-owned companies – delayed the development of film production in the region.

(2) Post-independence Khaleeji cinema: 1960s to 1990s

The intersection of the Gulf States and the Western (mostly the UK and the USA) security interests until the late 1960s gradually reinforced 'a conservative political stance' for the Gulf States into the transition of fully-fledged independent states in the early 1970s (Ulrichsen 2015, p. 9). Ulrichsen argued that while the world exploded with popular and radical movements of national liberation among postcolonial entities between the 1940s and 1960s, the Gulf States adopted a "balancing act between their reliance on British protection and the need to appease politicized local groups within society" (2015, pp. 9–10). That was seen through the building of local capital class and adaptation of Western laws and commercial codes. Additionally, "with the massive influx of incoming revenues into the Gulf economies during the 1970s, the flows of oil rents provided the emerging state structures with the financial wherewithal to create redistributive or 'rentier' states" (Ulrichsen 2015, p. 20).

One of the first film regulatory measures in the Gulf region was promulgated right before the independence of the rest of Gulf States. The rulers of Kuwait, Bahrain and Qatar issued orders to form national film distribution and exhibition companies shortly before their transition into independent states. The Kuwait National Cinema Company was established by royal order in 1954, seven years before Kuwait got independence in 1961. The Bahrain Cinema Company was established by royal decree in 1968, three years before Bahrain got independence. The Qatar Cinema and Film Distribution Company was established by royal order in 1970, one-year before Qatar achieved independence in 1971. As these new national companies took advantage of the informal exchange and viewing of films that were prominent in the region, they were – as with the oil companies – granted with concessions to distribute and exhibit films, some of which reached 50 years. In the period between 1960s and 1980s, this enhanced what Fahad Bishara et al. describe as "the state's control over commerce" (2016, p. 211).

The late 1970s and early 1980s is a particularly significant period for understanding the increased imbrications between regional politics and the film industry in the Gulf States. As in Saudi Arabia, along with the other Gulf States, cinema was part of the state-led national broadcasting system, several regional political incidents that had occurred since 1978 altered the relationship between the state and the film sector.

The post Iranian revolution and intense demonstrations against the Al Saud rule in Eastern Arabia during 1979, the Soviet invasion of Afghanistan in 1979 and the seizure of the Grand Mosque in 1979, as explained by John Willoughby (2008), urged the adaptation of an extreme view of Wahhabism in the kingdom of Saudi Arabia (p. 196). Saudi Arabia attempted to strengthen regional links with other Arab and Muslim countries through formation of national and international Islamic organisations and regional networks in the 1970s and 80s, as argued by Ulrichesn (2015) to "counter left-wing or secular oppositional alternatives" and "extend transnationally, the kingdom's 'soft power'" (p. 11).

In foreign policy, Saudi Arabia responded to these incidents strengthening the alliance with the other Gulf States through the Gulf Cooperation Council (GCC) in 1981. A shared history, values and traditions, ruling systems and Islamic Sunni practice, were among the arguments that the Saudi's made to encourage harmony among the six GCC countries (Al-Hamad 1997; Partrick 2011). The GCC organisation was created as "a powerful defensive unified identity against potential regional enemies" (Al-Janahi 2014, p. 27). This new 'Pan Gulf' social identity modelled on the largest member state, Saudi Arabia, provided a more

powerful force in the fields of politics and economics than of the cultural discourse and literature of these Six Countries (Foley 2010).

Therefore, what was happening in politics mirrored and influenced for decades
the cinema position in the Gulf region. This resulted in strained relationships
between the Gulf States and cinema from the 1980s to end of the 1990s, when the
Saudi Arabia regime, through the GCC organisation, bypassed specific conservative pan-Gulf cultural productions. The Gulf States increased their control over the
production and exhibition of content through Prints and Publication laws since
the 1980s. The impact of culture and the 'older class' remained a dominant factor in
what was considered culturally 'safe' to expose the younger generations to. Despite
this, the GCC organization had developed some cultural initiatives that aimed to
foster this 'unified identity'. The Joint Program Production Institution was created
in 1984 to contribute to the promotion and celebration of the shared common
values and traditions of the Khaleeji. The Joint Program Production Institution
(JPPI) was an initiative proposed by the State of Kuwait, which during the 1980s
throughout the 2000s, had been thriving as the centre of Khaleeji TV-drama, music
and theatre. As such, the JPPI's initiatives were focussed merely on performing
arts in theatre, music, television soap opera and radio. The film culture across the
region was not seen of the utmost importance to the GCC organization as the Gulf
States were at that time suffering from ongoing regional struggles with Iraq and
Iran before joining the World Trade Organisation.

The development of film institution and production was not seen as serious
and ambitious as it was with radio and TV, and that became instrumental for the
Gulf States' cultural and national identity formations. As there were no formal
film strategies in the period that followed the Gulf States' independence, it is
essential to note that there were some film initiatives from the institutionalised
media authorities. There were several media ministries in the Gulf States that
planned and built film studios as part of their broadcasting studios. The Kuwait
Ministry, for instance, established the cinema and TV production department in
1965 – which was lobbied by Khalid Sadiq – but lived for few years only before
it was renamed Television production[3]. Although the Gulf States had acquired
advanced film equipment, these were mostly used to produce news and documentaries (Beayeyz 1989). The lack of nationally trained filmmakers could be
the reason behind this. When Khaled Sadiq produced his first feature film,
Bas ya Bahar 1972, he was able to utilise the Kuwaiti television's 35 mm movie

---

3   Similarly, the Saudi Media Ministry signed a contract with the American Film
     Company in 1974 to build a new film studio as part of the new site of Saudi broad-
     casting authority.

camera for his production. In the case of Saudi Arabia, the film studio and the movie camera were never used because of the ban over cinema in 1983. Hence, the development of local cinema across the Gulf region was stalled by regional incidents and the views of religious conservatives.

Another major development for the cinema in the Gulf region was the complete transformation of ownership of the oil companies from foreign corporations to national governments, which contributed to limit the development of cinema culture and industry inside zones only. With oil companies under the full control of Gulf states, the heirs of the traditional merchant families pursued business opportunities in other industries, mainly service and construction. In each state, the development of cinema was part of the state's control over the means of production and distribution, including oil and media. Thus, cinema in each state was developed under the control of few local merchant families who had a large share in state-led national companies in Kuwait, Qatar and Bahrain.

The building of the cinema infrastructure

Historically, the early years of the Kuwait National Cinema Company and the Bahrain Cinema Company's business growth were a result of a series of horizontal integrations. The majority of the traditional theatres in Bahrain and Kuwait were required by law to merge with their respective national companies. This significantly increased the level of concentration in the local markets since the 1970s.

Right after the Bahrain Cinema Company's (BCC) inception in 1967, the company acquired a series of theatres, which included Al Nasr Cinema, Al-Hamra Cinema and Awal Cinema. In addition to the acquisition of independent cinemas owned by Abdul Rahman Alawi, the father of cinema in Bahrain, BCC rented a few cinemas from the Bahraini government and Bahrain Oil Company. By the 1980s, BCC had six cinemas screens from six theatres, which attracted broad audiences from local and expatriate communities showing mostly Indian and Egyptian films (Ali 2008). With BCC single-screen theatres suffering several fires' incidents, BCC was able to renovate its theatres with air conditioning and larger seats starting with the Al Nasr Cinema in 1979, which also led to an increase of ticket prices (The Bahrain Cinema Company 2015). Early in the 1990s, BCC disposed Andalus Cinema to Bahrain Ministry of Information in 1989, sold its usufruct right of Al Jazeera Cinema and closed down many theatres, such as Sitra Gate Cinema and Awali Cinema (The Bahrain Cinema Company 2015). Also, with the widespread growth of home viewing culture in the 80s and 90s, BCC established five video stores which were closed between 2001 and 2004.

Film distribution business model in Dubai

The first formal distribution structures in the Gulf region appeared in the 1970s in Kuwait when Kuwait National Cinema Company (KNCC), the first exhibition and distribution company in the Gulf region, was involved in renting Egyptian films after finishing exhibiting them in Kuwait to the rest of Gulf cinemas. KNCC had been the sole source of Gulf cinema companies, which had the rights to distribute Arabic and Egyptian films in particular in the region until the late 1990s (Behind the Camera Program 2017).

However, the KNCC's model of distribution, despite its supremacy over GCC cinemas, was soon challenged by the gradual formalisation of film distribution companies in the UAE and Lebanon that capitalised on Hollywood and Indian studios more than just Egyptian films. In the UAE, the developments of the market were led by a few individuals, most of whom were foreigners. In the 1970s and 1980s, Dubai was home to many Lebanese, Iranian and Indian expatriates who set-up distribution and exhibition businesses with connections and links with Hollywood agents in the Middle East. Among those businessmen are the Iranian Ahmad Golchin and Lebanese Selim Ramia who started distribution companies in Dubai back in the 1970s and 1980s that became leaders in film distribution business in the region. Golchin established Phars Films in the 1980s and then partnered with Ramia to found Gulf Film in 1989. While Phars Films focused on Asian films, Gulf Film focused more on Major Studios' films.

By the 1990s, six distributors in Lebanon (Joseph Chacra & Sons company, Italia Film, Empire Film, Four Star Film, Jaguar Film and Eagle Film) had already secured exclusive distribution agreements with the Major and Mini-major studios that covered the Middle East and North Africa region (MENA). The Lebanese distribution companies dealt with the Gulf cinema market remotely. The distribution of the Major films in the Gulf cinemas was channelled through either an agent representing the Lebanese companies within each country or an agreement with a local distributor to sub-distribute for them.

Thus, film exhibition and distribution in each Gulf States was under the control of the few national companies, owned by merchant families and immigrants with link to rulers, and few migrants. These national companies and expatriates who worked in business developed survival strategies for cinema industry, which was increasingly shifting under US influence.

Tab. 1: Major Film distributors of the Middle East

Distribution company	Location	Distribution deals with Majors
Italia Film	Lebanon/Dubai	Exclusive sub-distributor of Disney films for Buena Vista International in the ME.
Empire International	Lebanon /Dubai /Bahrain	Exclusive distributor of Sony Films, 20th Century Fox, DreamWorks Animation and Fox Star Studios in the MENA.
Four Star Film	Lebanon	Exclusive distributor of Paramount Pictures and Universal Pictures in the MENA.
Jaguar Film International Distribution	Lebanon / Dubai	Exclusive distributor of Lakeshore Labels films and Summit Entertainment films in the ME.
Eagle Films	Lebanon	Exclusive distributor of Lionsgate films in the ME.
Selim Ramia & Co Holding	Lebanon	By title.

Source: information collected from distribution companies' official websites and complied by the author

Film production

Despite the role of national companies in the region, cinema was mostly perceived as a "Western tool" and few Gulf filmmakers produced feature films.
While cinema companies – owned by families with a history of commercial
and trade business in areas such as real estate and construction – experienced
fewer social pressures, as their work was legitimized by rulers, Gulf directors
and filmmakers at the time were more exposed to social pressures and the
rejection of cinematic activities. Besides, the lack of support from government
institutions and cinema companies enhanced the perception of cinema as a
Western tool to be cautious of. The few filmmakers who made films during that
era, were dealt with great caution by censorship and by the distributors.

The majority of the Gulf filmmakers, who self-financed their film projects
such as Abdullah Al-Muhaisan, Khaleed Sadiq, Bassam Al-Zawadi, relied on the
international film festivals' circuit. The film *Assassination of a city* 1977 won a
prize in the 10th edition of Cairo film festival. The ambition of most filmmakers
from the region to engage in the film profession gradually vanished after the
1980s. Nevertheless, most of the national filmmakers and those with degrees
in film secured full-time jobs in government television institutions and, at the

same time, were partially involved in film production through their own compa-
nies. For instance, Khaleed Sadiq worked as manager for the Kuwaiti Ministry of
Media's production department between 1984 and 1994. Also, Bassam al-Zawadi
worked as general manager for the Bahraini television channel. Abdullah Al
Muhaisen has been an advisor to the Royal Court since 2005. The Saudi Ali
Alhuiraini graduated in 1984 with a master's degree in film directing from
Colombia University and worked at the Saudi national radio channel. While the
public media sector paid attention to directors who graduated abroad, between
the 1970s and the 1980s, the cinema and the audiences of the region were more
influenced by the private sector and its imported, 'mass-culture' productions
which undermined local productions.

Hence, the absence of governments' regulation, and in case of Saudi a cinema
ban, the transfer of ownership from oil companies to governments, and the
exclusive control of few merchant families over film distribution and exhibition
business impacted and stalled the development of film production in and across
the region. The centralised control over distribution and exhibition networks
in the rest of Gulf countries made it hard for filmmakers to continue making
films with the ever-growing culture of American movies. For instance, although
the Kuwait National Cinema Company became the only official distributor of
Egyptian films in the Gulf region since the 1980s, it did not engage in the distribution business of any other Gulf films before 2001.

This period ends in the late 1990s with the increasing development of the
deeper processes of globalisation in which the Gulf States were able to "shield[ed]
domestic markets from the full force of intentional system" in the 1970s and 80s
(Ulrichsen 2015, p. 24). Although this period saw the consolidation of pan-Gulf
politics and interests, the majority of the cinema corporations, film productions
and filmmakers were operating at a national level. However, the emergence of
Pan-Arab entertainment TV channels, that were mostly owned by Gulf investors,
gave rise to the Khaleeji TV-drama production that has crystalized the transnational flows and connections in pan-Gulf popular culture.

(3) Khaleeji cinema post 2002 to 2017

Between 2002 to 2017, Khaleeji cinema went through a period of a revitaliza-
tion that resulted in the beginning of a film production infrastructure while
the distribution and exhibition sectors in the Gulf region experienced an economic growth and expansion. These developments were shaped by several economic and political processes. First, the spread of radical Islamic movements

that threatened the political and economic system of the Gulf States. Kristian Ulrichsen (2015) notes that "the evolution of Islamist narratives of resistance to globalization in the years immediately before the September 11, 2001" was disruptive for Gulf States' oil rents and state-business relations as "they intersected with international financial and corporate networks" (p. 24). This resulted in Gulf governments, corporations and independents' constant attempts to break away from the influence of Hollywood representations of Arab culture as 'fundamentalist', by embracing and promoting open discussions with Western cultural values and productions.

Second, the economic integration into the world through membership in international organisations such as the World Trade Organization (WTO), which covers Trade-Related Intellectual Property Right (TRIPS), The World Intellectual Property Organization (WIPO), and the Berne Convention. The integration into the world economy provides the Gulf States with excellent economic opportunities to open trade, liberalisation of the market and to attract foreign direct investments, all of which have supported the economic performance of these countries, and to ease government dependence on oil economies. Also, Gulf government introduced national plans to gradually end dependency on oil revenues. The instability of oil resources that first hit Dubai in the late 1990s resulted in a series of socio-economic plans to move to a post-oil era. Abu Dhabi, Qatar and Saudi Arabia followed the Dubai example of development in non-oil sectors, in which development included institutionalisation of cultural, entertainment and creative industries.

At national level, Gulf governments started to pay attention to the WTO and WIPO's requirements. Most of Gulf States introduced amendments to legislations- such as the protection of intellectual property rights and Print and Publication laws- to follow the international standards for the protection of all aspects of intellectual and literary creativity (General Secretariat of the Gulf Cooperation Council, 2017). The UAE and Qatar shifted their position on film medium from only regulating content (through censorship) to providing economic stimuli. Natalie Knwalik and Philippe Meers (2017) highlight that membership in international organisations resulted in the emergence of new political actors participating to decisions related to areas of media and cultural policy, which included content regulations, trade and tariffs (2017, p. 248). For instance, Abu Dhabi legislated more than 110 laws and 75 decrees between 2005 and 2006 only to implement the government's restructuring as a catalyst for economic growth rather than an obstacle (Alittihad.ae 2007). In this sense, small states such as UAE and Qatar increased collaboration and co-production with major film players, which strengthened Hollywood's position over international markets, including their national film policies and infrastructure (Miller et al., 2005).

At transnational level, The GCC established two important multilateral treaties as direct reactions to WTO's and GATS obligations to liberalise national markets. The introduction of Customs Union in 2003 has upgraded the level of integration and increased commodity movement across the six countries. The establishment of the Common Market in 2008 extended the same rules of customs unions to the free movement of people, capital, goods. The Custom Union and Common Market sought to eliminate restrictions to the free circulation of GCC local products, capital and people in GCC countries (GCC citizens are eligible for free education, health services, business activities, social security claims and retirement benefits). The Common Market rule imposed 5 per cent tariffs on foreign commodities and non-GCC local commodities at the port of entry (GCC General Secretariat 2009).

The UAE and Qatar's cultural and film policies have benefited from GCC attention to 'authentic' native locals and businesses[4]. As the percentage of Gulf non-nationals grew from 2 million in the 1970s to more than 20 million in 2010, especially in Qatar, Abu Dhabi and Dubai, the three states were exposed to a radical increase of expatriate communities with nationals representing less than a quarter of the overall population. Abu Dhabi, Dubai and Qatar reacted to this 'transnational flow' of people and cultures by directing funds and grants "at those who can prove citizenship of a GCC nation as a sign of racial privilege, social status, and exclusive entitlement" (Mirgani, 2017, p. 5).

The GCC as a regional organisation did not have any influence in the shaping of Khaleeji cinema except for defining the geographical boundaries of what to consider *Khaleji* and what not. GCC was the organiser of three editions of the GCC film festival, which was hosted and financed by Doha in 2012, Kuwait in 2013 and Abu Dhabi in 2016. The GCC's attempt to construct a collective transnational filmmaking community through number of joint works and initiatives did not steadily materialise because the coupling of art and state politics at GCC level increases the influence of state politics on GCC cultural

---

4   Khaled Abdulkarim (2017)'s thesis *Crystallizing a Discourse of" Khalijiness": Exclusion and Citizenship in the Arab Gulf States* highlights how the UAE and Kuwait state-sponsored discourse of "Khalijiness" helps form and foster imagined communities among the local Arab Gulf citizens through the exclusion of non-national populations from state-sponsored national identities, as manifested through citizenship rights.

strategy (Mirgani 2017). Thus, Khaleeji cinema emerged more promptly not through the GCC organisation, but the special status of GCC filmmakers and businesses at film festivals, film training, and co-production opportunities in the UAE and Qatar.

The UAE and Qatar's top-down efforts to restore and take advantage of the Khaleejness involved many artists and inhabitants in the region, followed the trend of film festivals in those countries and offered an alternative space for national interaction and discussion about the use of the small circuit of indigenous Khaleeji filmmakers and producers in Bahrain and Saudi Arabia as example. The Saudi Film Festival's editions benefited extensively from the cir-cuit of Khaleeji film industry including film producers, festival's organisers and screenwriters – such as Bahraini filmmaker Mohammed Buali, DIFF's artistic director Massoud Amer Allah and Emirate screenwriter Mohammed Hassan. Also, the board members of the Digital production department of private-owned Effat University include filmmakers and other professionals from Gulf countries.

Development and production of films

The UAE and Qatar emerged as powerful players and contributors in the effort to develop Khaleeji production away from the influence of Saudi government. In the period of 2004 to 2017, these states created new infra-structure and large-scale studios and production companies designed to develop the production sector, including Dubai Studio City (2005), Abu Dhabi TwoFour54 Intaj (2008), Abu Dhabi Image Nation (2008), Doha Film Institute Production (2010). These new specialised infrastructure and film commissions in Dubai, Abu Dhabi and Doha have changed the direc-tion of most regional production from the historical production centres in Lebanon and Egypt, making the UAE and Qatar the base of Arab and Khaleeji film production. These state-owend large studios, companies and infrastructures have supported pan-Arab television, commercials and film productions industry. However, given that film production sector is new in the Gulf region, the majority of the productions that have used and benefited from these studios, incentives and commissions/institution were non-Gulf productions and films.

The UAE and Qatar governments' assistance and special treatment of the film industry have two cultural and economic justifications; one is to preserve national culture through finding locals and new voices; another is to benefit

Tab. 2: Number of pan-Gulf film initiatives in the Gulf region between 2006 and 2017

Initiative name	Organized by
Gulf Muhr competition from 2006 to 2017	Dubai International Film Festival
Gulf Film Festival from 2008 to 2013	Dubai International Film Festival
IWC Award for Gulf filmmakers in 2011–2017	Dubai International Film Festival
Gulf Development Unit in 2012–2015	Doha Film Institute
The Hazawi fund for producer and director of GCC nationalities 2013–2017	Doha Film Institute
DIFF DFC Award 2014–2017	Dubai International Film Festival

Source: information collected from the official websites and complied by the author

the local economy through more regionally focused commercial initiatives. Hjort and Petrie (2007) observed that "under globalisation, state support has been influenced by a new international division of cultural labour, with economics competing with, at time eclipsing, culture as the primary rationale for funding" (p. 16). Therefore, the Khaleeji cinema and industry has developed under two conflicting visions, "favouring subsidies for film as both culture and a vehicle for a politics of recognition" and "market-oriented investment in cultural industries allied to other potential sources of foreign earnings, such as tourism" (Hjort and Petrie 2007, p. 16). The majority of khaleeji films operated outside this unit-based studio system. Between 2004 and 2017, the GCC nationals benefited greatly from the UAE and Qatar's state-driven film initiatives and festivals through training and workshops, grants for development and production, distribution opportunities and awards.

In 2006, the Dubai International Film Festival (DIFF) announced the launch of Gulf Muhr competition. In 2008, the Gulf Film Festival, a subsidiary of Dubai IFF, was created to support Khaleeji cinematic movement and existed for only six editions. In 2012, the Doha Film Institute announced the launch of the 'Gulf Development Unit' to organise film education and training initiatives for filmmakers in Qatar and the GCC region. In 2013, Doha Film Institute created 'the Hazawi fund' for producer and director of GCC nationalities (Doha Film Institute 2012). A large number of short and feature films in the Gulf countries were produced from these initiatives. Although these events and awards were unsystematically designed to stimulate the cinema of the region, they also acted as national gatekeepers of the filmmaking outputs.

The Emirati and Qatari model of international film festivals between 2004 and 2012 had a significant influence on short-lived Khaleeji's cultural contexts, fostering the culture of film production and promoting the distribution of films. These international film festivals allocated exclusive spaces and financial support for producers and directors of Gulf Arabian origin, including Iraq and Yemen. Between 2004 and 2017 more than 90 national feature films (and many short films) were produced from the six Gulf States, and the majority of these films relied on the circuit of Khaleeji film festivals.

Khaleeji feature films participation to the festivals' circuit generated interests from local and regional distributors. Dubai International Film festivals represented a fundamental platform in the way it packaged the films for distributors. Friendly agreements between Dubai International film festival and theatrical distributors created a short-term system for the exchange of selected films, which was mainly focused on national cinema and sometimes on selected GCC cinema. Most Emirati feature films produced between 2009 and 2017 were distributed by Vox Cinemas, which was strategical partner of DIFF' Dubai Distribution Programme.

Informal circuit and film production

The context of 'Khaleeji' cinema is not only the formal economics of film, but also the numerous mutual influences and interactions occurring at more informal levels – such as online platforms. The advent of inexpensive digital technologies and their availability in the Gulf market – especially in Dubai- replaced the old concept of expensive production equipment. In addition, digitisation has empowered easy-access and exposure to local content online and outside the traditional circuit of film festivals and commercial cinemas. In fact, digital content in the Gulf region, such as YouTube videos, have facilitated the scholarly analysis of the GCC state's role in 'redefining' the concept of Arab cinema, beyond the influence of popular Egyptian cinema (Hudson 2015).

One of the early players in the development of Khaleeji cinema was the grass-roots activities that occurred at Cinemac.net, a website created by the Saudis in 2004 as the first movie buff website. This website has become the main platform for most Gulf emergent filmmakers between 2004-2010, including filmmakers, journalists and critic from around the Gulf countries such as Haifaa al-Mansour, Abdullah Al-Eyaf and Abdullah Hassan Ahmed. Cinemac.net played important role to "foster virtual film communities and cultivate film-related activities in real life" (Ciecko, 2011, p. 7). The majority of the website's users used the virtual space to engage with film competitions and festivals around the region. For instance, Haifaa al-Mansour's *Wadjda* (2012) benefited from the circuit of film festivals in the UAE and Qatar between 2008 to 2010 to develop and fund her script. However, the easy access to the Internet and digital technologies had limited impacts on the business model of filmmaking in the region, as most of the production used to be short films designed for film festivals' circuit. Access to digital and inexpensive equipment did not lead to transfer the whole value chain of film in the virtual space and to produce, distribute and exhibit these films online.

If we analyse film production model in the region away from only feature films, we find that the production of Saudi short films in YouTube began as the work of freelancers which were very active in posting original short films before establishing their own production companies to make feature films. Since 2011, Saudi Arabia has been enriched with the culture of short comedy films on YouTube in particularly from Telefaz11 and Myrkott, in addition to a number of independent content makers. Their online successes on YouTube opened for them business opportunities toward feature film projects with cinema chains. For instance, Vox Cinemas signed a distribution deal in early 2018 with Myrkott, a Saudi production company behind the YouTube animated hit *Masameer* which has attracted more than 700 million view across social media[5].

Thus, UAE and Qatar's globalisation-driven strategies based on the development of big-budget films and co-production (studio-system movies) did not stimulate large market demands for these films while new films produced on a limited budget but with multiple sequels instead of one film actually did. This model is based on the idea that profit is achieved by increasing exposure to the films as a brand by featuring prominent social media influencers to drive traffic and sales to a product (usually in commercial cinemas). These sequels trend was followed by Abu Dhabi-based Dhabi Films which produced mystery/horror movies sequels *Grandmother's Farm Part* 2013/*Grandmother's Farm Part-2* 2015 and action/adventure movies sequels *Hajwala: The Missing Engine* 2016/*Hajwala-2* 2018. The Bahrain-based AK Studios produced comedy movies sequels *Swalef Tafash: Jazeerat Al Halamaya* 2016/*Tafash We Arb3een Harami* 2017. The Abu Dhabi-based Xmovies produced comedy movies sequels of *Edhay fi Abu Dhabi* 2016/*Edhay fi Thiland* 2017/ *Edhay fi Aldawam* 2020.

---

5   https://www.majidalfuttaim.com/en/Media%20Centre/Press%20Releases/2018/03/VOX%20Cinemas%20Saudi%20Arabia%20Signs%20exclusive%20distribution%20deal

Economic growth of GCC exhibition sector

The introduction of the GCC Custom Union and Common Market rules have influenced the business of film distribution and exhibition in the Gulf region. The GCC's Custom Union and Common Market offer Gulf-based distributors an exemption from customs fees when exporting or importing to the six GCC countries. These rules allowed the expansion of cinema chains in the Gulf region. Many leading cinema companies extended their businesses to another country in the Gulf region, shaping a new era of a few corporations with greater control of the GCC cinema market. Bahrain Cinema Company extended its cinema brand CINECO to Qatar in 2010, Gulf Films extended its exhibition arm, Novo Cinemas, to Bahrain and Qatar, MAF extended its VOX Cinemas to Oman, Bahrain, Kuwait, Qatar and Saudi Arabia.

In terms of industry concentration levels, the theatrical exhibition industry in the Gulf has marked a massive increase in the number of cinema companies from 5 to 16 companies in 1996 and 2016 respectively. UAE has the largest number of cinema chains in the GCC region, which accounts for ten companies in 2016. The highest number of cinema screens in Gulf region in 2016 was located in the UAE with 374 screens, followed by Kuwait with 98 screens, Bahrain with 76 screens, Qatar with 56 screens, Oman with 52 screens (Northwestern University in Qatar 2016). The table 3 clearly shows the acceleration of exhibition concentration, from 255 to 600 screens in 2006 and 2016, with 70% controlled by the big four companies, Vox Cinemas, CINESCAPE, CINECO and Novo Cinemas. Vox Cinemas has doubled its share in the GCC market from 15% to 26% in 2006 and 2016, before it reached 45% in 2018.

Vox Cinemas dominates Oman exhibition industry (with 95% shares of screens) since 2016. The purchase of Oman Arab Cinema Company by Vox Cinemas left Omanis cinemagoers with no alternative for cinemas. Thus, Vox Cinemas developed a monopoly in Oman exhibition market but operates in an oligopoly market in a larger Gulf geographical area.

Conclusion

This chapter discusses the three stages in the development and political-economic relations of the cinema business of Gulf countries. It explores how the rise of foreign oil companies in the 1930s and 1940s helped the business of local cinemas and filmmakers to fluorish. It shows that between the 1970s and

Tab. 3: The four large cinema chains in the GCC

Timeframe	Chain	Number of sites	Number of Screens	Proportion of screens located in multiplexes	GCC Market share
2006	9783631799512_ C006_inl_001	4 cinemas in UAE	40 screens	100%	%15
2016	9783631799512_ C006_inl_002	13 cinemas in UAE and Oman	167 screens	100%	%26
2006	9783631799512_ C006_inl_003	5 cinemas in UAE	96 screens	100%	%37.7
2016	9783631799512_ C006_inl_004	15 cinemas across UAE, Bahrain and Qatar	136 screens	100%	%21
2006	9783631799512_ C006_inl_005	5 cinemas In Bahrain and Qatar	38 screens	85%	%14
2016		10 cinemas in Bahrain and Qatar	91 screens	100%	%14
2006	9783631799512_ C006_inl_006	12 cinemas in Kuwait	39 screens	74%	%15
2016		11 cinemas in Kuwait	54 screens	99%	%8
GCC cinema Market shares	In 2006–255 screens				%81
	In 2016–656 screens				%69

Sources: *arabianbusiness.com, Cineco's financial statements, Cikescape's financial statements, Novo website, MAF's press releases, screendaily.com[67] and complied by the author.*

1990s, the concept of cinema development remained problematic as the Gulf States strengthened regulations over the imported films. Thus, the building of cinema infrastructure, industry and culture was concentrated in the hand of a few state-led cinema companies. The chapter highlights the shift in the third

---

6   https://www.screendaily.com/exhibition-middle-east-gulf-starts-to-widen/4034819. article

7   http://www.alraimedia.com/Home/Details?Id=b8c28168-aeb0-4763-ba2f-0d1ac0f28988

period and how it revives the concept of cinema development in line with the UAE and Qatar's national government projects. Although each government strives to develop film festivals through which the legislation of film institutions has subsequently crystallized, Khaleeji and GCC nationals constitute essential components of these development plans. Hence, the recent economic openness of the Gulf States and economic cooperation among themselves - represented by the Gulf Cooperation Council - indirectly contributed to the rise and development of Khaleeji production, distribution practices and cinema chains in the Gulf region between 2002 and 2017.

The third stage of development of cinema across the Gulf region would be incomplete if we focus only on the formal circuit of film. The chapter focused on the formal and informal circuits of film, and their influence on the broad Khaleeji production and exhibition. The ambition of this analysis is to facilitate the understanding of power relations in contemporary Khaleeji cinema, exposing some of the prevailing conceptions about ownership and control. Another ambition of this analysis is to contribute to the development of a theory about the formation of Middle East cinema as argued by Hamid Naficy (2008) through contextualisation of similarities and shared features between regional societies and their cinematic productions.

The year 2017 is the end of the third period of Khaleeji cinema influenced by recent political and economic conditions. The Qatar-Gulf crisis has hindered the business and industry of the Gulf cinema and market since mid-2017. The Saudi government's announcement of cinema licensing in the late 2017, and the dismiss of Dubai International Film Festival in April 2018, brought Saudi Arabia back to a powerful position over the Khaleeji film industry. With Vision 2030, the Saudi plan to become a regional player in the Middle East film industry and to have 2000 screens by 2030, which could significantly influence the business of production, distribution and exhibition in the region, thus marking the beginning of a fourth phase of Khaleeji cinema that need further examination.

References

Abdulkarim, Khaled A. *Crystallizing a Discourse of "Khalijiness": Exclusion and Citizenship in the Arab Gulf States*. University of Pennsylvania, 2017.

Ajel.SA. *(Arabic) Saudi Cinema: Launched from the Beasts and Destroyed by the Movies of the Seventies* [Online]. 2017. Accessed October 21, 2018, https://ajel.sa/m5837V/.

Al-Hamad, Turki. "Will the Gulf Monarchies Work Together?" *Middle East Quarterly* 4, no. 1 (1997): 47–53.

Al-Janahi, Buthaina Mohammed. *National Identity Formation in Modern Qatar: New Perspective.* Qatar: Qatar University, 2014.

Al-Nouwairy, Imad. *(Arabic) Spotlight on Cinema in GCC.* Kuwait: Kuwait Magazine, 2011.

Ali, S. "(Arabic) Cinema Activity in Bahrain Is Parallel to the Spread of Cinemas." *AlRayu* (2008 November 6).

Alittihad.ae. *(Arabic) Restructuring the Government* [Online]. 2007. Abu Dhabi. Accessed November 14, 2017, https://www.alittihad.ae/article/126769/2007/1-إعداد-قلكي ه-ل حكوه.

Armes, Roy. *New Voices in Arab Cinema.* Bloomington: Indiana University Press, 2015.

Beayeyz, Ibrahim A. *An Analytical Study of Television and Society in Three Arab States: Saudi Arabi, Kuwait, and Bahrain.* Columbus: The Ohio State University, 1989.

Beeman, William O. "Gulf Society: An Anthropological View of the Khalijis— Their Evolution and Way of Life." In *The Persian Gulf in History*, edited by E. Potter, 147–159. New York/London. Palgrave MacMillan, 2009.

Behind the Camera Program. *(Arabic) Interview with Hisham Al Ghanim, President of the International Film Distribution Company* [Online]. YouTube. 2017. Accessed January 10, 2018, https://www.youtube.com/watch?v=5Oziwt9uX8Y.

Bishara, Fahad Ahmad, Haykel, Bernard, Hertog, Steffen, Holes, Clive, and James Onley. "The Economic Transformation of the Gulf." In *The Emergence of the Gulf States: Studies in Modern History*, edited by John E. Peterson. London. Bloomsbury Publishing, 2016.

Ciecko, Anne. "Cinema "Of" Yemen and Saudi Arabia: Narrative Strategies, Cultural Challenges, Contemporary Features." *Wide Screen* 3, no. 1 (2011): 1–16.

Doha Film Institute. *Hazawi Gulf Short Film Production Fund.* Doha: DFI, 2012.

Dönmez-Colin, Gonul. *The Cinema of North Africa and the Middle East.* London: Wallflower Press, 2007.

Foley, Sean. *The Arab Gulf States: Beyond Oil and Islam.* London. Lynne Rienner Publishers, 2010.

GCC General Secretariat. *Objectives and GCC Cultural Development Plan.* [Online]. 2009. Accessed November 1, 2018, https://www.gcc-sg.org/en-us/

CooperationAndAchievements/Achievements/MediaCooperation/Pages/
JointCulturalAction.aspx.

General Secretariat of the Gulf Cooperation Council. *WTO's Agreements
and Their Implications for the GCC Countries*. Riyadh: Gulf Cooperation
Council, 2017.

Hjort, Mette, and Duncan Petrie. "Introduction." In *Cinema of Small Nations*,
edited by Mette Hjort. Edinburgh: Edinburgh University Press, 2007.

Hjort, Mette. "Small Cinemas: How They Thrive and Why They Matter."
Mediascape: UCLA's Journal of Cinema and Media Studies (2011): 1–5.

Hudson, Dale. "Review of Transnational Cinema/Media Studies Conference."
Transnational Cinemas 6 (2015): 84–96.

Hudson, Dale. "Locating Emirati Filmmaking within Globalizing Media
Ecologies." In *Media in the Middle East*, edited by Nele Lenze, Charlotte
Schriwer, and Zubaidah Abdul Jalil. Switzerland: Palgrave MacMillan, 2017.

Khatib, Lina. *Filming the Modern Middle East: Politics in the Cinemas of
Hollywood and the Arab World*. London: I.B. Tauris, 2006.

Knwalik, Natalie, and Philippe Meers. "South African Post-Apartheid Film
Policy: Shifting Discourses on Film, National Identity and Cultural/Creative
Industries." In *Reconceptualising Film Policies*, edited by Nolwenn Mingant
and Cecilia Tirtaine. London: Routledge, 2017.

Manama story. *(Arabic) Manama Constructed the First Cinema in the Gulf!
Despite the Opposition of Older People under the Pretext of Corruption*
[Online]. 2017. Accessed November 20, 2018, https://manamastory.
com/المنامة-شيّدت-أول-سينما-في-الخليج-ر-غم/.

Marks, Laura U. *Hanan Al-Cinema: Affections for the Moving Image*.
Cambridge, MA/London, England: The MIT Press, 2015.

Mirgani, Suzi. "Introduction: Art and Cultural Production in the GCC." *Journal
of Arabian Studies* 7 (2017): 1–11.

Mosco, Vincent. *The Political Economy of Communication: Rethinking and
Renewal*. London: Sage Publications, 1996.

Naficy, Hamid. "For a Theory of Regional Cinemas: Middle Eastern, North
African and Central Asian Cinemas." *Early Popular Visual Culture* 6
(2008): 97–102.

Northwestern University in Qatar. *Media Industries in the Middle East 2016*.
[Online]. 2016. Available: http://www.mideastmedia.org/industry/2016/

Partrick, Neil. "The GCC: Gulf State Integration or Leadership Cooperation?"
In *Kuwait Programme on Development, Governance and Globalisation in the*

Gulf States Research Papers. London: The London School of Economics and Political Science, 2011.

Sarhan, M. *(Arabic) The History of Cinema in Bahrain*. Bahrain: Al Ayam Press & Publishing Est, 2005.

Shafik, Viola. *Arab Cinema: History and Cultural Identity*. Egypt: American University in Cairo Press, 2007.

The Bahrain Cinema Company. *Annual Report 2015*. Bahrain, 2015.

Ulrichsen, Kristian Coates. *The Political Economy of Arab Gulf States*. [Online]. 2015. James A. Baker III Institute for Public Policy University. Available: https://www.bakerinstitute.org/media/files/files/a9688a6e/CME-pub-PoliticalEconomy-050815.pdf.

Willoughby, John. "Segmented Feminization and the Decline of Neopatriarchy in GCC Countries of the Persian Gulf." *Comparative Studies of South Asia, Africa and the Middle East* 28, no. 1 (2008): 184–99.

Part 2   Local Cinema and Globalization: Struggles, Survival and Sustainability

Xiaofei Han

Production of Main Melody Film in Post-Socialist China: A deconstruction of *Wolf Warrior 2*

Abstract Main melody film, a particular genre in Chinese cinema initiated by the state, is to wrap up the dominant ideology of a socialist China with pleasurable entertainment and is among the most important parts of the state ideological apparatus in promoting nationalism. By deconstructing the phenomenal commercial success of a recent film that belongs to this genre, *Wolf Warrior 2* (战狼2), this chapter examines how the production of main melody films has been transformed by the triangular interplay among the rapidly commercialized Chinese cinema, the state's virtually split attitude towards foreign (primarily Hollywood) films, and the sophisticated business and financial strategies adopted by local film producers and investors since 1990s. Remarkably, the production of main melody film, in line with many other types of Chinese films, is marked by the vigorous financialization process of film industry and featured by practice such as Valuation Adjustment Mechanism (VAM). Introduced from financial market and not commonly seen in other film markets like Hollywood, VAM has effectively mobilized large volume of private capital and injected to the production sector of main melody films such as *Wolf Warrior 2*. Further, local filmmakers in China have also maximized state's administrative protection of domestic films as well as the techniques and styles learned from – and meanwhile assimilated by – their Hollywood rivalries on their way to meet investors' expectations.

Keywords: Chinese film industry, main melody film, financialization of media, globalization, political economy

Introduction

In the summer of 2017, *Wolf Warrior 2*, a Chinese action movie broke into the top 100 worldwide grosses of all time at 54th – the first and only non-English language film listed so far (Box Office Mojo 2017). Since its July 27th debut in China, *Wolf Warrior 2* took the market by storm and surpassed 5.5 billion RMB (US$830 million) after just five weeks, which has made it the top-grossing film in China of all time and the second-highest-earning film in a single territory in history, just behind *Star Wars: The Force Awakens (2015)* in North America (Frater 2017). Given its phenomenal commercial success, *Wolf Warrior 2* is one of the "main melody films" in China, a particular genre

in Chinese cinema initiated by the state, which combines the dominant ideology of a socialist China with pleasurable entertainment and it is among
the most important parts of the state ideological apparatus in promoting
nationalism (Liu 2005; Ma 2013; Su 2011, 2014). *Wolf Warrior 2* features "a
muscular, adrenaline-fueled story" (Frater 2017) whose unstoppable hero is
a former member of a fictitious Chinese special troops unit called the Wolf
Warriors going to a fictional African state in the middle of a civil war to rescue
Chinese workers and their African comrades. As a main melody film, *Wolf
Warrior 2*, however, embeds the structure of the "hero myth" in its story, a
theme that features individualism and American supremacy – a commonly
recurring trope in Hollywood blockbusters (Chen 1998; Lawrence and Jewett
2002; Wang 2009).

Focusing on its unprecedented commercial accomplishment as a main
melody film that features Hollywood narrative and theme, this chapter looks
into the reasons behind the success of *Wolf Warrior 2* in Chinese market.
Through the theoretical lens of critical transculturalism proposed by Marwan
Kraidy (2004, 2005), this paper highlights the triangular interplay among the
commercialized Chinese cinema, the state's virtually split attitude towards
Hollywood films, and the business strategies adopted by the producers and
investors behind *Wolf Warrior 2*. By looking at three dimensions, financialization of the film, discursive construction of state's ideology through hero myth,
and marketing strategies for distribution, this chapter further discusses how the
production of main melody film has been challenged and complicated by the
market dynamics imposed by China's tighter integration into the global capitalist system since 1990s.

The analysis indicates that the grand success of *Wolf Warrior 2* should be situated within an accumulative process of the state's selective opening up of limited space for Hollywood films and the marketization of domestic cinema since
1990s. Remarkably, the production of main melody film is no longer the state's
project but has become the market's project with the vigorous financialization
process of film industry featured by the practice such as Valuation Adjustment
Mechanism, which is rarely seen in Hollywood production while becoming
increasingly phenomenal in Chinese film industry. Effective mobilization of private capital, the lessons drawn from the popularity of Hollywood films regarding
production styles and themes, and the sophisticated marketing strategies which
maximized the administrative protection of domestic films from the state are
the factors that combine to create the phenomenal success of *Wolf Warrior 2* as
a new main melody film.

Critical transculturalism: From domination to globalization

There are two traditionally opposing theoretical frameworks when it comes to conceptualizing global cultural flows, especially regarding the cultural influences of the U.S. over other localities. The global triumph of Hollywood is often considered as evidence of how the process of globalization is really the imposition of a single homogeneous system that is characterized by economic and cultural convergence and the universal and standardizing values of cultural imperialism. Leading scholars of this thesis, such as Herbert Schiller (1991, 1992) and Armand Mattelart (1983, 1994), believe that the U.S. enjoys a cultural supremacy over other countries which reflects the power structure of global capitalism. Cultural products, such as Hollywood movies, contribute to the colonization of global audiences and the emergence of a hegemonic culture that threatens the sustainability of other cultures and the creation of alternative values and life styles (Schiller 1989, 1992; Kraidy 2004; Su 2010a, 2014). For the cultural imperialism approach, culture is perceived as holistic, organic unity which is closely associated with the nation-state with its underlying stress on national "cultural authenticity" while overlooking the cultural diversity and fusion that commonly exists within most nation-states (Kraidy 2004, 2005). By contrast, a second strand of researchers questioned the idea of global cultural uniformity and paved the way for theories of cultural globalization as an alternative to cultural imperialism (Appadurai 1995; Tomlinson 1996, 1999). Narratives of cultural globalization denied the simplistic causal relationship between institutional power and the homogenization of culture. Whereas the term "imperialism" reflects an intentional and systematic endeavor, "globalization" is employed as the guiding framework for understanding the more complex and not necessarily intentional processes of cultural globalization. The latter, moreover, conveys a process of interlocking sub-national, national and supra-national forces as well as the tension between global forces of cohesion and local reactions of dispersal (Appadurai 1995; Tomlinson 1996; Kraidy 2005).

Ultimately, however, neither of these two approaches – cultural imperialism versus cultural globalization – offers a well-rounded theoretical framework for the analysis of *Wolf Warrior 2*. This is because, on the one hand, although *Wolf Warrior 2* embeds the story structure rooted in the hero myth, a typical narrative of Hollywood blockbusters which has been influenced by decades of China's opening up toward Hollywood movies, it cannot be simply considered a product embodying the Hollywood dominance over Chinese domestic film production because there is a powerful presence of the state's ideology within *Wolf Warrior 2* as a main melody film, which is recognized and supported by the party-state in various ways. On the other hand, however, to apply the framework of cultural globalization to the production and distribution of *Wolf Warrior 2* is likely to downplay the role of the Chinese government as well as local and global capital in cultivating the politico-economic habitat which has yielded the film. Given the significance of the discursive and deliberate insertion of state ideology into the commercial production of transnational cultural flows, the liberal underpinnings of cultural globalization theory are fatally compromised because it fails to capture the broad structures of power that define the processes of globalization as well as the powerful role of the state and the neoliberal market in the socio-cultural dynamics at localities. The interaction of these forces fundamentally shapes cultural flows in our current juncture. Given all this, the success of *Wolf Warrior 2*, and its deployment of Hollywood narrative conventions in conveying nationalism, must be examined in a way that simultaneously captures the Chinese state's attitude toward Hollywood films, the marketization of the domestic film industry and, finally, the liberalization of the financial market as a part of China's integration into the global system. The analysis of *Wolf Warrior 2*, thus, calls for a more integrative framework that emphasizes the political-economic aspects of international communication, while eyeing the complex, uneven and interlocking processes of global cultural flows and the discursive construction within the film.

Critical transculturalism, a relatively recent theoretical framework proposed by Marwan Kraidy (2004, 2005), provides a blending of political economy and cultural studies approaches with an emphasis on "the multiple and integrated levels of both structure and agency" (Comor 2002, p. 320). Such an approach is particularly pertinent to how we approach the analysis of *Wolf Warrior 2*. While sharing the broad concerns about the relation between power and cultural changes that have long animated the cultural imperialism approach, it also looks into the cultural hybridity and discursive construction that are central concerns in the cultural globalization thesis. In particular, Kraidy (2004) contends that it is essential to view cultures as synthetic entities whose hybrid components are shaped by both structural and discursive forces (Kraidy 2004, 2005). It is noteworthy that hybridity, as the cultural logic of globalization, is not post-hegemonic; rather, there are casual links between politico-economic power and cultural hybridity in many instances (Kraidy 2004, 2005). Yet the processes and implications of hybridity are too convoluted to be explained by an always already direct politico-economic causality. Instead, and therefore, by focusing on both the historical politico-economic context in which the film is situated *and* the discursive construction of nationalism embedded in the story through the utilization of abundant Hollywood elements, critical transculturalism provides a tenable theoretical approach to reveal the complexity of the grand success of *Wolf Warrior 2* and thus moves beyond the commonplace model of domination and resistance. In the next section, before entering the critical examination of the film *Wolf Warrior 2* itself, this chapter will provide a historical review of main melody film as a particular film genre in Chinese cinema and how it has adapted to the market mechanism as the commercialization of the domestic film market deepens. The key to understanding *Wolf Warrior 2* and other attempts to produce blockbuster films in China for both domestic and global markets, in other words, is to simultaneously grasp that they are both a highly commercialized commodity yet still laced with ideological significance.

Production of main melody film in China: A prehistory of *Wolf Warrior 2*

Birth of main melody film

Cinema has functioned as an important vehicle for the maintenance and reinvention of nationhood, while adding substance to people's imagination, helping to create a distinct image of the nation overtime (Anderson 2006; Bourdieu, Wacquant, and Farage 1994). As a critical component of China's cultural policies, the state has adopted a split attitude towards Hollywood movies (Su 2010a, 2011, 2014). In short, it has attempted to maximize the economic gains from Hollywood films while trying to minimize its ideological influence. The central policy regarding Hollywood films can be summarized by an eight-word principle: *yi wo wei zhu, wei wo suo yong* (all films imports must serve China's needs and national interests and should be made use of for China's gains and goals) (State Administration of Radio Film and Television 2001, article 2). On the one hand, the state aimed to lift the domestic film industry by filling the gap between a planned film production and a huge market demand by approving the annual quota for foreign hits with a revenue-sharing system starting from 1994 (Zhu, 2003; Wang 2009; Su 2010a, 2014; Nakajima 2016). In 1990s, the domestic film industry slid into deep difficulties due to the rapid commercialization of the market, low levels of productivity, the shortage of production capital and the growing diversity of new entertainment choices available to Chinese audiences (Su 2010a, 2010b, 2014). The revenue-sharing system of foreign imports was designed to boost the distribution sector as well as to use the earnings from the shared revenue of Hollywood films to support domestic film production (which I will discuss in more details later). Such treatment was effective, as reflected by the box office which soared immediately after this system was implemented. In 1994, for example, the state opened room for ten foreign imports to start with, and the Hollywood imports permitted entry into Chinese theatres resulted in $7.2 million (USD) in film revenue, which constituted 60% of the total annual revenue in Chinese cinema (Su 2010a). In 1998, the phenomenal film *Titanic* received 360 million RMB (US$60 million) and it alone accounted for 40% of the annual box office in China (Rosen 2002; Editorial Committee of China Film Yearbook, 2011). Hollywood imports had pulled Chinese audiences back to cinema.

On the other hand, despite of the thriving domestic box office, there were deep-rooted worries about the unprecedented influence of Hollywood movies from both policy-makers, intellectuals and domestic film producers. Those concerns, in turn, were soon reflected in yet further changes in the state's central policy regarding Hollywood films (Su 2010a, 2011). There were concerns, for instance, that the American values and life styles represented in Hollywood films would be instilled in Chinese people, that they would threaten Chinese cultural traditions, and that they might even endanger the country's national identity. The state used the rhetoric of "dancing with wolves" (Su 2011, p. 101) to describe how to manage the relation between Hollywood and domestic films. The state's decision to allow a limited number of foreign imports, however, was built on the gambit that, by doing so, the Chinese side's share of the revenue could be plowed into new economic tools to develop and modernize the domestic film industry. Despite this instrumentalist attempt to harness Hollywood to domestic industrial policy strategy for the Chinese film industry, the prevalent hostilities and anxieties felt towards Hollywood were far from being subdued. Indeed, responding to the mounting influence of Hollywood imports, the state made even greater efforts to underscore the ideological function of domestically produced films. Both measures – that is, increased economic resources for the film industry *and* sterner ideological resolve –worked hand-in-hand to help justify the Chinese government's ruling status and to build an enduring and robust sense of national identity (Su 2010a, 2014). In short, "global Hollywood" was harnessed to Chinese industrial and ideological ends.

This split attitude from the state had significant implications. First and foremost, it has led to the birth and adoption of the so-called main melody film as a primary strategy to minimize Hollywood influences. The term of main melody film was initially mentioned in a proposal by then-director of Film Administrative Bureau, Teng Jinxian, to support domestic film production which "highlight main melody while encouraging diversity" (Ma 2013; Su 2010a) in 1987. According to then-president Jiang Zemin, main melody films "promote patriotism, socialism and collectivism and resolutely resist money-worship, hedonism and excessive individualism" (Su 2014, p. 101). This definition was later extended to all movies that are conductive to social progress and Chinese people's well-being. As a particular film genre, main melody film serves as one of the most important parts of the state ideological apparatus in convincing audiences of the inevitability and the validity of a socialist China while reinforcing a sense of national identity and the leadership of the party-state as being "of its people and for its people".

Following the eight-word principle as the basis of its film policy, the state sought to use the shared revenues from Hollywood hits to support the production of domestic films, the main melody film in particular (Su 2010a, 2011, 2014). For example, starting from 1996, 5% of box office revenue from all films has been allocated to the Special Fund for National Film Development (Ministry of Finance & State Administration of Radio Film and Television 2006). That fund, in turn, is designed to "sponsor the production of feature film projects promoted by the state" (Article 2). One other aspect of this approach during 1990s and early 2000s was that the production and distribution of main melody films were fully state-sponsored projects. Through a special committee composed of party bureaucrats, the state participated in the different stages of film production, from financing, to screenplay writing, to actual film making and theatrical distribution (Wang 2009; Su 2014). In terms of the distribution, in particular, audiences – workers from state-owned enterprises and students especially – were organized to go to the cinema by administrative orders with tickets issued by the government instead of attendance based on voluntary purchases at the box office (Su 2010a).

In addition to directly resulting in the birth of the main melody film genre, the opening up of the Chinese film market toward Hollywood films also introduced some changes in domestic audience tastes (Wang 2009; Nakajima 2016). Chinese audiences were rapidly catching up with their global counterparts in terms of being assimilated by Hollywood's aesthetic style (Wang 2009; Nakajima 2016). Such change was further advanced by the increasing quota for foreign mega-productions each year, which rose from ten to twenty in 2001, just before China joined the WTO, and to thirty-four during President Xi Jinping's visit to the U.S. in February 2012 (Su 2014). Most of these films were Hollywood blockbusters. Some argue that the unique profundity and sensibility that have long defined Chinese cinema, and which are based on its people's most intimate experiences of and reflections on life, humanity, history and nationhood, have been (and continue to be) gradually reshaped by "the dramatic yet fleeting stimulations of MTV-style and Hollywood-style entertainment" (Wang 2009, p. 313). Such transition is evident from the common adoption of Hollywood techniques and themes in domestic commercial film production in recent years.

Furthermore, it also imposed great challenges on main melody films which in many cases appeared to be dogmatic and to lack creativity and spectacular scenes, compared with its Hollywood – and even domestic commercial – rivalries. As a particular genre directly responding to China's encounter with Hollywood in the post-socialist era, main melody film has increasingly become a cultural product which consumed huge resources yet gained little market profits in general. However, the crisis of main melody film does not lead to its elimination, but the rise of an upgraded sub-genre as the marketization process of the domestic film industry deepens, the "new" main melody film, to continue to serve as state's ideological apparatus.

Marketization of the Chinese film industry and the "new" main melody film

Reform of the film industry in China took place almost simultaneously with the state's selective opening up to Hollywood films. The reform officially began in 2000 with Document 320 issued by the State Administration of Radio Film and Television (SARFT) and the Ministry of Culture (State Administration of Radio Film and Television & Ministry of Culture, 2000). Between 2001 and 2005, the SARFT and the State Council promulgated several documents and supplementary regulations, which opened the gate for foreign and private capital to enter film production and theatre construction (State Administration of Radio Film and Television 2001, 2003; State Administration of Radio Film and Television & Ministry of Commerce 2004; the State Council 2005). The state especially encourages private capital to take an active role in boosting the film industry by removing many of the restrictions regarding ownership and operations. According to the *Provisional Regulation of the Entry and Operation Qualification of Enterprises in the Film Industry* co-released by SARFT and the Ministry of Commerce in 2004, private enterprises are encouraged to enter the film production sector with the Permit for Film Production issued by the SARFT, without necessarily affiliating with any state-owned enterprises.

The effective mobilization of private capital has contributed greatly to a burgeoning domestic film industry with a consecutive annual growth rate of over 25% for ten years between 2006 and 2016 (National Bureau of Statistics of China 2017). The main melody film is no exception regarding the marketization process of the film industry and has experienced a major transition from the state's dominance to market dominance. Private capital and enterprises have become the primary financial source for an increasing proportion of main melody films. They now are no longer state-sponsored projects and, consequently, filmmakers are growingly concerned about market reaction and audience tastes. This, in turn, has given rise to an emergent type of commercialized main melody films – sometimes called the "new main melody films" (Nakajima 2016, p. 98):

> These films 'conspire' [hemou] successfully in the aspects of commerce, art and the state ideology, and differ significantly from past main melody films [which focus solely on the promotion of state ideology], and hence can be called 'new main melody films'. (Zhao 2012, p. 18)

Compared with the previous generation of main melody films, new main melody films are a sophisticated hybrid of both the state's ideological influence and commercial pressures. Producers are increasingly solicitous about the film's profitability, which urges them to keep pace with popular Hollywood hits by borrowing filmic techniques from Hollywood studios, the introduction of more entertainment elements, and the adoption of the Hollywood style scenes and narratives (Su 2010b). According to *Liberation Daily* (Jiefang Ribao), the official daily newspaper of the Shanghai Committee of the Communist Party of China, the production of main melody films has moved into a brand new stage along with the marketization of the domestic film industry in the past several years. Such trends are exemplified in films like *Operations Mekong*[1] (2016) and *Wolf Warrior 2*, both of which have become the products of the "market autonomy" dominated by commercial logics, instead of the state (Zeng 2017).

The commercially successful new main melody films have demonstrated a close coordination between the commercial logics which has dominated local film production since 2000s, on the one hand, and the state's aim to perpetuate socialist ideology, on the other. Remarkably, the market has replaced the state to become the dominant institution in producing new main melody films and the assimilation of Hollywood blockbusters has contributed immensely to effectively delivering the state's ideology to audiences, as reflected by the grand success of *Wolf Warrior 2*. In the next section, I will deconstruct the film *Wolf Warrior 2* into three parts: the financialization of the film, the discursive construction of nationalism through the hero myth, and the marketing strategies adopted for the distribution of the film. The thrust of the analysis is to showcase how the new main melody film embeds multilateral and interlocking processes of transnational communication flows, which are defined by a complex ensemble of structural and agency considerations.

---

1   *Operation Mekong* is a Chinese-Hong Kong crime action film which is based on the 2011 Mekong River massacre, released in China on September 30, 2016.

Deconstructing *Wolf Warrior 2*

1. Financialization of the Chinese Hollywood style mega-production

The financing of *Wolf Warrior 2* is highly market-driven. This is exemplified by two practices. Firstly, private capital played a primary role in financing *Wolf Worrior 2*. Tab. 1 below provides a full list of production and distribution firms that played a part in bringing the film to the screen. As Tab. 1 shows, twenty-one enterprises were involved altogether, including fourteen production companies and seven distributors. China Film, which is controlled by the SARFT, and Deer Pictures, which is controlled by CCTV, are the only two state-owned companies in the production sector on the list, but it is crucial to note that they participated as part of the joint production team only. In other words, they had a relatively minor status in providing financial support. In addition, there is only one publicly-owned enterprise in the distribution sector: YingDu Cultural Invest Development, which is owned by the Office of Beijing State-Owned Cultural Assets Supervision and Management. Most of the companies are from the commercial film and culture industry, led by China's leading firm in this domain, Wanda Picture, and two companies controlled by Wu Jing, the director and leading actor of the film. The e-commerce giant, Alibaba, is also behind the production and distribution of the film.

Secondly, in addition to the injection of capital primarily from the private sector, the production of *Wolf Warrior 2* was largely shaped by the adoption of a practice borrowed from financial market – the Valuation Adjustment Mechanism (VAM) agreement, a tool that has fundamentally enabled the broader liberalization of the Chinese financial market. As early as in August, 2016 when *Wolf Warrior 2* was still in preparation for filming, Beijing Jingxi Culture and Tourism Co., Ltd (Beijing Culture) and UEP Media, the primary distributors for the film, signed a VAM agreement with the primary production enterprise, Beijing Dengfeng International Media Co., Ltd (Dengfeng), which is actually controlled by Wu Jing (Beijing Jingxi Culture and Tourism 2016).

A VAM agreement, usually translated as a "dui du" ("Bet-on") agreement in Chinese, is commonly used in mergers and acquisitions. A buyer/investor and a seller/financer sign a contract setting out the value adjustment triggering conditions before the acquisition, with the seller/financer getting higher payments if the goals are achieved while the buyer/investor will be compensated if the goals are not met (Qin 2017). When applied in the film market, the VAM works a little differently. A distributor is an investor in a film project and the production company is a financer. The two sides agree on a box office goal based on the perceived potential of the film and then the

Tab. 1: Production & distribution companies of *Wolf Warrior 2*

Category	Name of Enterprise	Ownership	Actual Owner/ Affiliation
Production	Beijing Dengfeng International Culture Communications Co., Ltd	Private-owned	Wu Jing
	Spring Era Film Co., Ltd.	Private-owned	
	Jetsen Culture Industry Group Co., Ltd	Private-owned	
	Chao Feng Pictures, LLC	Private-owned	
	Horgos Orange Image Media Co., Ltd	Private-owned	Beijing Enlight Media – Hangzhou Ali Venture Capital – Alibaba Group
	Khorgos Dengfeng International Culture Communication Co., Ltd	Private-owned	Beijing Dengfeng International Media (Wu Jing)
Joint Production	China Film Co., Ltd	State-owned	China Film Group Corporation – SARFT
	Deer Pictures Co., Ltd	State-owned	CCTV
	Bona Film Group Company Limited	Private-owned	Dongyang Alibaba – Alibaba Group
	Beijing Jingxi Culture & Tourism Co., Ltd	Private-owned	
	Wanda Media Co., Ltd	Private-owned	Beijing Wanda Investment
	I Verge Information Technology (Beijing) Co., Ltd	Private-owned	Youku – Hangzhou Ali Venture Capital – Alibaba Group
	Jiahui Culture and Media Co., Ltd	Private-owned	
	Star Era Movie & TV Culture Media Co., Ltd	Private-owned	Jetsen Techonology

(*continued on next page*)

Tab. 1: (continued)

Category	Name of Enterprise	Ownership	Actual Owner/ Affiliation
Distribution	Beijing Culture and Tourism Co., Ltd	Private-owned	
	UEP Media	Private-owned	
Joint Distribution	Beijing Qi Tai Ocean Culture & Media Co., Ltd	Private-owned	
	Wuzhou Film Distribution Co., Ltd	Private-owned	Wanda Pictures
	YingDu Cultural Invest Development Co.Ltd	State-owned	Office of Beijing State-Owned Cultural Assets Supervision and Management
	Shanghai Tao Piao Piao Movie & TV Culture Co., Ltd (Online film ticket retailer)	Private-owned	Alibaba Pictures – Alibaba Group
	Beijing Hero Film Pictures Co., Ltd	Private-owned	

Source: Author's compilation of data from corporate annual reports, enterprise announcements, National Enterprise Credit Information and Publicity System, online corporate data aggregator platform Tianyancha.com, and the film Wolf Warrior 2.

production company's income based on the box office goal will be calculated and paid by the distributor(s), usually before or soon after the theatre debut of the film (Chen 2016; Cao 2016; Qin 2017; Xu, 2017). The distribution company will enjoy a much larger slice of box office revenue for the part that exceeds the target. The VAM agreement effectively helps to alleviate the financial risk borne by the production team by transferring it to the distributor(s) since the production cost is likely to be covered regardless of the actual box office. This is precisely why the VAM agreement of a film project is also called "bao di" (minimum cost guarantee) agreement in Chinese. In other words, it often guarantees the coverage of the production cost of the film (Beijing Jingxi Culture and Tourism 2016).

While rarely observed in the film production in Hollywood studios, the VAM agreement is becoming a significant phenomenon in Chinese film production in recent years. Such agreements began to make their mark when a couple of

VAM financed domestic films made it into the top 10 annual box office China in 2013 and 2014, such as *Journey to the West: Conquering the Demons and Monkey King* (2013), the annual box office champion, while a year later *Breakup Buddies* (2014) ended the year in the second place in domestic box office revenue (CBO 2013, 2014; Chen 2016). In 2016, possibly stimulated by these successful cases, the number of domestic films that adopted the VAM significantly increased, and there were four films which broke into the top 10 box office rank that year, including *Mermaid* (2016), the then-top-grossing film of all time in the Chinese market with total receipts of nearly 3.4 billion RMB revenue (CBO 2016; Chen 2016; Cao 2016). That all-time high, however, was quickly surpassed by *Wolf Warrior 2* just nineteen months later.

Behind the triumphant cases above, there were many other films that failed to meet their target in the VAM agreement and resulted in great loss for investors, mirroring the long-standing trend in Hollywood and across the cultural industries, especially books and music, for blockbusters to be a one-in-ten phenomenon while the rest barely break even or flop completely from a strictly commercial point of view (Xia 2017). However, distribution companies still aggressively seek opportunities to sign VAM agreements with producers for two primary reasons. First, as mentioned earlier, if the film selected by the distributor(s) becomes a real blockbuster and surpasses the target box office, the income for distributor(s) will dramatically increase (Chen 2016; Cao 2016). According to the VAM agreement of *Wolf Warrior 2*, for instance, the box office goal for the film was negotiated at 800 million RMB (US$ 120 million) and the income for Dengfeng, the production company controlled by Wu Jing, would be 217.6 million RMB, or about 31% of the net box office,[2] if that happy turn of events transpired. The two primary distributors, on the other hand, will receive 12% of the net box office, which is around 86.4 million RMB, based on the 800 million RMB target. If the box office outstrips the target but remains below 1.5 billion RMB, the revenue-sharing proportion for distributors will increase to 25%. For the box office revenue segment that surpasses 1.5 billion RMB, the distributors will collect 15% of the revenue. Such revenue-sharing system is more favorable for the distributors if the goal is met, since the proportion for the distribution sector of domestic films usually

---

2   According to the corporate announcement of Beijing Culture, the target box office for the film is the 800 million RMB, while net box office is the remaining revenue after taxation, contribution to the Special Funding of Domestic Film (which is 5% of the total box office) and other administrative costs. Local theatre chains will claim approximately 57% of the net box office while the remaining 43% of net box office is the gain for producer and distributor to split.

ranges between 5% and 15% of the net box office on average – that is, if without a VAM agreement (Chen 2016; Qin 2017).

The other handsome return that most companies can hardly resist when signing a VAM agreement is its potential on effectively elevating the companies' stock price, which can far exceed the profits earned from a single film's box office. After *Wolf Warrior 2*'s debut in theatres, the stock price of Beijing Culture, the primary distributor which invested the most in the film, soared from 13.53 RMB to 22.5 RMB per share and the total trading value of the corporation expanded by 5.5 billion RMB within just ten days (Li 2017). The adoption of a VAM agreement for *Wolf Warrior 2* (and many other domestic films) and the risk that film investors are willing to take in order to exchange for returns in financial market, therefore, reveals an increasingly strong link between the film market and the financial market in China. This, in turn, indicates the trend of the financialization of Chinese cinema. The financialization of media, according to Winseck (2016), refers to a condition where business strategies in different sectors of media and communication are driven by financial capital and financial models. The wide adoption of mechanisms, such as the VAM agreement, has been enabled by the steady liberalization of Chinese financial market – as part of the nation's integration into the global capitalist system – and as part of an aggressive search for new modalities of capital accumulation, especially against the background of slowing economic growth in China over the last five years.

Wolf Warrior 2 is an especially interesting case here for two reasons. First, it showcases the breadth and depth of the financialization process, which has created significant impacts on, and has been embraced by, the production of not only commercial films but the popular main melody film which was once the state's exclusive preserve. Second, the financing model of *Wolf Warrior 2* as a new main melody film again reminds us of how transnational cultural flows and cultural production at localities are constantly shaped by interlocking processes of globalization as well as the convoluted interactions between politico-economic structure and local players, such as investors and producers, and the flagrant tendency for all of these aspects, players and interest to trespass willy-nilly across conventional borders between different sets of actors and different markets in the pursuit of commercial success and astonishingly high profits (even though many such efforts will eventually fail, recalling the ration of blockbuster successes to filmic flops).

The financialization process of the film has also created profound impacts at the levels of production of *Wolf Warrior 2*. The VAM agreement financially ensured the adoption of Hollywood production tactics in the film. According to the agreement, the production team received first payment of 70 million RMB from the distributors while the film was still in shooting (Beijing Jingxi Culture and Tourism 2016). The total budget for the film was more than doubled from 80 million RMB to 200 million RMB after the agreement was signed (Weboss 2017). Also, the VAM agreement imposed pressure on the production team to cater for the taste of as wide a range of audiences as possible in order to hit the target box office figure being sought, even though their investment was already reimbursed. In an interview after the film was released, Wu Jing admitted that he experienced exceptional stress and anxiety in the production process due to the VAM agreement; and regardless of the total box office of 5.8 billion RMB, Wu Jing confessed that his happiest moment was when the box office met 800 million RMB target (Chen 2016). The deep concern for market reaction and box office performance of the film, together with a deep pocket, explains, and also encouraged, the adoption of the Hollywood tactics and commercial elements incorporated into the film. For example, Wu Jing recruited a team of professionals with rich experience in producing Hollywood action films for *Wolf Warrior 2*. Altogether, this production team consisted of 1,700 people comprising nine languages and hailed from 27 countries (Sun 2017). Sam Hargrave from *Captain America: Civil War* (2016) was invited to serve as action director and fight coordinator for the film. From the shooting stage to post-production, the film demonstrated top quality Hollywood-level technical accomplishments/skills. The successful delivery of Hollywood-caliber action sequences, such as a *Fast & Furious*-type chase with tanks, or a six-minute long shot of a fierce, underwater fight, are considered one of the major reasons behind the movie's record-shattering success. Yet, the impacts of Hollywood did not stay on the technical level but also penetrated to the discursive layer of *Wolf Warrior 2* in constructing nationalism and patriotism.

2. Discursive construction: Building nationhood of China through Hollywood story

Just like main melody films which are vehicles for the construction of an enduring national identity of China, Hollywood movies are considered by many the vehicles of American culture and values supported by U.S. political and military power (Chen 1998; Schiller 1992; Su 2011). The connection between the mythic fantasy of the hero and the US democratic political ideals are established through a two-steps structure of the hero myth. The first step is the manifestation of the U.S. as the world police and world-savior with exaggerated American-style glory and dreams (Chen 1998; Su 2011). The second step-structure is to introduce mysterious, idealized heroes, which serves the construction of the first structure, and to portray the U.S. as a paradise where freedom, equality and fraternity are achieved, and justice being served by heroes (Chen 1998; Lawrence and Jewett, 2002). The purposes and ideals of a hero are always correct, representing the wish of not only the Americans but also of people of all nations. Also, heroes are the embodiments of their nation, the legitimacy and justification of their actions thus become transferrable to justify the purposes and exertions of the U.S. Essentially, the hero myth refers to a magic dream, a long-lasting ideological illusion which masks "the exploitation and pillage, the huge disparities between the rich and the poor, between the classes, nations and genders" (Su 2011, p. 193). This cheating illusion aims to promote Americanism to a global audience, which aids in establishing the hegemony of the American system. *Wolf Warrior 2* has borrowed such hero myth in its storyline as a key structure for the discursive construction of Chinese nationhood in an increasingly globalized world.

The story of *Wolf Warrior 2* is based on two evacuations of Chinese citizens, from Libya in 2011 and Yemen in 2015 respectively, which were organized by Chinese state (Wang, 2015). The first structure of the hero myth in the movie is the manifesto of China and its profound influences in Africa, where the hero's mission takes place. China, above all, is the only nation in the film which stays to provide assistance to the evacuation of their citizens when the fictional African state fell into civil war. It fully demonstrates the state's commitment to protecting and supporting their nationals in a caring and efficient manner, especially compared with the U.S., which vacated its embassy immediately after the war erupted. Furthermore, as the story unfolds, it unveils China's prevalent influences on various social facets of the fictional African state. China-led investment and construction, such as local hospitals and huge camps for factories, and vigorous and entrepreneurial overseas Chinese, such as Chinese store owners, Chinese factory managers, Chinese doctors, are all portrayed as highly beneficial, providing jobs for African workers, developing local infrastructure, bonding with local Africans and powering the local economy. Meanwhile, given an established role in local society, the nation yet does not overstep and remains respectful of the sovereignty of African states in handling their interior affairs as well as the international political order. For example, the Chinese Navy and vessels only wait at the portal since they will not enter war zone without permission from the United Nation. China being constructed here is a powerful, responsible country but still with restraint, which mirrors the path and diplomatic policy of "peaceful rise" insisted by the Chinese Communist Party since 2003 (Gu 2004; Hsu, 2007).

The structure of hero myth is further established through the actions delivered by a fearless, righteous hero, Leng Feng. As a former soldier of special troop unit Wolf Warriors, Leng Feng is expelled from the army due to his intervention in a forced, violent eviction in a Chinese village. And later, when Leng Feng is sent off by the People's Liberation Army (PLA) Navy to rescue Chinese workers in local factories in Africa, he has no access to any support from the PLA since he no longer serves in the military. Such setting features individualism which is very rare in main melody films as they almost always promote collectivism as one of the core components of socialist values. However, regardless of individualism, Leng Feng's choices and actions still reflect the film's aim at persuading domestic audiences about the country's righteousness, as well as both the growing influences and responsibilities at international level. For example, the initial task for Leng Feng is to help with the evacuation of Chinese workers in the factory; however, Leng Feng decided to rescue all the Africans employees as well and eventually bring them on board of the PLA Navy vessels. Leng Feng's choice underscores the humanitarianism carried by the Chinese authority, which serves to consolidate the manifesto of China established in the first structure.

The construction of nationalism of a rising China and the stimulation of patriotic sentiments from audiences reach the climax in the scene where Leng Feng guides a group of multiple nationals to pass through the crossfire zone occupied by rebellion army. In order to convince the rebellion army that they are just civilians, Leng Feng drops the weapon and lifts up a national flag of PRC instead, to inform the rebellion army who they are. "Hold your fire, it's Chinese!" Convinced that if they hurt Chinese citizens, Chinese government will take serious actions, the commander of rebellion army asks the soldiers to hold fire and let Leng Feng and his companions pass safely. The scene of Leng Feng holding up the national flag of China is strikingly symbolic. With the Five-Starred Red Flag fluttering high and bright at the top of the scene, people of different nationalities unite under – and are sheltered by – this flag. The illusion of American supremacy established by hero myth in Hollywood films is replicated here and adjusted to the discursive construction of China's nationhood. It is not American supremacy but Chinese supremacy being formulated in the film, which highly resonates with the state's ideology and foreign policy.

The deployment of hero myth in constructing nationalism and patriotism of China in this film embeds the contradiction that cannot be fully cupped by the thesis of either cultural imperialism or cultural globalization. The anxiety about the cultural and ideological influences of Hollywood on China reflects not only the ideological confrontation between the U.S. and China. At the deeper level, it is also about China searching for a new national culture, a new national identity and even a Chinese alternative modernity in a rapidly globalized world (Su 2011). Yet, it is the well-established, typical Hollywood hero myth structure that the local producer has adopted when it comes to the discursive construction of China's own national identity. It reveals the profound influences of Hollywood movies in local cinema after China's decades' of opening up towards foreign imports. However, the adoption of hero myth structure in fact does not eliminate the function of *Wolf Warrior 2* as a main melody film. By contrast, it effectively contributes to the delivery of an updated and enduring nationhood of a rising China and the construction of a responsible, confident authority which is capable of protecting its citizens and even other nationals. In this sense, this film neither exemplifies Hollywood's dominance over local cinema nor mirrors the utopian view of the creation of plural cultures led by free-willing agencies at localities in globalization process. This film is, instead, a synthetic cultural product within which the boundary between state's ideology and the strong marks left by Hollywood are shaped by both the structure and agency.

3. Marketing strategies: Domestic film protection month and national campaign for Army's day

In addition to the high quality of production and the affective discursive structure and mise en scène that stimulate patriotic sentiments from Chinese audiences, both the producers and distributers of *Wolf Warrior 2* have deliberately clung into two major events for marketing purposes, which contributes tremendously to its historic box office record. The first event is the "domestic film protection month" implemented through administrative order from the SARFT. In each July and August, there are six to eight weeks when most of the foreign films will be shut out from theatres so there will be more screens open up for domestic films (Tartaglione 2015). It initially started in 2004 to support the domestic movie *House of Flying Daggers* directed by Zhang Yimou, which was welcomed in oversea theatres but experienced frustration in home market (Tartaglione 2015). After that, the "domestic film protection month" lives on as a tradition and it has become increasingly connected to the Army's day of PLA, which is August 1, by state's patriotic campaign – essentially, to celebrate Army's Day and to support domestic films to over pass their Hollywood rivalries are both gestures of patriotism. This was particularly the case in 2017 due to the 90th anniversary of the founding of PLA. There was national patriotic campaign in July and August, and a grand military parade took place on July 30, 2017 (Lu 2017).

Aiming to take the advantages of both the screening schedule that favored domestic films and the affective patriotic discourses of national campaign of

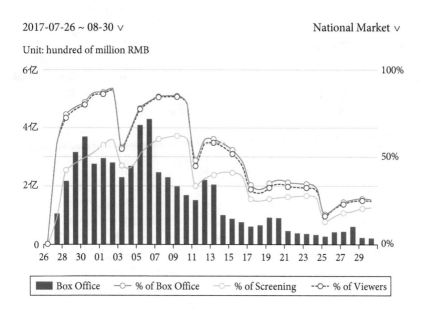

2017-07-26 ~ 08-30 ∨   National Market ∨

Unit: hundred of million RMB

Chart 1: Performance of *Wolf Warrior 2* in the First Five Weeks within Chinese Market
Source: Mobile app of Yi En Film Database

PLA anniversary that perfectly resonates with its story, *Wolf Warrior 2* picked July 27 as its debut date. Such arrangement was clearly stated in the VAM agreement signed between Dengfeng and Beijing Culture when the film was still in shooting: Beijing Culture requested Dengfeng to meet the production schedule of *Wolf Warrior 2*, and to ensure that the film would be ready for release within the period between July 1 and August 18 in 2017 (Beijing Jingxi Culture and Tourism 2016). Chart 1 above maps out the performance of *Wolf Warrior 2* in Chinese market in the first five weeks since its debut, which collected over 90% of its aggregate box office. The chart demonstrates that *Wolf Warrior 2* took up over 50% of the screens in most days in its first two weeks' showing, thanks to the "blackout" of foreign movies in July and August, which locked its Hollywood competitors out of the market.

The domestic film protection month reveals the still powerful role of the state in post-socialist China. Although the state has stepped down from the leading position in producing new main melody film such as *Wolf Warrior 2* – largely due to decades of marketization of film industry and the opening and reform in other sectors of the national economy – it still provides strong support in maximizing the film's screening schedules by administrative order. Meanwhile, the production team and investors of the film explicitly exploited the administrative protection and the patriotic campaign carried out by the state, in order to achieve the box office goal as part of its business strategies which were carefully planned ahead. Such efforts reveal a close synergy between the state's aim in promoting nationalistic and patriotic discourses, and the market dynamics actively anticipated by producers and investors in their pursuit for maximum profits.

Conclusion

The case of *Wolf Warrior 2* has demonstrated how the production of main melody film has been reshaped under the influences from not only Hollywood films but the integration of China's national economy into the global capitalist system on multilateral level. First of all, the hybridity between Hollywood blockbusters and main melody film is enabled, and greatly advanced, by the financialization of the film industry with practices such as VAM agreement, which is the result of decades of liberalization of Chinese financial market. In particular, it has showcased the process of how the conventional borders between different markets and dimensions of globalization are trespassed by various actors, from the state to the local film producers and investors in cultural industry. Cultural product at localities against the backdrop of globalization is neither the result of a dominant culture and/or value from few superpowers overriding other alternatives nor the creation of diverse and plural cultures that mirror local agencies' free will and innovative potentials. Instead, it is a battlefield in which different players and institutions both compete and coordinate with one another in their pursuit of maximized capitalist revenue within the ideological boundary set by the state.

Secondly, *Wolf Warrior 2* reflects the state's surprisingly accommodating and adaptive capacity for opening up selective space for global Hollywood and incorporating both market forces and private capital into the film production and state mechanism. Likewise, it demonstrates the adaptive capacity for local producers and investors too in terms of maximizing their monetary returns through exploitation of the state's support, market mechanism, and audiences' demand. Together, in the pursuit of their distinctive aims, the state, market and investors, however, eventually coalesced to make a main melody film the top-grossing of all time in Chinese cinema, which was keenly watched by at least 140 million Chinese.

At last, the hybridity between the Hollywood narrative of hero myth and state's ideology in *Wolf Warrior 2* reveals the complexity of transnational cultural flows. On the one hand, main melody film as a particular genre was initiated by the state to minimize the Hollywood influence but, as exemplified by the case of *Wolf Warrior 2*, main melody film now in fact aims to replicate Hollywood style from production tactics to the storytelling in order to satisfy market and investors. On the other hand, under the profound impacts of Hollywood films, *Wolf Warrior 2* still successfully achieved its goal as a main melody film, which is to construct an enduring and up-to-date national identity of China as an international heavyweight and an indispensable nation, delivered by the cliché of the hero myth. As reminded by Su (2011), at the much deeper level, the debate of China's policy toward Hollywood films is essentially about a post-socialist China searching for a new national culture, a new national identity and even a Chinese alternative path to modernity in a rapidly globalized world. The popularity of the movie *Wolf Warrior 2* in its home market also allows us to glimpse a confusing, and sometimes even painful, process of modern Chinese trying to figure out what does it mean to be a Chinese, along with a thirst of being recognized by the larger part of the world. Just as Frank Grillo, the American actor who plays the primary antagonist in the movie, said in an interview conducted by *The Hollywood Reporter*: "People say this movie is nationalistic and it's propaganda, and in a sense, it is. But this pride in China is real, and the audience wants to believe that being Chinese means something special" (Sun 2017).

References

Anderson, Benedict. *Imagined communities: Reflections on the origin and spread of Nationalism*. (Revised eds.). 2006. London: Verso.

Appadurai, Arjun. "The production of locality". In Fardon, Richard. (Eds.), *Counterworks: Managing the diversity of knowledge*. London: Routledge. 1995. pp. 204–225.

Beijing Jingxi Culture and Tourism. No. 2016-118 corporate announcement regarding investment and connected transaction (disclosed with the contract of distribution and partnership of film *Wolf Warrior 2*). 2016, August 5. Retrieved from http://disclosure.szse.cn/finalpage/2017-08-01/1203745755.PDF

Box Office Mojo. "All Time Worldwide Box Office Grosses". (2017). Retrieved November 06, 2017, from http://www.boxofficemojo.com/alltime/world/

Cao, Jun. "2016 zhongguo dianying shichang: shenhua de pomie" [Chinese film market 2016: Miracle shattered]. *Financial Times*. December 6, 2016. Retrieved September 2, 2018, from http://www.ftchinese.com/story/0010705 27?full=y&archive.

CBO Chinese Box Office. *Records of annual box office 2016*. 2016. Retrieved August 17, 2018, from http://www.cbooo.cn/year?year=2016

CBO Chinese Box Office. *Records of annual box office 2014*. 2014. Retrieved August 17, 2018, from http://www.cbooo.cn/year?year=2014

CBO Chinese Box Office. *Records of annual box office 2013*. 2013. Retrieved August 17, 2018, from http://www.cbooo.cn/year?year=2013

Chen, Changye. "Jinxia baodi faxing ji jin quanbai, cuo zai nali?" [Bet-on distribution mostly failed in this summer, why?]. *36Kr*. August 22, 2016. Retrieved August 17, 2018, from https://36kr.com/p/5051593.html

Chen, Xiaoyun. "Meiguo dianying: Huayu baquan he yishixingtai shenhua [American films: Hegemony of discourse and ideological myth]. *Dangdai dianying* [Contemporary Cinema], 2, 1998, p. 39–44.

Editorial Committee of China Film Yearbook. *China film yearbook*. Beijing: China Film Press. 2011.

Comor, Edward. "Media corporations in the age of globalization". In W. B. Gudykunst & B. Mody (Eds.), *Handbook of international and intercultural communication* (2nd ed.). Thousand Oaks, CA/London: Sage. 2002, p. 309–324

Frater, Patrick. "Wolf Warrior II's massive success forces studios to rethink China approach." *Variety*. August 31, 2017. Retrieved November 6, 2017, from http://variety.com/2017/biz/news/china-wolf-warrior-ii-1202543266/

Gu, Ping. "Weida minzu fuxing de daolu xuanze – lun zhongguo de heping jueqi." [A path to national rejuvenation – discussion of China's peaceful rise]. *People's Daily*. February 17, 2004.

Hsu, Kevin Fan. "China finally has its own Rambo: the ultra-nationalist fantasy *Wolf Warrior 2* is making crowds – and government officials – happy". *Foreign Policy*. September 1, 2017. Retrieved December 10, 2017, from http://foreignpolicy.com/2017/09/01/china-finally-has-its-own-rambo/

Kraidy, Marwan. *Hybridity, or the cultural logic of globalization*. Philadelphia: Temple University Press. 2005.

Kraidy, Marwan. *"Critical Transculturalism"*. The 55th Annual International Communication Association Conference. New Orleans, LA, May 27–31, 2004.

Lawrence, John S., and Robert Jewett. *The myth of the American superhero*. Grand Rapids, MI: Eerdmans. 2002.

Li, Manning. "Zhanlang 2 chixu gaoshao, beijing wenhua gaoguan shandian kaichu tuishaoyao" [As *Wolf Warrior 2*'s heat continues, senior executives of Beijing Culture cooled the stock market]. *Zhengquan shibao* [Securities Times]. August 9, 2017. Retrieved on September 12, 2018, from http://company.stcn.com/2017/0809/13545339.shtml

Liu, Fusheng. *Lishi de fuqiao: shiji zhijiao "zhuxuanlü" xiaoshuo yanjiu* [Historical floating bridge: A study of "main melody" fiction at the turn of the 21st century]. Kaifeng, China: Henan University Press. 2005.

Lu, Hui. "Military parade held to mark PLA 90th birthday (Part I)". *Xinhua Net*. July 30, 2017. Retrieved December 11, 2017, from http://news.xinhuanet. com/english/2017-07/30/c_136484187.htm

Ma, Weijun. "Chinese main melody TV drama: Hollywood and ideological persuasion". *Television & New Media*, 15(6), 2013, p. 523–537.

Mattelart, Armand. *Transnationals and the third world: The struggle for culture*. South Hadley, MA: Bergin and Harvey. 1983.

Mattelart, Armand. *Mapping world communication: War, progress, culture*. Minneapolis: University of Minnesota Press. 1994.

Ministry of Finance/State Administration of Radio Film and Television. *Revision of the management methods of the special fund for national film development*. August 17, 2006. Retrieved from http://www.mof.gov.cn/gp/ xxgkml/kjs/200806/t20080624_2499145.html

Nakajima, Seio. "The genesis, structure and transformation of the contemporary Chinese cinematic field: Global linkages and national refractions". *Global Media and Communication*, 12(1), 2016, p. 85–108.

National Bureau of Statistics of China. "Annual statistics of broadcasting and film development: 2006-2016". 2017. Retrieved from http://data.stats.gov.cn/ easyquery.htm?cn=C01

Qin, Qian. "How much money has *Wolf Warrior 2* made and who gets it?" *China Film Insider*. August 2, 2017. Retrieved July 12, 2018, from http:// chinafilminsider.com/chinasplaining-how-much-money-has-wolf-warrior-ii-made-and-by-whom/

Rosen, Stanley. "The world at the door: Hollywood and the film market in China". In E. Heikkila & R. Pizarro (Eds.), *Southern California and the world*. Westport, CT: Praeger. 2002, p. 49–77.

Schiller, Herbert. *Mass communication and American empire* (2nd ed., Updated). Boulder: Westview. 1992.

Schiller, Herbert. "Not yet the post-imperialist era". *Critical Studies in Mass Communication*, 8(1), 1991, p. 13–28.

Schiller, Herbert. *Culture Inc.: The corporate takeover of public expression*. New York: Oxford University Press. 1989.

State Administration of Radio Film and Television & Ministry of Commerce. (2004, October 10). *Provisional regulation of the entry and operation qualification of enterprises in film industry*. Retrieved from http://www.sarft. gov.cn/art/2004/11/10/art_1588_26368.html

State Administration of Radio Film and Television . *Opinions of promoting the broadcasting and film industry development.* December 30, 2003. Retrieved from http://www.51wf.com/print-law?id=1101756

State Administration of Radio Film and Television. *The detailed regulations to implement the structural reformation of the mechanism of film distribution and presentation.* December 13, 2001. Retrieved from http://www.sarft.gov. cn/art/2001/12/13/art_106_4376.html

State Administration of Radio Film and Television & Ministry of Culture. *Document 320: Several opinions regarding the deepening of the reform of film industry.* June 6, 2000. Retrieved from http://www.gov.cn/gongbao/ content/2001/content_60781.htm

Su, Wendy. "Cultural policy and film industry as negotiation of power: The Chinese State's role and strategies in its engagement with Global Hollywood 1994–2012". *Pacific Affairs*, 87(1), 2014, p. 93–114.

Su, Wendy. "Resisting cultural imperialism, or welcoming cultural globalization? China's extensive debate on Hollywood cinema from 1994 to 2007". *Asian Journal of Communication*, 21(2), 2011, p. 186–201.

Su, Wendy. "To be or not to be? – China's cultural policy and counter hegemony strategy toward global Hollywood from 1994 to 2000". *Journal of International and Intercultural Communication*, 3(1), 2010a, p. 38–58.

Su, Wendy. "New strategies of China's film industry as soft power". *Global Media and Communication*, 6(3), 2010b, p. 317–322.

Sun, Rebecca. "Meet the Director Behind China's Highest-Grossing Film of All Time". *The Hollywood Reporter.* December 8, 2017. Retrieved December 10, 2017, from https://www.hollywoodreporter.com/features/ meet-director-behind-chinas-highest-grossing-film-all-time-1064322

Tartaglione, Nancy: "'Monster Hunt' seizes China record; Blackout pics begin to close gap with H'wd." *Deadline.* July 27, 2015. Retrieved December 11, 2017, from http://deadline.com/2015/07/ monster-hunt-china-record-blackout-hollywood-1201485542/

The State Council. *The state council's several decisions regarding the entry of non-public assets into cultural industry.* April 13, 2005. Retrieved from http:// dy.chinasarft.gov.cn/html/www/article/2011/012d78fcc59905cd4028819e2d 789a1d.html

Tomlinson, John: "Globalization and Cultural Analysis". In David Held/Anthony G. McGrew (eds.): Globalization Theory: Approaches and Controversies. Polity: Cambridge. 2006, pp. 148–168.

Tomlinson, John. *Globalization and culture.* Chicago: University of Chicago Press. 1999. p. 1–27.

Wang, Kevin. "Yemen evacuation a strategic step forward for China." *The Diplomat.* April 10, 2015. Retrieved December 11, 2017, from https://thediplomat. com/2015/04/yemen-evacuation-a-strategic-step-forward-for-china/

Wang, Ting. "Understanding local reception of globalized cultural products in the context of the international cultural economy: A case study on the reception of Hero and Daggers in China." *International Journal of Cultural Studies*, 12(4), 2009, p. 299–318.

Weboss. "How much money has *Wolf Warrior 2* made? Let's do the math…" *Sohu News*, August 1, 2017. Retrieved on July 24, 2018, from https://www. sohu.com/a/161479550_808541

Winseck, Dwayne. "Financialization and the "crisis of the media": The rise and fall of (some) media conglomerates in Canada". *Canadian Journal of Communication*, 35(3), 2016, p. 365–394.

Xia, Tian. "5 bu dianying 4 bu kui, weihe baodi faxing hai qianfuhouji?" [4 Out of 5 films that adopted VAM did not meet their target, why VAM is still being used commonly?] *PE Daily*. August 15, 2017. Retrieved August 10, 2018, from http://news.pedaily.cn/201608/20160815401710.shtml

Xu, Lu. "Who are the investors behind *Wolf Warrior 2*?" *WeChat Public Account: Entertainment Capital*. August 1, 2017. Retrieved November 30, from http://news.pedaily.cn/201708/20170801417945.shtml

Zeng, Yuli. "zhanlang2 de juli yu jianjundaye de juxing". [Cohesion of values in *Wolf Warrior 2* and starring in The Founding of the army], *Jiefang Ribao [Liberation Daily]*, August 3, 2017. Retrieved July 3, from https://www. shobserver.com/journal/2017-08-03/getArticle.htm?id=25885

Zhao, Lan. "Shangye, renwen, guojia xingxiang de 'hemou': Guanyu Zhongguo xinxhuxuanlü dianying" ['Conspiracy' among commerce, art and state ideology: On Chinese new main melody films]. *Zhongguo Dianying Shichang [Chinese Film Market]*, 7, 2012, p. 18–19.

Zhu, Ying. *Chinese cinema during the era of reform. The ingenuity of the system.* Connecticut and London: Westport. 2003.

Daniel Lindblom

In the land of Finnish Swedish cinema: A look into the political economy of local cinema in Finland

Abstract Globalization and digitalization presents Finno-Swedish cinema with formidable challenges. While Finnish cinema is already struggling to survive as "small cinema", the challenge for Finno-Swedish cinema is even harder. In this chapter I discuss the main features of this challenge and offer some reflections to address it.

Keywords: Finnish Swedish cinema, local culture, Hollywood, cultural dominance, diversity, European cinema

Introduction

This chapter looks into the current situation and possible future of Finnish Swedish cinema, as well as at local film and local stories in general. In other words, how "small cinema industries", like the Finno-Swedish one, continue to stay alive and evolve while being quite invisible for the rest of the world and not being a part of the so-called Hollywood empire. In this chapter I will also look at the process of change affecting the film industry and to some of its implication for Finno-Swedish cinema.

Universal stories

Local stories have always been able to be universal. We can start by looking at a Hollywood classic like Casablanca (1942). Technically speaking, that film is not local cinema, since it was a major Hollywood production, but if we look at the story itself, it could as well be a French, Italian, Swedish, African or an Iranian story, or even a Finno-Swedish one, with a universal connotation. Casablanca hardly needs any bigger introduction. It is one of the most if not the most famous movie of the Golden years of Hollywood, right there alongside Gone with The Wind (1939). But the story of Casablanca, based on Murray

Burnett's and Joan Alison's unpublished play Everybody Comes to Rick's, is universal. Not just American. It is, in fact, about the situation of the world at that point when the movie actually was made. War was going on in Europe, terror, fear and turmoil, concentration camps. The famous story is about the American Rick, a New Yorker in exile, who pretends not to care about the state of world and has started a bar and restaurant in Casablanca, Ricks, where he has found a kind of place on the side of the world, as if he has retreated there, while the war goes on in Europe. But in his heart Rick has solidarity to the righteous cause and those people in need; he will choose to fight against the Nazis, one can understand from the end of the movie. And at the same time the city Casablanca is ruled by the Germans. So, this story could be of any country at that time. Although it would not have become so famous, we can assume, if it had not been for that it was a big Hollywood production and a big hit, with stars as Humphrey Bogart and Ingrid Bergman.

Finno-Swedish cinema, and Finno-Swedish culture, are part of the Finno-Swedish community. A community of a minority: Swedish-speaking Finns in Finland. Now, a Finno-Swedish story is a local story, in the sense that it is a story told by or about a minority. This is at least how most Finno-Swedish filmmakers and film scholars, and even film students of today, see Finno-Swedish cinema. But why is Finnish and Finno-Swedish cinema so invisible outside its own country? By invisible, I mean that Finnish cinema has very little reputation, neither good nor bad, except for Aki Kaurismäki, outside its own country.

There are other countries, countries that are so to speak outside the Hollywood domain. These countries are many, but let's take two examples, since we are talking about universal stories. The Russian director Andrey Zvyagintsevs films Leviathan (2014) and Loveless (2017) were both Oscar nominees and also won numerous awards around the world (Loveless won the Jury prize at Festival de Cannes), and since the movies were not only very good, but important movies about contemporary Russia, Putin's Russia, and critical of that society, Hollywood gave them attention. Another local film that got much attention was the Turkish-French film Mustang (2015) by Deniz Gamze Erguven. A film about a family of five girls, living on the eastern side of Turkey. The girls are ruled by their patriarchal uncle (which symbolises president Erdogan of Turkey) and after the girls one day play with boys by the sea, the girls are locked inside the house, forbidden to leave it, and then the older sisters (all in their teens) are forced to enter marriages, which leads to some of the girls committing suicide. This is a story, the screenwriter-director Gamze Erguven said, about what it is to be a girl in Turkey (Zolads, Lindsay, Vulture, 22.2.2016).

The films mentioned above are films that are, so to speak, approved by Hollywood. Or in other words, approved by the West. And one could argue that the cinema of the West lives, more or less, on Hollywood's mercy. The films mentioned are all quality films, but they also serve the West by telling about the violence and the corruptness of Russia and Turkey: important stories, but also what the world wants to see, Russia is bad, Turkey is bad, and this is what Hollywood, The United States and the West want to sell to audiences all over the world. This does not mean it is Western propaganda, on the contrary: these films are both, in their own way, beautiful, important and heart-breaking. But it is important to see that they can also be used as tools by Hollywood and the West.

Now, Finnish cinema does simply not only serve Hollywood – like films made by dissidents – but remains quite invisible because it has not at all the quality that other Nordic and European countries, and Eastern countries, have. And now the industry has changed a lot in the last ten years and is changing still more rapidly than ever. How will this affect European cinema? And local cinemas?

In the Nostradamus report of 2018 – a report on the current and future situation of the film and TV industry, put together by Finnish Swedish journalist and author Johanna Koljonen, the reality is that the industry changes: "Storytelling changes hearts and minds, but it will rarely change reality back to how it was before." it says in the report (Koljonen 2018). Netflix is of course a reality nobody can ignore. And as of December 2017, Netflix has 117.58 million subscribers. And the frightful fact is now that a third of the world's population owns a smartphone. The report clearly dictates that the content – much of what is on Netflix, and HBO then – must fill a need in people's life. It cannot be any other way. And this is the way it has always been (the industry lives on capitalistic terms). Digital services, like Netflix and HBO, have a direct consumer relationship, and therefore access to data: this leads to the fact that the streaming services know straight away, and in detail, what their consumers are watching, how much and what the majority of people want. The digital services will of course also – on their channel, consumers' personal channel – "suggest" TV-series and films for you. In that way the industry controls the audience; feeding them things that are similar to want they have seen before; soon the audience will only watch the same stuff. Freedom is gone. Only at the cinemas, when people go out in the world to enjoy cinema culture, there is still a freedom of choice. According to the Nostradamus report (Koljonen 2018), "…in 2023 the industry will not have grown smaller, but the industry will be leaner, and a new order have started to take shape." We will see what that order will be.

The Nostradamus report also states that European cinema is not doing well, and a new system is required so that the industry in Europe can grow to be better and compete with Hollywood. Top European hit films are required, to be able for the industry to stay on the market. Making right decisions is now more important than it was five or ten years ago. Although, the film industry is changing more slowly than the TV industry, because there are still mastodons (Hollywood bosses with enormous power in the business, in Hollywood and overseas, one could imagine) that hold on to the old system.

But Hollywood films and European films, and even more, of course, all "local" films (most of all films from countries on the side of the Hollywood empire, like Finland) are a quite different thing. Different things in many ways, and it is an understatement. This starts at the cinema. Both in Finland, the Nordic countries, and in other countries in Europe. Small films, or foreign films, local films (films that have little budgets also when it comes to marketing) are not getting nearly as much time in cinemas (some just a few months, some only three months or so, before no one even gets the time to go and see these "more European, more difficult films") while *Star Wars* and other blockbusters get more cinema-time, of course because the studios can pay the movie theatres more. So, people don't get to see, or even get to read about the ("much better, more important") films in the paper before they are put away. And then all we can see is *Star Wars* and *Fast & Furious 7*. And the new Quentin Tarantino movie.

The room of Finnish Swedish cinema

If Finnish cinema has only a few ways to be funded, Finno-Swedish cinema and TV has even more difficulties. In Finland, the state funds the films. The Finnish Film Foundation gives the biggest support. The two foundations that give funding for Finno-Swedish film and TV – the project has to have a Finnish Swedish connotation, and most often the language is in Swedish – are Svenska Kulturfonden (The Swedish culture foundation) and Konstsamfundet (The Art Foundation) which is a part of the Swedish Literature society (Finno-Swedish). There are also some other foundations, but these two gives most of the money to cinema and TV. Apart from these two, the other two big cinema and TV funders are, always, Svenska Yle and of course, The Finnish Film Foundation.

In the last twenty years, there have only been made a few Finnish Swedish films and TV-series. In 2000, the film *Kites over Helsinki* (*Drakarna över Helsingors*) was made by Peter Lindholm. The film is based on the best-selling Kjell Westö novel by the same title from 1996, now a modern Finno-Swedish (and Finnish) classic. It is important to notice that this film is based on a famous novel, because the next big film, of the same budget (even though *Kites over Helsinki* was not an historical epic, it still was a big Finno-Swedish film) was a film based on another Kjell Westö novel: The 2006 Finlandia Prize winner *Where We Once Walked* (*Där vi en gång gått*). The novel was made into a movie that had its premiere in 2011. And at the same time, this full feature movie, made for the cinema, with a budget of approximately one million euro, was, with the same money, no extra, made into a TV mini-series by the same name, the same story, same actors, at the same time. Why was this decision made by the financiers? Because of money, no doubt. Or rather, the lack of more money. The next bigger production that was made, was in 2016, when the mini TV-series (eight episodes) *Lolauppochner* (in English, Lolauppanddown) was made by director Ulrika Bengts. The TV-series is also based on a best-selling novel by Finno-Swedish Monika Fagerholm. The budget for the whole TV-series was 1,385,000 euros, the same as director Ulrika Bengts last movie, but as she said in an interview in Hufvudstadsbladet in 2016 (Hällsten 2016), her last movie, *The Apprentice* (2013), was a 90 minutes film with five roles, while Lolauppochner has thirty-five roles and is six hours long. At one point, it seemed that this TV-series was never going to see the light of production, since first Nordisk Film & TV-fond withdrew their funding, and after that also The Finnish Film Foundation, which is crucial for a bigger production in Finland. But Svenska YLE gave just enough support so that the TV-series could be made. Now, of course, compared to international budgets, and budgets of other Nordic TV-series or films, this money was even for Finnish standard very little. Since the Film Foundation backed out, there was hardly enough money to make a TV-series of that size. Still, *Lolauppochner* was made and got some pretty good reviews as opposed to some other Finno-Swedish big production dramas.

An even more recent TV-series that is not only Finno-Swedish but in two languages (which plays a part to bring more audience) was the TV-series *Aktivisterna* (*The Activists*, 2018) by screenwriter and director Lauri Majala who has mostly worked in theatre. *Aktivisterna* is about a group of people in Helsinki during the beginning of the 1900s, not unlike, when it comes to the period theme, the Claes Olsson movie *Colorado Avenue* (2007) based on Lars Sunds novels *Colorado Avenue* (1991) and *Lanthandlerskans son* (1997) and the movie and the TV-series *Where We Once Walked*. The reviews of all these period pieces have all said more or less the same thing, yes, some praises to, but mostly: Finnish period drama does simply not work – not the setting, not the acting, not the script and, above all, it lacks the boldness to tell stories that really gets the viewers' attention. One review, written about *Aktivisterna* in *Helsingin Sanomat* by Lena Virtanen (2019), said that it was "foolish to wish for a Finnish period drama series" and that it would have been better that nothing would have been made. So, what is the problem with Finnish and Finno-Swedish film? It is a broader question, which we shall not linger on too long here. But we can only say that the lack of money and the lack of doing are the reasons why Finnish and Finno-Swedish cinema and TV does not hold to international, or even Nordic, standards. Journalist Lena Virtanen also asked, after stating that Aktivisterna could as well have been a TV-series from the 1990s: Have we learned nothing in twenty years? (Topelius, 2019)

Well, perhaps there might be some hope, since there have been some quite successful Finnish Swedish TV-series made for children. Like Elin Grönbloms' children-TV-series: *Fanny* (2014), based on NRK Supers TV-series *Sara* (2008–2009) as well as Grönbloms' TV-series *Sommarkollo* (2017) and most recently *Steffi* (2018), a drama series about a teenage girl who tries to cope with her best friend's death. These TV-series got better reviews, and although it is clear that the lack of proper production money is also a problem here, the TV-series for children are of better quality than TV-series and films made for older viewers.

Maria Lundström, who is producer for culture, documentaries and drama at Svenska YLE, talks warmly about TV-drama made for children and young people. According to Lundström, the production of Finno-Swedish TV-drama and film is very thin, there are not made much TV-series and films. According to Lundström, a big part of the problem for this – and the lack of quality in Finno-Swedish drama – is because the market and the industry are so small that there is no competition among the Finno-Swedish filmmakers. And still it is expected that a Finno-Swedish film or TV-series is coming out now and then, and when that one comes out, it should be good. In the best of worlds, so good that it could compete on the Nordic or even international market. Unfortunately, the scripts that come in seldom have the quality YLE is striving for.

Local film is important, yes, and it is important that Finno-Swedish film and TV address local topics and stories, but Lundström, who is making the decisions for the Finno-Swedish TV, also thinks that it is a non-profitable thinking that Finno-Swedish film should only be made for local audience. When she reads scripts, she always compares them with what is being done on Finnish, Nordic and international level.

Based on this, one can draw the conclusion that all the production has, of course, a lot to do with resources and finances. Also, the lack of time and quality. But when it comes to TV-drama made for children and youth, there is light at the end of the tunnel. Compared to drama made for grown-ups, when it comes to drama made for children and youth, there are interesting ideas, interesting scripts, interesting makers and new name's, and this is fantastic to notice, says Lundström.

So, if there is a problem with Finno-Swedish TV-drama for grown ups, it is the scripts. There is a great need for better and unique ideas. And in Finland there is a lack of script development, unlike in Sweden, where there are functions and specific companies that only work with script development. Needless to say, it would be good to see something of that in Finland.

Historically, there has always been a huge difference between Finnish and Swedish – Danish cinema and TV-drama and now, in the last ten years or more, also Norwegian. But when we discuss local films and language, it is a fact that two-languages productions can reach more audiences. Since the Swedish-speaking community is definitely not all we got to aim for. But to create something – in Finland, in Finnish or Finno-Swedish TV – like the Norwegian *Skam*, or a very popular drama-TV-series for young people, is of course challenging, but not impossible. It is all about having the right skilled and talented people to get together at the same time around a unique idea. Also, there has not yet been, as in Denmark with the Dogma-boom, any similar boom in Finland (Schepelern, Kosmorama 2013).

And one important thing to know, is that *Skam* is not a one-time hit, but a long development of stories and a work of a lot of people with experience. In order to have the Finnish language or Finno-Swedish TV-drama do something remotely similar, there needs first to be more TV-series productions, more chances for people, for young people, in the TV-field to get to work and get experience, and above all, perhaps boldness. Boldness and a deeper cooperation between scriptwriters, producers and funders (Stokel-Walker, The Telegraph 2017) .

Another fact is that compared to Finnish TV (the Finnish side of YLE), Svenska YLEs budgets for TV-shows and films are of a whole different world; much smaller than on the Finnish side. Still, change is possible. Change in stories and change in the way stories for TV are being told. Especially now, when society has undergone and is undergoing more changes, changes towards more openness for ethnic and sexual minorities. Lundström hopes that a change in Finnish Swedish drama will happen soon. And specifically, stories that address diversity, representation and equality.

Since stories can no longer be told in the same, traditional way, they need to change. And Lundström says it is problematic when the scripts still are behind the change occurring in the rest of society. And there is the difference one can see between TV for grown-ups and TV for children: the scripts for children-TV are updated, fresher and braver.

Then comes the question of streaming services: the enormous challenges they set for local streaming channels, and local film and TV everywhere – since no one longer watches TV. Netflix is competing with YLE. But a fact is that in Finland, YLE Areena – a streaming service with all YLEs programs, available of course to anyone in Finland – is, according to a poll that the research company AudienceProject made, more popular than Netflix. Even among young people. So, it is crucial to offer programs that are good enough, that can compete with the other Nordic and even international TV-programs, to keep the young people. And in this day and age, that means TV-series.

Join the Empire or vanish?

Audience has always been everything when it comes to entertainment and cinema business. And we can ask if, in the near future, there will be a sort of Nordic Netflix. Or will Netflix buy all Nordic TV-shows to some extent? It has already streamed a lot of these. Netflix rules a lot of the entertainment industry – the film and TV part – right now. It is as if international streaming service channels, ruled from Hollywood, gives Europe and local films an ultimatum: join us or die!

Then we ask: Is there a reason to "fight" Netflix and other similar international streaming services that are widening their empires? What reasons, and how?

Another question is: Do we really need to fight against Hollywood, why? This is a bit more an ideological question, than a question of money or industry. But still a bit of both.

Stories from Hollywood – films and TV-series – are not special, not unique, they are merely following trends, as always. If more films and TV-series about sexual minorities are made, it is only, in Hollywood (and in Hollywood's ghettos, like in France, Spain and Italy), because they sell; because they want to fool the audience. And fooling the audience, is what Hollywood and Netflix are very good at. Now, we also want to be fooled, and want to escape. How easy is it not to be able to switch one's thoughts? But it is also, in the long run, foolish and even dangerous.

Local film – different people making different stories, even though they can resemble each other – is important. This leads to more diversity. Everyone who has Netflix, or has gotten familiar with it, knows that Netflix, just as Hollywood blockbusters, offer shows "specially for You", easy shows that you "love" to watch.

Like candy. Or fast-food. Netflix offers fast-food for you, over and over again. This may seem like a radical opinion, and it is a protestant attitude that we must give something – as when we read a difficult book – and give our thoughts, try to think, to be able to enjoy a TV-series. It is still only entertainment? Yes, but what about all the talk about feministic ingredients in children's books, different gender and ethnicity in stories? If we want people in our society to think a bit differently, and most important of all, build their own opinions, we need to produce and create stories for TV that are a bit different and that still attract young people as audience. And we must give the young people the chance and the courage, the boldness, to tell these new stories.

A lot of people in the field in Finland wish people were bolder. But it is both the makers – screenwriters, directors, producers, cinematographers and sound artists – and the funders who need to take risks, be bolder, and "fight" against what is popular. Since American culture – as Wim Wenders have said – and in my opinion, also Hollywood, has inhabited our consciousness.

Now, early this winter, YLE made a promise that they will have a new strategy for domestic film and TV-series development. That there will be changes, and new staff that deals with these new developments. One can only hope that this brings real changes, and not only talk. In order so that local film can develop and survive, and so that new voices, local voices that tell non-Hollywood but still universal stories, can be heard.

References

Hällsten, Annika. "Flickorna i Flatnäs intar tv-rutan". Hbl, 18.12.2016. Retrieved 7.8.2019, from https://www.hbl.fi/artikel/flickorna-i-flatnas-intar-tv-rutan/

Koljonen, Johanna. Nostradamus report. 2018, p. 7–14. Retrieved 7.8.2019, from https://goteborgfilmfestival.se/en/nostradamus/2018-nostradamus-report/

Stokel-Walker, Chris. "Skam: How a web-based Norwegian teen drama is changing how we watch TV". The Telegraph, 5.12.2017. Retrieved from https://www.telegraph.co.uk/tv/2017/12/04/skam-web-based-norwegian-teen-drama-changing-watch-tv/

Stocchetti, Matteo & Lindblom, Daniel. "Nationell film finns inte". Ny tid, 20.1.2017. Retrieved 7.8.2019, from https://www.nytid.fi/2017/01/nationell-film-finns-inte/

Schepelern, Peter. "After the Celebration: The Effect of Dogme on Danish Cinema". Kosmorama, 13.12.2013. Retrieved 7.8.2019, from https://www.kosmorama.org/en/kosmorama/artikler/after-celebration-effect-dogme-danish-cinema

Topelius, Taneli. "Missä kuljimme kerran". Iltasanomat, 28.10.2011. Retrieved 7.8.2019, from https://www.is.fi/tv-ja-elokuvat/art-2000000444084.html

Virtanen, Leena. "Suomen poliittisen historian kootut kliseet – Lauri Maijalan Aktivistit ei tuo historialliseen tv-draamaan mitään uutta". Helsingin sanomat, 3.2.2019. Retrieved 7.8.2019, from https://www.hs.fi/kulttuuri/art-2000005986075.html

YLE Press Release. "Suomessa Yle Areena on edelleen suosituin suoratoistopalvelu, muualla Netflix voittaa". 24.1.2019a. Retrieved from https://yle.fi/aihe/artikkeli/2019/01/24/suomessa-yle-areena-on-edelleen-suosituin-suoratoistopalvelu-muualla-netflix

YLE Press Release. "YLE vahvistaa elokuvien hankintaa". 5.2.2019. Retrieved 7.8.2019, from https://yle.fi/aihe/artikkeli/2019/02/05/yle-vahvistaa-elokuvien-hankintaa

Zolads, Lindsay. "Mustang Filmmaker Deniz Gamze Ergüven on Women in Film and Her Oscar-Nominated Feminist Escape Movie", Vulture, 22.2.2016. Retrieved 7.8.2019, from https://www.vulture.com/2016/02/conversation-mustang-director-denize-gamze-erguven.html

(A part of this article is based on an interview the author made with Maria Lundström, head of Drama at Svenska Yle.)

Movies and TV-series

Casablanca (1944, Michael Curtiz)

Colorado Avenue (2007, Claes Olsson)

Fanny (2012, Elin Grönblom)

Gone with the Wind (1939, Victor Fleming)

Kites over Helsinki (2001, Peter Lindholm)

Leviathan (2014, Andrey Zvyagintsev)

Lolauppochner (2016, Ulrika Bengts)

Loveless (2017, Andrey Zvyagintsev)

The Activists (2018, Lauri Maijala)

The Apprentice (2013, Ulrika Bengts)

Skam (2015–2017, Julia Andem)

Sommarkolo (2017, Elin Grönblom)

Where We Once Walked (2011, Peter Lindholm)

Natàlia Ferrer-Roca

Art against the odds
The struggles, survival and success of New Zealand local cinema

Abstract New Zealand is well-known as being able to produce some of the most successful high-budget Hollywood 'blockbuster' productions, such as *The Lord of the Rings* or *The Hobbit*, despite its comparatively small population and remote location. However, little is known about its own bottom-tier films, their funding problems and sustainability challenges. Bottom-tier films, those productions that are made with small-budgets and the domestic audience foremost in mind – which are also known as 'local cinema' – generally face significant economic challenges when confronted with a small domestic media market. This paper provides a critical analysis to fill this knowledge gap by applying a political economy of communication perspective and drawing on findings derived from review of academic literature and secondary data, policy analysis, archival research and expert interviews with key personnel in industry and state agencies. Precisely, it builds on Dunleavy & Joyce (2011), Lealand (2013) and Ferrer-Roca (2015). In the first part, the paper will provide a value chain analysis – development, budget and institutional objectives, production, domestic distribution (including piracy) and international distribution – of three New Zealand bottom-tier productions that have achieved unusual success, in critical and/or commercial terms. These three case studies are used to examine the distinguishing factors of bottom-tier films will be *Sione's Wedding* (2006), *Boy* (2010) and *The Orator* (2011). The second part will offer a comparative analysis of the three bottom-tier case studies previously presented. The value chain structure will allow to provide a thorough examination of the current problems concerning the funding and sustainability of New Zealand local cinema, as well as how digitalization and globalization (i.e., piracy) is directly affecting the financial sustainability of bottom-tier productions. Based on the New Zealand case, the paper concludes with a set of recommendations regarding policy and institutional arrangement from an analytical approach of critical political economy, which might be useful for other small countries with lack of economies of scale aiming at strengthening their local cinema.

Keywords: local cinema, bottom-tier films, film value chain, political economy of communication, New Zealand

Introduction

Due to digitalization and globalization, the traditional business practices of local cinema and industry structures of feature films around the world are changing and facing new challenges. New Zealand is a perfect case study to analyse this phenomenon because, despite its comparatively small population and remote location, it is a country well-known for being able to produce some of the most successful high-budget Hollywood 'blockbuster' productions, such as the trilogies of *The Lord of the Rings* and *The Hobbit*. However, little is known about its own local cinema productions, their funding problems and sustainability challenges.[1] Local cinema – or 'bottom-tier films' (Ferrer-Roca 2017), are those productions that are made with small-budgets and the domestic audience foremost in mind, and generally face significant economic challenges when confronted with a small domestic media market (Ferrer-Roca 2015).

This chapter aims to provide a critical analysis to fill this knowledge gap by applying a political economy perspective. Precisely, within the New Zealand feature film literature, it builds on Dunleavy & Joyce (2011) and Lealand (2013). In the first part, the chapter provides a value chain analysis – development, budget and institutional objectives, production, distribution – of three New Zealand bottom-tier productions that have achieved unusual success, in critical and/or commercial terms. These three case studies used to examine the distinguishing factors of bottom-tier films are *Sione's Wedding* (2006), *Boy* (2010) and *The Orator* (2011). The second part offers a comparative analysis of the three bottom-tier case studies previously presented. The value chain structure allows to provide a thorough examination of the problems concerning the funding and sustainability of New Zealand local cinema,[2] as well as how digitalization and globalization (i.e., piracy) are directly affecting the financial sustainability of bottom-tier productions.

Approach

This chapter takes an institutional political economy approach of communication, which essentially considers media "as commodities produced by capitalist industries" (Murdock and Golding 1973; as quoted in Wasko 2008). By moving across the value chain of feature films, the interests of institutional actors are explained. This approach aims to critically analyse the relationships with their environment which, according to Wasko (2008), is sustained by political power,

---

1   See Muñoz Larroa's chapter in this volume for more about the sustainability of the New Zealand film industry, with special focus on Wellington.

2   See Ferrer-Roca (2018) for an examination on the institutional ecology of New Zealand's film funding institutions, as well as the public funding schemes funded by the NZFC to assist domestic productions along the value chain steps of development, production, post-production and distribution.

media industries and other economic sectors. In other words, as Thompson puts it (2011, p. 3), institutional interests are regarded to be shaped contextually over time in relation to "their roles, interactions with other institutional agents, and their negotiation of macro-level forces".

Methodology

Drawing on findings derived from review of academic literature and secondary data, policy analysis, archival research and expert interviews with key personnel in industry and state agencies, this chapter takes an institutional political economy perspective to illustrate some of the main challenges that bottom-tier films are facing in contemporary New Zealand. Using three case studies as part of my research strategy has proved particularly useful as it allows to not only understand processes but also their contexts (Hartley 2004). Together with the institutional political economy perspective central to my work and the semi-structured interviews conducted with filmmakers, the aim is to understand the motives, priorities and interests of key actors in each case study. Attempts to ensure a larger degree of validity has been supported by the process of methodological data-triangulation, including documentary/archival data, case study and interviews.

Bottom-tier films

This chapter uses the term bottom-tier productions to describe feature films that have "significant New Zealand content" as outlined in the New Zealand Film Commission Act (NZFC 1978). These productions are characterised by being low budget and, most of them, need major financial support from New Zealand public institutions and funders, especially the New Zealand Film Commission (NZFC), in order to be developed, produced and, in some instances, even distributed (Ferrer-Roca 2015; Muñoz and Ferrer-Roca 2017). According to the former head of the NZFC, Graeme Mason (RadioNZ 2013), the public funding support for most bottom-tier feature films used to be between 70 and 90 percent of the production's total budget (Ferrer-Roca 2017). This means that most bottom-tier productions are not economically sustainable on their own.[3] Nevertheless, as these productions contribute to the expression of New Zealand cultural identity, they can also gain minor funding support from other New Zealand screen funding agencies.

---

3   Coinciding with Muñoz Larroa's (2015) findings.

From a political economy perspective, bottom-tier feature films can be regarded as forming "the foundation upon which the whole New Zealand film industry stands and can be sustained" (Ferrer-Roca 2017, p. 6). These productions can be regarded as the core of the national film industry because, as Mason (2012) pointed out, it is in this tier that the largest proportion of New Zealand film industry creative personnel operate. In other words, the ongoing activity of bottom-tier films "provides the basic infrastructure that sustains the other two tiers. Middle- and top-tier films, such as *The World's Fastest Indian* or *The Hobbit,* respectively, would be unlikely to have been made in New Zealand if the professional skills and infrastructure had not already been developed via a continuing flow of bottom-tier feature film productions." (Ferrer-Roca 2015, p. 226).

Consequently, bottom-tier films are pivotal not only because they are culturally specific to New Zealand, but also because they have the capacity to provide vital industry training as well as the basic infrastructure and specialist expertise for the rest of the industry. In this context, it can be argued that the success development of "the New Zealand film industry is the result of more than 35 years of continuous filmmaking made possible through the flow of public support received from the NZFC and the Government" (Ferrer-Roca 2017, p. 6).

Case studies

Case Study of *Sione's Wedding* (2006)

> Infectiously energetic, so drenched in joy and so bloody funny that to give it less than a top rating would be churlish. It is, whatever its shortcomings, impossible to imagine it being done better.
>
> Peter Calder (2006, para. 5–6)

Sione's Wedding[4] is a 97-minute romantic comedy feature film. Directed by Chris Graham, co-written by James Griffin and Oscar Kightley, and produced by John Barnett and Chloe Smith, *Sione's Wedding* was made with a total budget of NZ$3.95 million. Production company South Pacific Pictures (SPP) had the advice of executive producer Paul Davis and worked in association with the NZFC, New Zealand on Air (NZoA), Village SKYCITY Cinemas and Joseph P. Moodabe.

---

4   Official website: www.sioneswedding.com

Story, concept and development

Sione's Wedding is a feature film about four Samoan-New Zealand best friends, who face the challenge of finding a serious partner, or being refused permission to attend their friend's wedding. The film is set in Auckland, the city with the world's largest Polynesian population. The original idea behind *Sione's Wedding* emerged when producer John Barnett suggested writer James Griffin to develop a feature film set in the Samoan community of Auckland. The Pacific Island community in Auckland represents almost 14 percent of the city's population, a sufficient size to create "its own world within the city" and consequently establish parallelisms with other international large migrant groups (SPP 2005, p. 22). Even though the influence of Polynesian culture in New Zealand played an important role in the genesis of the film, the main themes of love, respect and friendship were expected to be universal (ibid., p. 6), suggesting that the feature film production could achieve export appeal without compromising its cultural objectives and distinctive Samoan-New Zealand identity.

The development process of *Sione's Wedding* differs from the following two case studies in that, while *Boy* and *The Orator* feature films required NZFC's funding for its development process, *Sione's Wedding*'s screenplay was developed with minor NZFC financing.[5] The film production company, South Pacific Pictures (SPP), is one of the biggest and most successful private television and film production companies in New Zealand. Due to the company's infrastructure and cash-flow from producing feature films, drama series, mini-series, tele-movies, and more recently entertainment, reality programming and documentaries (SPP 2008), SPP is able to have its own development fund to produce screenplays in-house before submitting the project for NZFC funding consideration (Barnett 2013). By diversifying outcomes and producing several audio-visual products concurrently, a production company not only reduces commercial risk and becomes economically more sustainable in the face of market uncertainties, but also leverages the skills and resources between two audio-visual sectors, television and feature films. Such a connection is common in New Zealand, because the television production sector offers, unlike film, ongoing employment.

Being able to offer an internal development fund has consequences in terms of the value chain of feature film productions. A sizable and well-established production company is far less economically dependent on public institutions like the NZFC for the initial finance to develop a feature film project. Fig. 1 illustrates

---

5   NZFC Script Development for *Sione's Wedding* was NZ$30,000 (2002/03). Source: NZFC Past Funding Decisions.

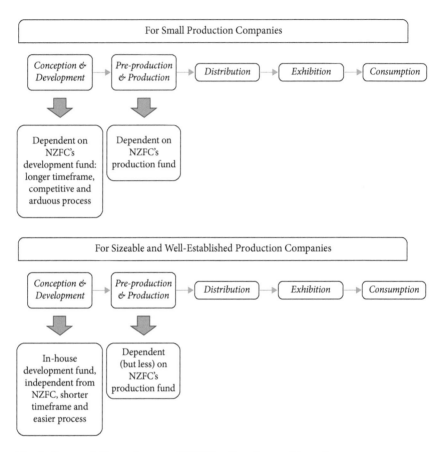

Fig. 1: Economic Dependency on NZFC Funding. Source: The author.

how big production companies that develop a feature film screenplay independently from public institutions can access such funding in-house in a faster and easier manner, bearing in mind that the timeframe for decision-making within private companies can be more flexible than that for a public institution like the NZFC, where specific deadlines for development applications are an established and necessary practice.

There is also the capacity for feature film projects developed outside public funding deadlines and processes to be less dependent on NZFC finance into their production phase. This is because completed screenplays are easier to sell and thus can seek and successfully obtain additional external funding in advance of production. In contrast, small, privately-owned New Zealand production companies are heavily dependent on NZFC financing, because it is the only New Zealand public agency that provides financing for developing a feature film. In the absence of this, an independent project is forced to continue without funding, creating a precarious employment situation for the scriptwriter and producer involved in what is usually a bottom-tier project. This situation lengthens the timeframe of the film production and completion process as well as ultimately increases the project's economic dependence on NZFC finance.

The story of *Sione's Wedding* was an original screenplay. However, it was inspired by the popularity of the *Naked Samoans*, a comedy theatre group that since 1998 has been entertaining New Zealanders not only on stage, but also on television with the animated show *bro'Town* (dubbed *Simpsons of the South Pacific*), which won Best Comedy at the 2005 New Zealand Screen Awards. Most of the *Naked Samoans* group members starred in the comedy feature film *Sione's Wedding* and one of them, Oscar Kightley, was also involved as a co-writer. Although neither story nor the characters of *Sione's Wedding* were established prior to this film, the group of actors and their distinctive brand of Samoan comedy had already an audience. This might have minimised commercial risk for all the parties involved in the filmmaking process, be they public funders, filmmakers or investors.

Budget and institutional objectives

The total budget for *Sione's Wedding* was NZ$3.95 million. The feature film drew its finance entirely within New Zealand, thanks to the collaboration between the NZFC (NZ$2.5 million) and NZoA (NZ$300,000), with support from television channel TV3, as well as financing from Village Sky City Cinemas. *Sione's* also was the first New Zealand film ever to receive investment from a theatrical exhibition chain (SPP 2005, p. 26). UK-based sales agents Hanway Films, the international distribution company, also participated in the financing of the film with a considerable sales in advance (NZ$800,000) (ibid.). According to producer Barnett, two circumstances helped to diminish investor anxieties about the commercial risk. In his view, not only was the recoupment structured in a way that was attractive to private investors, but also the previous successes of the actors and cast assured them that "there was clearly going to be a market" (Barnett 2013). In other words, success in other platforms (in this case television and theatre) was used to predict the likely success of a feature film that featured the same group of actors.

Public funders not only invested in *Sione's Wedding* due to its anticipated success, but also because it met many of the public funder's key values and institutional objectives. First, it was a New Zealand story told from a young Polynesian perspective, offering "unprecedented representations of Samoan community life and mores in multicultural, Twenty-first Century Auckland" (Dunleavy and Joyce 2011, p. 228). Second, all 'above-the-line' as well as 'below-the-line' creative personnel and crew were from New Zealand. Additionally, the expectation of both producers and funders was that the film would connect with its targeted audience, notably the large Polynesian (especially Samoan) community that exists in New Zealand.

Domestic distribution

From a box office perspective, the domestic distribution of *Sione's Wedding*, handled by Village SKY CITY and South Pacific Pictures (SPP 2005, p. 26), was commercially successful.[6] The film stood out for its strong box office performance with a total of NZ$4,090,321 million (Moore 2013), an amount that, according to Barnett, allowed the production company SPP to recoup a higher revenue than the filmmakers of the feature film *Boy* ever did (Barnett 2013). Even if *Boy's* box office takings (NZ$9.3 million, see next case study) were more than double those for *Sione's Wedding*, the distribution deal was more favourable for the latter production, assisted by Barnett and SPP's extensive experience in this business. Distributors and exhibitors consider feature films made by first-time directors to be more commercially risky, as there is no prior data to predict box office figures. As a result, the conditions offered by distributors and exhibitors to smaller independent productions like *Boy* are less beneficial for the filmmakers than the terms negotiated with bigger production companies like SPP with a history of success in both TV-drama and feature film production.

The distribution terms and conditions for *Sione's Wedding* differed from the following two case studies in that, first, the feature film was produced by one of the biggest and most successful production companies in New Zealand. This offered reliability and business experience, supported by an established 'track record' of screen production accomplishments. Second, distributors and exhibitors considered the commercial risk of the film to be minimised by the fact that the group of actors and their distinctive brand of Samoan comedy had already an audience. Both circumstances allowed production company

---

6   NZFC Theatrical release support for *Sione's Wedding* was NZ$75,000 (2005/2006). Source: NZFC Past Funding Decisions.

South Pacific Pictures to negotiate a more favourable distribution deal than the filmmakers of *Boy*.

Sione's Wedding opened in New Zealand cinemas in March 2006 and became the top-selling DVD on release that same year (SPP 2008). The commercial success of *Sione's Wedding* was enough warranty to make a sequel six years later, with *Sione's 2: Unfinished Business* in 2012. Even though the sequel was not as commercially successful as the first feature, taking NZ$1.8 million at the domestic box office,[7] stands out as the second New Zealand sequel of all time and the first in the Twenty-first Century.[8]

Piracy

Piracy of *Sione's Wedding* involved some distinctive components. A long-time employee at the Auckland post-production company where the film was edited was found guilty of copying and distributing a pre-production copy of the feature before its theatrical release (NZFACT 2007). While not specifying how the figures are calculated, Barnett, as film producer and CEO of SPP at this time, estimated the piracy had cost between NZ$700,000 and NZ$1 million. These included NZ$300,000 in lost box office return to the company, a further NZ$200,000 in DVD sales, the equivalent percentage for distributors and exhibitors, the revenue from the New Zealand taxpayers through its major public investor, the NZFC, and additionally the loss of tax and GST on the film's legitimate revenues (Bull 2006). Furthermore, the pirated version found its way to the USA, the UK and Germany, extending the possible damage to the film's potential international returns. The person who pirated the film was convicted and sentenced to 300 hours of community service (NZFACT 2007). It was the first time a New Zealander had been convicted of breaking copyright law in the film industry (ibid.). As a result, the case was widely covered in nationwide media, raising public awareness of the massive revenue losses caused by piracy.

International Distribution

The international critical response to *Sione's Wedding* was positive even though the production did not win any significant awards. It screened at five international film festivals, the main ones being the Montreal Film Festival in 2006

---

7   Figures taken from Motion Picture Distributors Association of New Zealand(MPDA, 2012a).

8   *What Becomes of the Broken Hearted?* (1999) is the sequel of *Once Were Warriors* (1994).

and the Hawaii International Film Festival in 2007 (Graham 2009). Noteworthy is the fact that the film was chosen by the NZFC and the Ministry of Foreign Affairs and Trade to screen at the celebration of the fifty years of Samoa's independence, which included a celebration of the signing of the Treaty of Friendship with New Zealand, in August 2012 (NZFC 2012). The Samoan independence celebration included a special New Zealand Film and Television Festival broadcast on Samoa's TV3 channel, which opened with the Samoan-New Zealand comedy *Sione's Wedding*.

Renamed *Samoan Wedding* for its international release as a way to highlight its cultural distinction to foreign audiences, the feature film was theatrically released in Australia and the USA,[9] among other countries. Indicative of its popularity in foreign markets is that, in its opening week in the Italian theatrical cinema market, *Samoan Wedding* managed to achieve seventh place at the national box office (SPP, n.d.).

Case study of *Boy* (2010)

> Beneath the quirkiness and silliness of "Boy", there's a legitimate artistic presence on display. Waititi wrote, produced, directed and starred in the film, which goes beyond [its] coming-of-age story structure, to become something much richer and deeper that still leaves a smile on your face. (John Lichman 2012b, para. 5)

Released in 2010, *Boy*[10] is a 90-minute feature film that mixes comedy and drama. Written and directed by Taika Waititi and produced by Ainsley Gardiner, Cliff Curtis and Emanuel Michael, *Boy* was made with a total budget of NZ$5.6 million. The two production companies, Whenua Films and Unison Films, had the advice of associate producer Richard Fletcher and worked in association with the New Zealand Film Production Fund Trust (FF1), the NZFC, NZoA and Te Māngai Pāho.

Story, concept and development

Boy is set in 1984 on the rural East Coast of New Zealand, in Waihau Bay. The main character is an eleven-year old boy, who has two heroes, Michael Jackson and his father Alamein. When Alamein returns home after seven years in prison, *Boy* is forced to confront the father he imagined with the harsh reality of the

---

9   *Sione's Wedding* took A$343,068 at the Australian box office and US$72,244 in the USA. Figures taken from www.boxofficemojo.com.
10 Official website: http://boythefilm.com

man. Whereas the film is a drama because it features "neglected children, absent fathers, bullying, minors running drugs, gang members, violence, swearing, sexual references, kids boozing and smoking dope and a mother dying in child-birth" (Geary 2012, p. 10), it is also a comedy because it uses a very particular humour, with lots of satire and irony, to deal with these serious issues (Perrott 2010). Waititi summarises the main theme as "the painful comedy of growing up and interpreting the world" (Marriner 2010, p. 30). *Boy* has an original screen-play and is also autobiographical.

Budget and institutional objectives

Boy's total budget was NZ$5.6 million, a reasonable amount for a bottom-tier New Zealand feature film. Funding entirely raised within New Zealand, made possible by the collaboration between New Zealand public institutions and funds, specifically the New Zealand Film Production Fund Trust (FF1) (NZ$2.5M), NZFC Screen Production Incentive Fund (SPIF) (NZ$1.8M), NZ on Air (NZ$400,000), the NZFC (NZ$250,000), Te Māngai Pāho (NZ$150,000) and Māori TV (NZ$50,000), as well as private investor Unison/Andromeda (Ivancic 2013, 2015). The film met many of the NZFC's key values and institu-tional objectives. First, it was a Māori narrative characterised by 'significant New Zealand content', which reflected New Zealand and New Zealanders in an orig-inal and ingenious way (Geary 2012). Second, the NZFC's expectation was that it would connect with its targeted audience, New Zealand viewers, and also that it would achieve good domestic sales, as well as critical acclaim (Mason 2013). However, *Boy* easily surpassed all expectations, becoming the highest grossing New Zealand feature at the domestic box office.[11]

The potential for *Boy* to develop the careers of the filmmakers involved was a key consideration for the NZFC, given its statutory obligations in this area. However, Watiti already had a successful record of accomplishment prior to the release of *Boy*. His short film *Two Cars, One Night* (2003) was nominated for an Academy Award in 2005 and won eight prizes in the international film festival circuit, including Best Short Film at the Berlin, Seattle, Oberhausen, Hamburg and American Film Institute (AFI) festivals. His first feature film *Eagle vs Shark* (2007) attained domestic box office sales of NZ$905,604 (MPDA, 2007) and his

---

11 Theatrical film tickets usually go up over time, so while this affirmation is true in absolute terms, on an inflation-adjusted chart *Once Were Warriors* (1994) is still the highest grossing New Zealand box office ever.

talent was already recognised abroad with his script being accepted at the prestigious Sundance Writer's Lab in 2005.

In view of these accomplishments, the NZFC's Board not only saw the potential to develop Waititi's filmmaking career further by funding his next feature film, but also used an institutional risk reduction strategy by backing a filmmaker with a nationally and internationally recognised profile. This risk reduction strategy was further encouraged by the involvement of skilful and qualified above-the-line creative personnel. Producers Cliff Curtis and Ainsley Gardiner added credibility to the project, due to their extensive portfolios and experience, while Emanuel Michael, a producer based in the USA, provided the link for distribution within the American market. Associate producer Richard Fletcher also increased the film's credibility by bringing to the project his extensive producing experience and his work in the film distribution business, plus his expertise as NZFC's former Head of Business Affairs.

Domestic distribution

From a commercial perspective, there is no doubt that the domestic release and distribution strategy of *Boy* was a big success. It made NZ$9.3 million at the New Zealand box office, "making it the second highest grossing film behind James Cameron's *Avatar*" in that year (Wood 2010, para. 4).[12] The domestic critical reaction to *Boy* was very positive. *Boy* was nominated for thirteen awards at the 2010 New Zealand Qantas Film and Television Awards, winning seven of them, including Best Film, Best Director, Best Supporting Actor and Best Screenplay (NZFC 2010a, p. 16). The film was released on DVD immediately afterwards and, according to the Video Association of New Zealand, was the third highest-selling DVD in 2011 (*OnFilm* 2012, p. 7).

When *Boy* was funded, the NZFC used a different policy for distribution than the one it has now. At that time projects had to have a distribution deal in place to be eligible for development and production funding. Several anonymous sources have confirmed that the NZFC's sales person at that time pushed *Boy*'s filmmakers to accept a less than ideal distribution deal.[13] The public funder's rationale was understandable, because it is generally very hard for New Zealand bottom-tier films to get a distributor interested prior to production.[14] Apart

---

12 See previous footnote about inflation-adjusted chart.
13 The exact details of the distribution deal cannot be published due to being commercially sensitive data.
14 See Muñoz Larroa (2017) for more information on film distribution and delivery outlets in New Zealand.

from that, no one expected to be distributing the all-time highest grossing New Zealand feature release, so the initial distribution deal was considered to be satisfactory. Consequently, the filmmakers who wrote, directed and produced *Boy* have not yet been able to earn any money from their film.

Piracy

Online copyright theft of feature films is a contemporary global problem and New Zealand productions are no exception. In terms of value chain, the piracy problem can emerge during post-production but generally begins just after the domestic theatrical distribution of a feature film, like in this case. Within days of its domestic release, and before being released overseas, *Boy* was made available on a peer-to-peer file-sharing site. The NZFC (2010b) published a press release stating that they were unable to quantify how much this pirated release could damage *Boy*'s planned DVD and international prospects. NZFC Chief Executive, Graeme Mason, explained that:

> Ultimately piracy hurts not only those directly involved in making the film, but those who work in the wider industry. Strong returns on movies such as *Boy* enable the NZFC to invest more money into developing more New Zealand stories that resonate not just with Kiwis, but with audiences around the world. That's a good thing for the industry and for New Zealand as a whole. (ibid., para. 7)

Although not all illegal copying/streaming translates into lost box office or DVD sales, piracy reduces the expected recoupment – which is almost impossible to quantify – that investors and funders are entitled to on the basis of their initial investment. Accordingly, one impact of the piracy of NZFC-funded features is that it reduces the quantity and quality of future productions, at the same time reducing the potential returns on public investment in New Zealand feature films.

International distribution

Bottom-tier film *Boy* was screened at more than fifty international film festivals during 2010 and 2011, and also was nominated to compete at the prestigious Sundance Film Festival in 2010. Also noteworthy were the World Cinema Audience Award at AFI Film Festival (NZFC 2011a), the Audience Award at the Berlin International Film Festival, and the Best Fiction Feature Film Award at the Sydney Film Festival, which was "the first time in 20 years that a New Zealand film won the award" (NZFC 2010b, para. 5). NZFC's sales arm, NZ Film, subsequently sold the film to distributors in nine countries.[15]

---

15 The USA, Canada, Australia, Sweden, Iceland, Poland, Turkey, Israel and Spain.

Even if the release of *Boy* broke all New Zealand box office records and won many awards both domestically and internationally, no distributor was willing to invest the necessary resources to release *Boy* in American cinemas. So the filmmakers and the USA distributor Paladin (Fleming 2011) decided to fund the release independently through Kickstarter.[16] The Kickstarter campaign called "Boy: the American release!" collected US$110,796 – a figure higher than the initial target of US$90,000 – from 1,826 anonymous backers. This allowed the film to be released in more than eighteen American cities[17] during March and April 2012 (Kickstarter Team 2012; see also Crossley 2012).

Some of its cultural content may have reduced the appeal and potential success of *Boy* in the American market. Two main problems for New Zealand feature films can be identified on the basis of *Boy*'s reception in the USA. First, it is likely that New Zealand's English accent – colloquially termed 'Kiwi' English – was not easy for American viewers to understand. This problem was confirmed at the American release during which Waititi, when asking about how well American viewers could understand 'Kiwi' accents, received affirmation that some had experienced difficulty (Lichman 2012a). What this shows is that, even though most New Zealand feature films aim for release and accessibility in foreign English-language markets, their 'Kiwi' accents – not to mention productions made in te reo Māori – still pose barriers to this achievement (Ferrer-Roca 2014). Second, and within its narrative and stylistic blend of comedy and drama, *Boy*'s story also used what might be regarded as 'characteristically Kiwi' style of humour which, once again, might not necessarily be fully understood by foreign viewers. Nevertheless, these two argumentations require to be further investigated, because the problematic reception of cultural specificity on the part of audiences unfamiliar with those cultural details is notoriously complex and difficult to objectively measure (Steemers 2004).

The potential to include cultural details that are identifiably 'New Zealandish', and as such will resonate with New Zealand audiences, are one of the main arguments for the production and public funding support of New Zealand's bottom-tier feature films. This cultural perspective suggests that if a feature production is primarily made for New Zealand viewers, the fact that it may not be exported should not matter. However, this argument, that large amounts of public money should be spent on feature films intended primarily for domestic

---

16 The New Zealand crowd-funding platform equivalent is www.pledgeme.co.nz
17 It has been impossible to confirm whether these were art house or mainstream multiplex cinemas.

viewers, is hard to justify if feature films (as well as TV-dramas) are regarded, or expected to operate, as an exportable product (Dunleavy 2005, p. 120). To the extent that 'exportability' is an expectation of these features, pressure arises for bottom-tier films and their main public funder, the NZFC, to compromise their cultural objectives and distinct identity in order to sell these productions on international markets (ibid., p. 10). As Dunleavy has argued (2005, p. 120 and pp. 268–70), when similar expectations are applied to costly forms of local TV-drama, reception problems have been evident, these arising from the very different requirements of domestic and international audiences that such productions are attempting to serve.

Case study of *The Orator* (2011)

> The first feature filmed entirely in Samoan, The Orator is a compelling drama with more to offer than just anthropological interest. An exploration of love, death and bitter family conflict that unfolds in sync with the relaxed rhythms of Pacific island life, this New Zealand production marks an auspicious feature debut for… Tusi Tamasese.
>
> Leslie Felperin (2011, para. 1)

The Orator[18] – *O Le Tulafale* in Samoan language – is a 110 minute dramatic feature. As suggested above, it was the debut feature for writer-director Tusi Tamasese, who worked alongside producer Catherine Fitzgerald and two associate producers Maiava Nathaniel Lees and Michael Eldred. With a total budget of NZ$2.5 million, the film was produced by two New Zealand companies, Blueskin Films Ltd and O Le Tulafale Ltd, in association with the NZFC.

Story, concept and development

As an 'art-house' feature which surpassed all the expectations of its funders and filmmakers, *The Orator* is an important film due to the rarity of its milestone achievements for Samoan cinema. Even though many feature films have been shot in the Samoan islands (mostly American-financed), *The Orator* is special as the first feature to have been written and directed by an indigenous Samoan, to be entirely spoken in the Samoan language, and to offer an entirely Samoan story that is performed exclusively by Samoan actors (MCH 2010).

    The Orator is a contemporary drama about Saili, a night-watchman at the local store who musters the courage not only to stand up to his wife's intimidating brother, but also to ultimately reclaim the chiefly status of his father. Very

---

18 Official website: http://theoratorfilm.co.nz

significantly, Saili is also a dwarf, his physical size and disadvantage rendering these achievements all the more heroic. The cultural perspectives underlying this unusual story owe a great deal to the Samoan experiences and origins of their creator, the Samoan-born Tamasese, who spent the first 18 years of his life in Samoa, before moving to New Zealand for university study. The location of his first feature film – *The Orator* – is Vaimoso, on the main island of Upolu, the village where he was born and where his family home remains (NZFC 2011a).

Budget and institutional objectives

The Orator was made with a final budget of NZ\$2.5 million.[19] The NZFC was the primarily financier with NZ\$2,313,000 million, and the film was also able to attract private investment from within New Zealand as well as additional finance from the Samoan government (NZ\$60,000) (Ivancic 2013). As a general approach, the NZFC is prioritising projects able to attract funding from external sources, as opposed to those which rely entirely on NZFC funding. Therefore, the fact that *The Orator* attracted investment from both private and public sources is likely to have been a positive indicator for the NZFC Board.

The filmmakers also emphasised in their NZFC production financing application why *The Orator* should qualify as a New Zealand film under the requirements of Section 18.2 of the *NZFC Act*. First, the most important 'below-the-line' and 'above-the-line' personnel, along with all equipment and facilities, the owners of the copyright, the production company and the majority of the total film finance were from New Zealand (Fitzgerald 2010). Additionally, and despite the Samoan location of the story and filming, the majority of the production spend would occur in New Zealand (ibid.). Second, there is a unique relationship and history between New Zealand and Samoa (ibid.). When Western Samoa gained independence on January 1, 1962, both countries signed a Treaty of Friendship, in which New Zealand agreed to "consider sympathetically requests from [Samoa] for technical, administrative and other assistance" (NZ Government, 1962, Article IV). Samoa is also the only country with which New Zealand has a Treaty of Friendship. Finally, there are currently 130,000 Samoan people living in New Zealand, comprising 50 percent of New Zealand's Pacific Island community (Fitzgerald 2010). This situation and the historical relationship that precedes it, has created stable links and solid ties between New Zealand and the sovereign state of Samoa (ibid.).

---

19 NZFC Script Development for *The Orator* was NZ\$73,000 (2008/09) and NZ\$20,000 (2009/2010). Source: NZFC Past Funding Decisions.

NZFC policy requires a completion guarantor where a production budget exceeds NZ$1 million, and *The Orator* was no exception. However, the filmmakers had to convince both the NZFC and the completion guarantor that such small budget – NZ$2.5 million – would be viable. As the completion guarantor of *The Orator* commented, "We were surprised at Catherine Fitzgerald's budget for *The Orator*, but then she explained how they were going to do it and the fact that Tamasese comes from where they were shooting, and had a lot of good relationships there. We then saw how it would work" (Parnham 2011). This also helped *The Orator* to meet the NZFC's 'value for money' funding criterion, when it considers whether or not the investment request is appropriate for the level of cultural and creative achievement. Overall, the performance expectations for *The Orator* were considerably high. When NZFC CEO Graeme Mason read the script, he said that he could picture himself seeing it at the Venice Film Festival. Even if this prediction put a considerable amount of pressure on the filmmakers (Fitzgerald 2013), it was proved to be realistic.

Production challenges

The Orator faced three main challenges during production, the first of which was shooting in Samoa, the second, working with a predominantly local untrained cast, and the third being the limitations of the film's small budget. Shooting a feature film in Samoa was not easy. Even though there is a growing television industry in Samoa, the infrastructure for a domestic feature film production remains limited (Hedley 2011). Additional challenges were presented by Samoa's unsettled and sometimes extreme weather conditions (ranging from torrential rain and floods, to extreme heat and mosquitoes), which caused daily inconveniences for both cast and crew (Rudkin 2012). Further challenges came from working with untrained and predominantly local actors, including Fa'afiaula Sagote, who played the main character Saili. After overcoming these obstacles, they had to cope with another unusual situation, which involved convincing "the older chiefs to stick with the words on the script and not use their own words" (Rudkin 2012, para. 6). The filmmakers had to manage all of the above challenges within the constraints of a low budget. As producer Fitzgerald explained, one way to overcome the funding challenge was to locate and hire talented individuals who could complete their tasks with maximum effect and efficiency, and who were also willing to work for lower rate of pay (Fitzgerald 2013).

This has been a perennial approach to the frequent problems of obtaining sufficient financing for New Zealand features and, testifying to the 'shoestring' budget tendency of domestic film productions, New Zealand crew members customarily earn far higher salaries working for Hollywood films than they can by working on New Zealand-financed production (Jones et al. 2003). The economic restrictions of working on New Zealand-financed films do tend however to find compensation in the potential for greater creative control and freedom for local filmmakers, a situation that is confirmed in the producing experience of Catherine Fitzgerald (Fitzgerald 2013). This infers that the makers of smaller budget films at least have the freedom to pursue the kinds of depictions and portrayals of New Zealand (or Samoan) culture they most value.[20] The real challenge, as Fitzgerald also acknowledged, is to produce films with both domestic and international audiences in mind (ibid.), given that the domestic market is simply too small to amortise the cost of film production, so that export sales are inevitable and essential (Dunleavy 2005, 2009; Dunleavy and Joyce, 2011).

Tamasese understands why his first feature film had to be low budget. First, they had to convince the NZFC to support the production of the first Samoan-language film ever (the NZFC had initially thought it would be in English) (NZFC 2011b). Second, Tamasese did not have a 'track record' as a feature film writer or director. His first short film, *Va Tapuia* (*Sacred Spaces*, 2010), was made with a very small budget to demonstrate to the NZFC that he could direct. Even though this film was selected for inclusion in the international film festival circuit, the NZFC was still doubtful and, bearing in mind the greater challenges entailed in directing a feature film, considered their investment risky due to lack of substantial previous achievements (Hedley 2011). Nevertheless, sometimes having a small budget is not as important as receiving the money at the right moment, a point that Fitzgerald emphasised during our interview by stating that: "I could have been more efficient with the money if I had got it when I needed it" (Fitzgerald 2013). This concern is by no means unique to New Zealand and underlines the inefficiencies of bureaucratic processes and acknowledges that these have real consequences.

Domestic distribution

The Orator took a total of NZ$766,758 at the domestic box office (MPDA 2012b).[21] Considering that a perfectly respectable New Zealand bottom-tier art film might be expected to earn upwards of NZ$300,000 domestically (a level at

---

20 Big budget films have strong commercial imperatives, which tend to diminish the creative freedom of the filmmakers involved.
21 NZFC Theatrical release support for *The Orator* was NZ$53,319 (2011/2012). Source: NZFC Past Funding Decisions.

which the distributor is not losing money),[22] *The Orator* can be regarded as very successful, even if the filmmakers have not made much of a profit from it to date.

Piracy

Piracy in the case of *The Orator* involved some unusual elements. The film was uploaded in its entirety on YouTube[23] in January 2012, three months after its New Zealand theatrical release. The culprit was neither a New Zealander nor a Samoan, but a person residing in Alaska (Fitzgerald 2013). Upon discovering this, producer Catherine Fitzgerald immediately contacted YouTube outlining and emphasising that the Alaskan individual had no right to upload this particular feature film on YouTube. Curiously, the person in Alaska went back and asserted that they did, so YouTube sent a letter to Fitzgerald asking for evidence of copyright ownership (Fitzgerald 2013). It seems that simply checking Fitzgerald's credentials in the credits of the film itself were not enough evidence for the YouTube team. With the NZFC unable to assist, Fitzgerald sought help from Australian-based Transmission Films, the film's Australasian distributor, a move which, in view of its international experience, networks and influence, was an important decision. As one of the main distributors for independent cinema, and the company who also distributed *The King's Speech* (2010) for example, Transmission Films had established the kind of reputation, international influence, and business relationships (including an output deal with Paramount) that gave them significant power in the higher circles of the international film business (ibid.). After Transmission Films challenged YouTube on the issue of copyright, YouTube was left with no option other than to remove the film from its website.

If Transmission Films had not been the official distributor of *The Orator*, or lacked the international reach and influence that it evidently did have, it is very likely that *The Orator* would still be available on YouTube. In terms of their ability to challenge and resolve acts of piracy, the cost of enforcement presents the greatest barrier for NZ producers. As Fitzgerald explained: "For me to employ a US lawyer to pursue this in Alaska would cost me considerably more money than I would ever lose from having it up on YouTube…I don't have the money" (Fitzgerald, 2013). In contrast, famous and internationally recognised

---

22 For a distributor not to lose money in releasing a feature film would require its revenue to be higher than the P&A and expenses spent prior and during the theatrical release of that feature film.
23 Producer Fitzgerald is not aware how the digital copy of The Orator was accessed.

filmmakers, such as Peter Jackson, are able to afford the cost of enforcement, as demonstrated when Jackson filed a *lawsuit* against New Line cinema claiming that he had not been properly paid. "The people who have the most power are the people who are the biggest players", emphasised Fitzgerald (ibid.).

International distribution

The international critical response to *The Orator* was overwhelming. The film's world premiere was held at the prestigious Venice International Film Festival, as NZFC CEO Graeme Mason had predicted. It screened in the Orizzonti Competition section of the Festival and received a Special Mention from the Orizzonti Jury along with two awards: the Art Cinema Award from the CICAE Jury of the Festival and the CinemAvvenire Best Film – *Il cerchio non è rotondo* Award from the Jury of the Associazione Centro Internazionale CinemAvvenire (*OnFilm* 2011). Subsequently, the film also screened at three of the main international film festivals worldwide: Sundance and Toronto in 2012, and Berlin in 2013. It won the Audience Award at the Brisbane International Film Festival and was the finalist for Best Performance at the fifth Asia Pacific Screen Awards. *The Orator* has also been screened in other major foreign international film festivals, including the New Zealand Film and Television Festival to celebrate fifty years of the Treaty of Friendship between New Zealand and Samoa (NZFC 2012).

Launching an international world premiere at one of the world's most prestigious film festivals, such as Venice, is a big achievement for any feature film. But it was not by chance. *The Orator* was permitted to enter the Venice festival thanks to the positive reaction to *Va Tapuia*, the previous short film by writer-director Tusi Tamasese. A year before, producer Fitzgerald sent this short film to the Venice Film Festival, whose director wrote her a personal letter advising that they were sorry not to be able to include *Va Tapuia* in the festival programme, but that they hoped she and Tamasese would submit more films in the future. A year later, NZ Film took *The Orator* promo-taster (not the official trailer, as they were still editing at this stage) to Cannes to show the footage. People from the Venice Film Festival recognised the distinctive voice of Tamasese in the film and were immediately interested (Fitzgerald 2013). This demonstrates how short films can actually be quite important in a longer term marketing strategy, and for the career development of feature producers, directors and writers.

Thus, even if a short film is not selected for screening at a big international film festival, it can still make a significant, lasting impression on festival selectors. However, this can also work in reverse. Festival selectors might reject a first feature film on the basis of their response to a first short film. Finally, *The Orator* was submitted as Best Foreign Language Film for the 84th Academy Awards, which was held in Hollywood on the 28th of February 2012.

Comparative analysis and conclusion

This final section offers a comparative analysis, following a value chain structure, of the three bottom-tier case studies analysed in this chapter. Any feature film project begins with the conception and then the development of a script idea. In the case of those three films, all stories are similar in that all are based on original screenplays. The cultural representations of each feature are nevertheless different. While the film *Boy* offers a Māori coming-of-age story, *The Orator* tells a story of power and struggle that is overtly Samoan in character, as well as being filmed on Upolu. Different again, *Sione's Wedding* offers a portrayal of Samoan community life in contemporary Auckland, the largest, most populated city of New Zealand.

The source of inspiration for each story was unique. On the one hand, *Boy* and *The Orator* screenplays emerged from first-hand life experiences of their directors and writers Waititi and Tamasese respectively. On the other, the feature film *Sione's Wedding* created its story using milieu that had been effectively 'tested' in earlier theatre and TV productions, with the film offering additional security to its investors through its deployment of the same group of demonstrably popular actors from these earlier productions. For reasons which these differences make clear, it can be suggested that the first creative strategy, used by *Boy* and *The Orator*, whose stories were entirely without creative precedent, entailed significantly greater commercial risk.

Be they producers, distributors or public organisation personnel, the one thing that most interviewees reiterated was the idea that knowing your audience in advance is fundamental to achieving a successful release. In Barnett's words, it is not about how much advertising budget you have, "it's about the fact that you connected with somebody" (Barnett 2013). In the case of the three bottom-tier feature films analysed, they all connected with their targeted audience, because they correctly identified it in advance and planned a subsequent distribution strategy to reach them. This seems to be a decisive aspect to ensure a successful film.

Regarding the final budgets of the three bottom-tier case studies analysed, *The Orator* had the lowest budget with NZ$2.5 million, followed by *Sione's Wedding* with almost NZ$4 million, and *Boy* with a budget of NZ$5.6 million. There seems to be, nevertheless, no correlation between the amount of financial investment and the international critical response. *The Orator* – with the lowest budget – received an overwhelming international critical reaction, premiering at Venice, screening at Sundance, Toronto and Berlin, and being submitted for the Best Foreign Language Film category for the 84th Academy Awards. Undoubtedly, good 'art-house' film productions can be made with small budgets and simultaneously receive international critical acclaim.

Interestingly, there does seem to be a correlation between budget and domestic box office results. On the one hand, the feature film *Boy*, with the highest budget, surpassed all expectations and became the highest grossing New Zealand feature at the domestic box office with NZ$9.3 million, an amount equivalent to 166 per-cent of its total budget. On the other, *Sione's Wedding* was able to equalise its final budget with its domestic box office result, having a budget of NZ$3.95 million and a box office revenue of NZ$4.1 million. Finally, *The Orator* film, with the lowest budget but with the best international critical response, had the lowest domestic box office result with NZ$0.76 million, which equals 30 percent of its total budget.

Nevertheless, any correlation between final budget and domestic box office numbers is inaccurate as it ignores not only the production circumstances under which each feature film was produced, but also its marketing budget.[24] As already explained in the case study analysis, not only was *The Orator* made partly thanks to the generous help of many Samoan people who participated in the production for no commercial compensation, but *Boy* was also made thanks to the help of Waititi's family and friends. If everybody involved in making those films had been paid at New Zealand rates, as was the case for *Sione's Wedding*, the real cost of producing *The Orator* and *Boy* would have been significantly higher.

From a business perspective, feature films are audio-visual products devel-oped to provide considerable economic returns to their investors. The amount of the final budget of a film production is, nevertheless, no equivalent security for economic success, as the analysis of the previous three bottom-tier case studies demonstrates. *Sione's Wedding*, with a medium budget of NZ$3.95 million, is the production that has been the most commercially successful for the filmmakers; compared to the other two productions, due to two circumstances. First, distributors and exhibitors were able to predict box office results more easily given the screenplay was based on already successful characters. Consequently, P&A spending for the theatrical release was based on recoupment expecta-tions and the advertising campaign was targeted and focused. Second, the

---

24 Due to being commercially sensitive, no private company or public institution make theatrical marketing budgets publicly available.

extensive business and creative experience of production company SPP allowed the filmmakers to negotiate more favourable theatrical distribution terms and conditions.

In theory, the lower the budget, the easier it should be to recoup the initial investment for the simple fact that there is less to recoup. However, the *Boy* case study showed that the distribution deal is a pivotal factor, in the sense that *Boy*'s filmmakers had to accept a less than ideal distribution deal partly due to their inexperience and partly due to pressures from the NZFC. Even if in absolute terms *Boy* has reached the highest grossing domestic box office of all times, the filmmakers did not earn much money beyond their normal production fee. The advertising budget was quite high and the distribution terms and conditions were mostly favourable to the distribution company. However, thanks to *Boy*'s success, next time a Waititi-directed film is on offer, it may expect far better terms from prospective distributors and exhibitors.

Piracy, unfortunately, was an issue for all three bottom-tier feature films. While both *Boy* and *The Orator* were made available online from unknown sources, a pre-production copy of *Sione's Wedding* was stolen by an employee of the Auckland-based post-production company. Although the offenders have not yet been revealed for *The Orator* and *Boy*, in the case of *Sione's Wedding* it was relatively easy to identify and convict the employee who pirated it. In *The Orator* case, producer Fitzgerald was able to claim copyright ownership to YouTube thanks to the reputation, international influence, and business relationships of the film's distributor, Australian-based company Transmission Films. Without such backing, *The Orator* would very likely still be available in its entirety on YouTube.

The NZFC's financial support has proven to be crucial for supporting the conception, development, production and even the distribution of bottom-tier feature films in New Zealand. As already mentioned, *Boy* and *The Orator* needed development funding from the NZFC in order for the screenplay to be completed. This necessity is underscored by the fact that these films came from small and/or newly established independent production companies. In contrast, *Sione's Wedding* was produced by one of the most successful and recognised New Zealand television and film production companies, which is able to develop its own projects in-house before applying to the NZFC for production finance. Additionally, while *Sione's Wedding* and *The Orator* were able to attract some private and external investment, the production of *Boy* was entirely financed by New Zealand public institutions, including NZoA, Māori TV and Te Māngai Pāho.

Significant for the overall research is the purpose underlying the exercise of the NZFC's supreme influence upon bottom-tier films within the New Zealand film industry. Due to economic and institutional contextual circumstances, the NZFC plays a pivotal role in the survival of bottom-tier films, not least because it is the only NZ public agency that significantly supports features in this tier. As a consequence of their dependence upon NZFC finance, most bottom-tier productions have to contend with and overcome the problem of a dearth of development and production funding.

One way to increase the productivity of the limited funds available is to increase the efficiency and effectiveness of the NZFC's financing process, especially by introducing greater flexibility around when its funding can be accessed by the filmmaker. Although some of the problem arises from the necessity of a competition between eligible film project proposals for a limited supply of NZFC funding support, it is clear that filmmakers could be more efficient with this funding if they were able to receive it when it is most needed. Nevertheless, in order to ensure transparency and accountability, government agencies like the NZFC cannot simply act as a bank to provide funding on request, instead needing to assess applications objectively and transparently in the context of their relative as well as their individual merits. Based on the comparative analysis between the three bottom-tier cases, there is no recurring correlation between the amount of financial investment involved and the national and international critical response or economic returns from theatrical distribution deals.

New Zealand public funders, especially the NZFC, are caught between Government Ministries with opposite, but at the same time, complementary aims – cultural and economic. These tensions shape NZFC's priorities by, hopefully, making decisions that will not only result in culturally meaningful films, but also economically successful ones. From an institutional point of view, supporting the filmmakers that achieve the highest domestic box office takings is a business strategy to reduce outcome uncertainty. Based on the New Zealand case, and from an analytical approach of critical political economy, these considerations regarding policy and institutional arrangements might be useful for other small countries with lack of economies of scale aiming at strengthening their local cinema.

References

Barnett, John. "Interview with John Barnett". Chief Executive Officer, South Pacific Pictures. Medium: Face-to-face. Auckland, New Zealand, 6 March, 2013.

Bull, Andrew. "Employee found guilty of Sione's Wedding film piracy". South Pacific Pictures. 2006, retrieved 8.8.2015, from http://www.

southpacificpictures.com/index.php?option=com_content&task=view&id=37&Itemid=2.

Calder, Peter. "Sione's Wedding". *The New Zealand Herald*. 2006, retrieved 31.8.2018, from http://www.nzherald.co.nz/lifestyle/news/article.cfm?c_id=6&objectid=10374260.

Crossley, Jazial. "Crowd funding, micro payments change face of films". *The Dominion Post*. 2012, retrieved 4.9.2018 from http://www.stuff.co.nz/dominion-post/culture/7977245/Crowd-funding-micro-payments-change-face-of-films.

Dunleavy, Trisha. *Ourselves on primetime. A history of New Zealand television drama*. Auckland: Auckland University. 2005.

Dunleavy, Trisha. "Public television in a small country: The New Zealand "experiment" 20 years on". *Flow TV* 9(13), 2009.

Dunleavy, Trisha, and Joyce, Hester. *New Zealand film & television; institution, industry and cultural change*. Bristol: Intellect. 2011.

Felperin, Leslie. "The Orator". *Variety*, 19 September. 2011, retrieved 5.11.2018, from http://variety.com/2011/film/reviews/the-orator-1117946168/.

Ferrer-Roca, Natàlia. "Business innovation in the film industry value chain: A New Zealand case study". In Robert DeFillippi and Patrick Wikström (eds.), *International perspectives on business innovation and disruption in the creative industries: Film, video and photography*. Cheltenham, UK/Northampton, MA: Edward Elgar. 2014. pp. 18–36.

Ferrer-Roca, Natàlia. "Multi-platform funding strategies for bottom-tier films in small domestic media markets: *Boy* (2010) as a New Zealand case study". *Journal of Media Business Studies*, 12(4), 2015, pp. 224–237, from DOI: 10.1080/16522354.2015.1099278.

Ferrer-Roca, Natàlia. "Three-tier of feature film productions: The case of New Zealand". *Studies in Australasian Cinema*, 11(2), 2017, pp. 102–120, from DOI: 10.1080/17503175.2017.1385135.

Ferrer-Roca, Natàlia. "Feature film funding between national and international priorities. How does New Zealand bridge the gap?". In Paul Clemens Murschetz, Roland Teichmann, and Matthias Karmasin (eds.), *Handbook of state aid for film – Finance, industries and regulations* (Media Business and Innovation Series). Cham, Switzerland: Springer. 2018. pp. 383–401.

Fitzgerald, Catherine. "Production financing proposal, *O Le Tulafale* (Orator)", submitted to the NZFC on 6 July, Wellington, New Zealand. 2010.

Fitzgerald, Catherine. "Interview with Catherine Fitzgerald". New Zealand Producer, Blueskin Films. Medium: Face-to-face. Wellington, New Zealand, 9 January, 2013.

Fleming, Mike. "Paladin acquires New Zealand pic "Boy". *Deadline.com*, 15 August. 2011, retrieved 4.9.2018, from http://www.deadline.com/2011/08/paladin-acquires-new-zealand-pic-boy/.

Geary, David. "Taika Waititi – Boy wonder!". *New Zealand Journal of Media Studies*, 13(1), 2012, pp. 9–16, from DOI: 10.11157/medianz-vol13iss1id24.

Graham, Chris: "Festival film history, *Sione's Wedding*". *Goodlifefilms.co.nz*. 2009, retrieved 10.8.2018, from http://goodlifefilms.co.nz/filmfest/.

Hartley, Jean. "Case Study Research". In Catherine Cassell and Gillian Symon (eds.), *Essential guide to qualitative methods in organizational research*. London, UK: Sage. 2004. pp. 323–33.

Hedley, A. "Q&A with director Tusi Tamasese – "The Orator"". *Flicks. co.nz*. 2011, retrieved 31.7.2015, from http://www.flicks.co.nz/blog/amazing-interviews/qa-with-director-tusi-tamasese--e2-80-93-the-orator/.

Ivancic, Mladen. "Film Data". Email conversation with Mladen Ivancic. Acting Chief Executive, NZFC, Wellington, New Zealand, 15 December, 2013.

Ivancic, Mladen: "Urgent Information Request". Email conversation with Mladen Ivancic. Head of NZFC Finance, NZFC, Wellington, New Zealand, 13 May, 2015.

Jones, Deborah, Barlow, J., Finlay, S., and Savage, H. "*NZ Film: A case study of the New Zealand film industry*". Wellington: Victoria Management School, Victoria University of Wellington. Competitive Advantage New Zealand (CANZ). 2003.

Kickstarter Team. "BOY: The American release! by Taika Waititi". *Kickstarter. com*. 2012, retrieved 4.9.2018, from http://www.kickstarter.com/projects/18395296/boy-the-american-release.

Lealand, Geoff. "A nation of film-goers: Audiences, exhibition and distribution in New Zealand". In Karina Aveyard, and Albert Moran (eds.), *Watching films: new perspectives on movie-going, exhibition and reception*. Bristol: Intellect. 2013. pp. 141–155.

Lichman, J. "Taika Waititi's "Boy" a whimsical & unique coming-of-age tale from New Zealand". *Indiewire.com*, 3 March, 2012a, retrieved 5.9.2018, from http://blogs.indiewire.com/theplaylist/review-taika-waititis-boy-a-whimsical-unique-coming-of-age-tale-from-new-zealand.

Lichman, J. "Taika Waititi talks about making the smash hit New Zealand film "Boy" and his plans to reunite with Jemaine Clement". *Indiewire.com*, 2 February, 2012b, retrieved 4.9.2018, from http://blogs.indiewire.com/theplaylist/taika-waititi-talks-about-making-the-smash-hit-new-zealand-film-boy-his-plans-to-reunite-with-jemaine-clement.

Marriner, K. "Father vs. son: a study guide to Boy". *Screen Education*, 60, 2010, pp. 26–33.

Mason, Graeme. "Thoughts on the Screen Industry". *OnFilm*, May, 2012, pp. 10–11.

Mason, Graeme. "Interview with Graeme Mason". Chief Executive Officer, New Zealand Film Commission. Medium: Face-to-face. Wellington, New Zealand, 30 July, 2013.

MCH. "Samoan feature film first". *Mch.govt.nz*. 2010, retrieved 4.9.2018, from http://www.mch.govt.nz/news-events/news/samoan-feature-film-first.

Moore, Brendan. "Box office figures please". Email conversation with Brendan Moore, Ratings Officer/Reporting Support, Film and Video Labelling Body (FVLB), Auckland, New Zealand, 24 September, 2013.

MPDA. "Eagle vs Shark box office". *Mpda.org.nz*, 17 October, 2007, retrieved 25.7.2018, from http://www.mpda.org.nz/reports/weekly.

MPDA. "*Sione's Wedding* box office". *Mpda.org.nz*, 15 March, 2012a, retrieved 10.8.2018, from http://www.mpda.org.nz/reports/weekly.

MPDA. "*The Orator* box office". *Mpda.org.nz*, 5 January, 2012b, retrieved 10.8.2018, from http://www.mpda.org.nz/reports/weekly.

Murdoch, Graham and Peter Golding. "For a political economy of mass communications". In R. Miliband and J. Saville (eds.), *Social register 1973*. London: Merlin. 1973. pp. 205–234.

Muñoz Larroa, Argelia. *Sustainability in the Film Industry: External and Internal Dynamics Shaping the Wellington Film District* (PhD thesis). Wellington: Victoria University of Wellington. 2015.

Muñoz Larroa, Argelia. "Film distribution and delivery outlets in New Zealand: A transnational phase and some implications for local films and diversity". *Studies in Australasian Cinema*, 11(3), 2017, from DOI 10.1080/17503175.2017.1397235.

Muñoz Larroa, Argelia and Natàlia Ferrer-Roca. "Film distribution in New Zealand: Industrial organisation, power relations and market failure". *Media Industries*, 4(2), 2017, from DOI 10.3998/mij.15031809.0004.201.

NZFACT. "*Sione's Wedding* pirate sentenced to 300 hours community service". *NZfact.co.nz*. 2007, retrieved 8.8.2015, from http://www.nzfact.co.nz/press_releases/Release_18July.pdf.

NZFC. "New Zealand Film Commission Act 1978". New Zealand: NZFC. 1978, retrieved 3.9.2018, from http://www.legislation.govt.nz/act/public/1978/0061/latest/DLM22640.html.

NZFC. "Boy". *NZfilm.co.nz.* 2010a, retrieved 3.9.2018, from http://www.nzfilm. co.nz/ film/boy.

NZFC. "Piracy of Boy illustrates threat to film industry". *NZFC Press Release,* 22 June, 2010b, retrieved 3.9.2018, from http://www.thebigidea.co.nz/news/ industry-news/2010/jun/71231-nzfc-piracy-of- boy-illustrates-threat-to-film-industry.

NZFC. "NZFC annual report 2010–2011". *NZFC.* 2011a, retrieved 26.7.2015, from http://www.nzfilm.co.nz/sites/nzfc/files/NZFC_Annual_Report_2010-11.pdf.

NZFC. "*The Orator* press kit". *NZfilm.co.nz.* 2011b, retrieved 9.8.2015, from http://www.nzfilm.co.nz/sites/nzfc/files/Orator_press_kit_International.pdf.

NZFC. "NZ official co-productions summary". *NZFC.* May 2012. New Zealand.

NZ Government. "Treaty of Friendship between New Zealand and Samoa. Signed in Apia, 1 August". 1962, retrieved 28.8.2015, from http://www. vanuatu.usp.ac.fj/library/online/texts/Pacific_archive/Samoa/Treaty_of_ Friendship.pdf.

OnFilm. "*The Orator* submitted for Academy Awards". *OnFilm,* September, 2011, p. 10.

OnFilm. "*Hallowed Boy* rivals Harry Potter on disc". *OnFilm,* February, 2012, p. 7.

Parnham, Peter. "Risky Business". *OnFilm,* November, 2011, pp. 20–22.

Perrott, Lisa. "Call and response: Taika Waititi's Boy". *Metro,* 2010, pp. 49–53.

RadioNZ. "Graeme Mason – Outgoing head of the Film Commission". *Nine To Noon.* 2013, retrieved 25.1.2019, from https://www. radionz.co.nz/national/programmes/ninetonoon/audio/2566746/ graeme-mason-outgoing-head-of-the-film-commission.

Rudkin, Francesca. "Interview with Tusi Tamasese". *RialtoChannel.co.nz,* 26 July, 2012, retrieved 4.9.2018, from http://www.rialtochannel.co.nz/blog/ id/106/interview-with-tusi-tamasese.

SPP. "*Sione's Wedding* goes top 10 in Italy". *South Pacific Pictures.* n.d., retrieved 7.8.2015, from http://www.southpacificpictures.com/index. php?option=com_content&task=view&id=29&Itemid=99999999.

SPP. "*Sione's Wedding* press kit". *South Pacific Pictures.* 2015, retrieved 6.8.2015, from http://www.nzfilm.co.nz/sites/nzfc/files/Press_Kit_3.pdf.

SPP. "*Sione's Wedding* – 93 mins feature film (2005) They made one little promise... not to spoil their boy's big day". *South Pacific Pictures.* 2008, retrieved 7.8.2015, from http://www.southpacificpictures.com/index. php?option=com_production&id=19.

Steemers, Jeanette. *Selling television: British television in the global marketplace.* London: BFI. 2004.

Thompson, Peter A. "Neoliberalism and the political economies of public television policy in New Zealand". *Australian Journal of Communication,* 38(3), 2011, pp. 1–16.

Wasko, Janet. "The political economy of communication". In Anders Hansen (ed.), *Mass communication research methods.* London: Sage. 2008, Vol. 2, pp. 3–25.

Wood, Stacey: "Kiwi movie *Boy* gets yet more acclaim with swag of awards". *The Dominion Post,* 20 September, 2010, retrieved 4.9.2018, from http://www. stuff.co.nz/dominion-post/culture/4144152/Kiwi-movie-Boy-gets-yet-more-acclaim-with-swag-of-awards.

Anne Lill Rajala

Market censorship and Finnish cinema

Abstract This chapter deals with the concept of 'market censorship' and the practical implications of it in the context of contemporary Finnish cinema. It consists of a limited literature review, as well as an empirical part based on interviews with Finnish filmmakers and from observations made from Finnish media articles etc. For mapping censorial actions and reactions, I have applied the classical model of communication (as suggested by Müller 2004). The results suggest that in Finland censorial actions come in forms of, for example, lack of transparency in the decision making, which further reflects on *who* gets financed in the first place and *what* are the stories that are regarded important enough to make (and *how*). Additionally censorial actions come from distribution and exhibiting companies, namely through which films get screened and how much or often, and with what volume they are marketed to audiences, making it even more difficult for small-nation cinema to be sustainable and self-reliant. Censorial reactions are often linked to all of these, yet often they are viewed as norms or 'just the way things are'.

Keywords: market censorship, censorship, Finnish cinema, freedom of expression, diversity

Introduction

One of the major values in democratic societies is 'freedom of expression' to assure a free flow of information (Dahl 2006). Film is sometimes seen as the most democratic form of art which can reach wide audiences (Sironen 2006, p. 76). As I shall argue here, this is far from true. In contemporary Western societies 'censorship' is often thought of as a practice belonging to a time in the past, perhaps the cold war or a distant geographical location with an authoritarian regime, and any claims of censorship in the present day are often opposed or treated with suspicion. Some softer forms of censorship, such as economic control and 'market censorship' are perhaps less aggressive or even visible than the 'traditional' or conventional forms of censorship, yet they might be as effective – if not even more effective – than the more straight-forward ways of restriction and repression. As the concept of market censorship is fairly unknown and contested, my attempt here is to discuss the definitions based on a limited literature review and suggest a comparison on how it differs from other forms of censorship, for example, 'self-censorship'. Additionally I will give examples of some of the practical implications of different forms of censorship in the contemporary Finnish filmmaking context. This empirical part or discussion is based on interviews with Finnish filmmakers and researchers conducted in the Media and Education in the Digital Age (MEDA) research programme in 2016–2018. And additionally I will discuss the topics in relation to other official Finnish research reports and media texts from that period of time. I have used the classical model of communication to map the censorial actions and reactions (Müller 2004, p. 15). In this model the analysis take into account six factors: the sender of the message, the receiver, the message itself, the code employed, the channel or medium, and the [socio-political] context (ibid.). The interviewees are anonymous due to the delicate nature of the topic. Specific filmmakers are mentioned only if their names have previously been published in an article or interview in the media.

The limited literature review mainly consists of texts by Beate Müller, Sue Curry Jansen, Helen Freshwater and Daniel Bar-Tal. Beate Müller writes about censorship through family resemblance and proposes a model for analysis based on the classical model of communication. Helen Freshwater proposes to extend the definitions of censorship to perceptions of censorship. Sue Curry Jansen deals with the history of the concept of market censorship, and Daniel Bar-Tal mainly discusses the concept of self-censorship. Other authors referenced to (besides the ones mentioned above) are referred to mainly when these previous ones have discussed their thoughts in their texts.

I will be using the term 'cinema' as an umbrella term for both fictive and non-fictional audio-visual content; namely 'film'. 'Film' refers to mainly full-length films, but occasionally also to short films, however, for example, commercial advertisement, trailers, and music videos are excluded. In the cases in which I discuss 'cinema' as a building or other physical space for exhibiting and viewing films, I will most often use the term 'film theatre'.

Towards a wider view of censorship

According to Beate Müller, up until the 1980s the term 'censorship' was commonly restricted to direct forms of regulatory intervention by political authorities, usually the state and the church (Müller 2004, p. 4). Müller writes (ibid.) that apart from 'self-censorship', two types of censorship were commonly distinguished:

(1) pre-publication censorship, or licensing, that is, the control of material before it is published, and
(2) post-publication censorship, which means restricting or restraining the distribution and reception of material after it has been published.

Since the 1980s there has been conceptual changes in our understanding of censorship. Proponents of 'new censorship' insist that apart from this kind of regulatory censorship, social interaction and communication is affected by constitutive or structural censorship (Müller 2004, p. 1). As a possible explanation to this development Müller suggests historical political turbulence, such as the fall of the Berlin wall, the collapse of the Soviet Union, and the opening of state archives throughout formerly socialist Europe leading to an increase in publications on censorship. Richard Burt has identified another possible reason: the 'right-wing agenda' of the Reagan/Bush administration and its attempts to limit some civil and aesthetic liberties in what cultural critics have called "the intense, prolonged assault on high and low modes of aesthetic production, circulation, and consumption beginning in the 1980s" (Burt 1994, p. xi). There are views that censorship used to divide the political right and left: the right being for it, the left against it; the right acting as an agent of censorship, the left is its victim (Müller 2004, p. 239). However, Freshwater says that it is not possible to conflate political affiliation with a stance on censorship (ibid.). Thus calls for the restraint of representation or silencing of expression are just as likely to come from the left as the right, for example, for regulation needed because of hate speech (ibid). Burt writes that "those on the left and the right occupy the same discursive terrain: both sides adopt the same rhetoric; both sides say they are against censorship and for diversity; each side accuses the other of trying to exercise censorship" (Burt 1994, p. xv). We also need to remember that there are often biases that censorship is inherently 'good' or 'bad', or that the censored message is 'valuable' (Müller 2004, pp. 238–239). Censorship is not only a 'negative force', a repressive exercise of power such as "destroying materials, blocking access to them, limiting [...] distribution and circulation, and assigning penalties for collecting and consuming forbidden materials" (Burt 1994, p. xv). Additionally Burt proposes that we adopt a view of censorship as an administrative power (1994). Michael Holquist in his turn claims that "to be for or against censorship as such is to assume a freedom no one has. Censorship *is*. One can only discriminate among its more and less repressive effects" (Holquist 1994, p. 16).

Müller says that since the 1980s "growing awareness of and debates about issues such as political correctness, 'hate speech', ethnic minorities, pornography, feminism, the canon, or the commodification of art, and the relationship of these topics to free speech and censorship, have led to a surge of academic publications in these fields" (Müller 2004, p. 3). There are however concerns that widening the concept 'censorship' carries the risk of equating censorship with, for example, any kind of social control (Müller 2004, p. 1). Despite these concerns, according to Freshwater it is possible to make strong arguments for a diverse conception of censorship. In contemporary society, "censorship can still appear in its most traditional guise, such as the intervention of a representative of a repressive institution, directly linked to the state: but it also materialises in the actions and decisions taken by those who administrate charitable foundations and local government, or corporate sponsors and sources of public subsidy" (Müller 2004, p. 241).

Müller proposes that we can use the classical model of communication to map censorial actions and reactions and to represent the various factors that may play a role in censorship (Müller 2004, p. 15). In this model there are six factors to take into account when analysing: the sender of the message, the receiver, the message itself, the code employed, the channel or medium, and the [socio-political?] context (ibid.). Rather than viewing censorship merely as a repressive tool used by an authority, this model helps us to understand that censorship is an unstable process of actions and reactions in the struggle for power, publicity, and the privilege to speak out (Müller 2004, p. 25).

Market censorship and self-censorship

According to Sue Curry Jansen (2010, p. 22), direct references to market censorship within the literature on censorship began in the 1980s and gained significant momentum in censorship scholarship in the following decades. In Jansen's view, the increased frequency in the use of the term 'market censorship' (and its synonyms) correlates with the end of the Cold War and the rise of neoliberalism. Jansen says that the concept still meets stiff opposition because "it breaks with established liberal legal and philosophical conventions, which treat censorship as an exceptional, even aberrant, practice in Western societies" (Jansen 2010, p. 12). Claims of market censorship are laden with ambiguity, and thus many scholars prefer to use the term 'self-censorship' (ibid.).

Daniel Bar-Tal describes that in self-censorship, for various reasons, "individuals decide not to reveal truthful information to their family members, close friends, fellow group members, members of organizations, media, leaders, or society members", and that in all of these cases, "they believe that there is cost in revealing the information, and therefore they choose to conceal it" (ibid). It is recognized that in certain cases self-censorship is necessary, yet in some cases it can be considered as a sociopsychological barrier which prevents "free access to information, obstructs freedom of expression, and harms free flow of information" (Bar-Tal 2017, p. 41). However, Bar-Tal focuses in his article specifically on censorship of *information* rather than opinions, yet in every-daily life a clear distinction between information and opinion is often difficult to make. Therefore for Bar-Tal self-censorship requires that a person believes that the possessed information is valid and truthful (2017, p. 42). Additionally Bar-Tal claims (2017, p. 42) that "the scope of self-censorship includes cases in which individual thinks that there are formal obstacles to sharing information, while in reality there are none." For him, individuals may *imagine* the existence of various types of formal censorship, however including these [imagined] cases in the definition would broaden the scope extensively without clear boundaries (ibid.). However, he mentions that there are cases in which "there may be social sanctions against sharing information without the existence of official obstacles" as the "social sanctions may be applied informally by individuals, groups, or social agencies that disapprove of information disclosure" (ibid.). Bar-Tal says that it is possible to differentiate between formally enforced self-censorship and socially enforced self-censorship (ibid.). While for Bar-Tal the former is excluded from the scope of self-censorship behaviour, the latter is included as there is a need to distinguish the socially enforced self-censorship from the formal sanctions that may regulate behaviour formally with rules and laws. "The other type of sanctions is of wide scope, and it is impossible to evaluate their subjective severity." (ibid.)

However, Freshwater mentions also the diverse *experiences of censorship* "which reflects the socio-historical specificity of instances of control, conditioning or silencing" (Müller 2004, p. 225). Censorship is for her "a process, realised through the relationships between censorious agents, rather than a series of actions carried out by a discrete or isolated authority" (ibid.). Considering this, perceived forms of, for example, market censorship leading further to self-censorship could, in my view, also be regarded as a form of market censorship.

The problem with using the concept 'self-censorship' as a synonym for or instead of 'market censorship' is for Jansen that it "locates agency in the individual artist, writer, publisher, producer or programmer rather than within the institutional structures and practices of systems of cultural production" (Jansen 2010, p. 12). The term suggests that the act of censoring is intentional, rational and voluntary suppression of information in the *absence* of formal impediments, such as laws and orders (Bar-Tal 2017, p. 37, 42). Thus for Jansen, the term self-censorship "may accurately describe some of the creative decisions individual cultural workers make: decisions in areas where they have the autonomy to make choices to include some things and exclude others, or to use one approach or genre rather than another", and such decisions may reflect the individual's personal moral, rational, aesthetic or emotional preferences (Jansen 2010, p. 13). Jansen says that it is however misleading to use the concept of self-censorship in order to describe how systems of cultural practices work, and it puts the blame on the victims (ibid.). Thus 'market censorship' is for her a more accurate description to the systemic censorship that plays an "increasingly prominent role in cultural production" (Jansen 2010, p. 12).

Jansen defines market censorship followingly (2010, pp. 13–14):

> Market censorship points to practices that routinely filter or restrict the production and distribution of selected ideas, perspectives, genres or cultural forms within mainstream media of communication based upon their anticipated profits and/or support for corporate values and consumerism. Such practices are reified, naturalized and integrated into the organizational structures and routine practices of media organizations and re-presented to the public as outcomes of consumer choices within a rational market system rather than as the result of calculated managerial responses to profit imperatives. Over time, these practices have become objectified, understood as 'just the way things are' or 'how things work', rather than as the historical outcomes of human decisions about how to organize the production and distribution of goods and services, and how to design, develop and deploy communication technologies. The veneer of inevitability that this phantom objectivity projects reinforces entrenched interests and makes the system highly resistant to change.

Jansen further explains that under these conditions, certain ideas get extensive exposure whereas others are marginalized, ignored, or deemed too controversial, risky or commercially unviable (Jansen 2010, p. 14). "In short, market censorship refers to the conditions of production and consumption that produce cultural hegemony" (ibid.). Additionally, already in 1981 Dallas Smythe suggested that "[t]he act of modern censorship is essentially a decision as to what is to be mass-produced in the cultural area" (Smythe 1981, p. 235). 'Market censorship' could also be used in a broad sense as a critical concept for analysing the dynamics of cultural production (Jansen 2010, p. 22). However, 'market censorship' is a leaky concept. According to Jansen, "criticisms of the concept of market censorship are not without merit. It is a provocative pairing of terms, a leaky concept without firm boundaries, which is too often deployed as well as rejected on ideological grounds. Market censorship usually operates behind closed doors and is therefore difficult to document" (Jansen 2010, p. 26). Another problem thus becomes the lack of transparency. "Without transparency, who can say for certain whether a manuscript was rejected because it failed to meet high editorial standards or because management insists on investing in and promoting works by authors with established 'brands'?" (Jansen 2010, p. 25).

Market censorship may additionally be hard to spot. For example, Pierre Bourdieu once wrote that "the more effective the process of regulation and repression is, the less apparent it becomes, as it begins to appear as the natural 'way of the world' (Müller 2004. p. 230). Thus "outsiders who did not grow up within Western democracies [...] seem to be able to spot [market censorship] more readily than insiders can" (Jansen 2010, p. 26). Bourdieu also draws attention to the fact that "[c]ensorship is never quite as perfect or as invisible as when each agent has nothing to say apart from what he is objectively authorised to say [...] he is [...] censored once and for all, through the forms of perception and expression that he has internalised and which impose their form on all his expressions" (Müller 2004, p. 230). Additionally Bourdieu discusses 'symbolic power' and writes that "symbolic power is that invisible form of power which can be exercised only with the complicity of those who do not want to know that they are subject to it or even that they themselves exercise it". (Bourdieu 1991, p. 164)

Jansen reminds that "[n]o form of censorship is ever fully effective: even under stringent forms of ecclesiastical or state censorship; some producers find ways around the system, whether by creative ingenuity (use of irony, esoteric language or forms, etc.), or by such means as exploiting loopholes in the rules, bribery, favouritism deriving from personal or political networks, and so on" (Jansen 2010, p. 24).

Jansen claims that in most cases, market censors and political authorities work in consonance with each other and their efforts are mutually reinforcing (ibid.). However, she discusses market censorship mainly in the US context and in relation to commercial corporations, which then comes with its own geographical and socio-political implications. Thus it is worth to note, as Freshwater suggests, that:

> Censorious events should be analysed with critical emphasis upon their socio-historical specificity: such an approach foregrounds the differences between different types of censorship and the decisions taken by numerous censorious agencies, as well as their interaction. Conclusions about censorship should surely be provisional, rather than fixed; plural, rather than singular; time and site-specific, rather than universal. Of course, responsiveness to charges of censorship should not obstruct investigation into the possible presence of complicitous relationships between censored individuals and censorious institutions. As Judith Butler proposes, it seems more appropriate to view censorship as a continuum, upon which it is possible to place the brutal extremes of incarceration or murder at one end, and the shadowy operations of constitutive exclusion at the other. Their connection is thus established, without negating their differences. (Müller 2004, p. 242)

The 'Finnish Case'

Finland is a country with a small population of approximately five and a half million people. The legal conception of free speech is roughly described as that everyone has the right to express, publish and receive information, opinions and other messages without any pre-prohibitions (Finlex online). The official national languages in Finland are Finnish and Swedish, Swedish being the mother tongue of approximately 5.4% of the population (Institute for the Languages of Finland online). There are also approximately 150 other small language minorities such as Saami, sign language and the Finnish Romani, albeit these languages are not considered national languages (ibid.). However, a citizen can have only one language registered as their mother tongue and thus official statistics do not reflect the multilingual and multicultural landscape properly (Westerlund 2019).

Finland being such a small market population-wise, the public subsidies are the lifeblood of the Finnish film industry (Ministry of Education and Culture online). Without this public support, perhaps only a handful of domestic films could be made each year. The main financial supporters are The Finnish Film Foundation (Suomen elokuvasäätiö) and the Finnish public broadcasting company, Yleisradio (later Yle).

The Finnish Film Foundation was founded in 1969 as an independent foundation operating under the supervision of the Department for Cultural Policy of the Ministry of Education and Culture (FFF online). The Foundation is the most significant film financier in Finland and its production support accounts for approximately 40 percent of the average production budget of feature films (ibid.). It supports an average of 70–80 film productions per year with over 20 million euros.[1] The Film Foundation receives its funding through the Ministry of Education and Culture from lottery and pools funds (ibid.).

The second most significant film financier is The Finnish public broadcasting company, which was founded in 1926 just four years after the world's first public broadcasting company BBC had been founded (Ylen historia online). Yle supports domestic film yearly with approximately 2 million euros usually buy buying the broadcasting rights [esitysoikeudet] in advance (Aromaa & Tuominen 2017). Albeit Yle participates in roughly 70% of the films that the Film Foundation finances, also their 'tastes' differ (ibid.), mainly suggesting that a project may be approved by the other institution but not the other. Yle is (or was at the time of writing this text, and this too appears to be changing) further divided in two departments, the Finnish and Swedish side. In 2014 the Swedish side of Yle was using 8% of the whole Yle budget (including news, drama and administration etc.) (Mankkinen 2015).

---

1 Twenty-four million in 2018 (Elokuvavuosi 2018/Facts & Figures 2018 [online]).

All in all, the governmental support for a long film funding is approximately 40% of a film's total budget, and the total yearly support is approximately 25 million euros (Pesonen 2017). The amount of governmental support is relatively small compared to other Nordic countries, for example, apparently in 2016 Norway supported domestic film with 44 million and Sweden with 35 million.

What many of the Finnish filmmakers we have interviewed find problematic is that overall, the Film Foundation and Yle funding system is a very conservative structure and it mainly supports well-established filmmakers and conventional storylines. The power to make the funding decisions is in the hands of only few, and according to the interviewees there is a lack of transparency in the decision making. Additionally the Film Foundation requires a 'good' distribution plan, and the interviewees claim that in practice this means that unless Yle is willing to participate in the funding and ensure broadcasting, there will be no funding from the Film Foundation either. According to the interviewees, this structure also makes it very difficult to get funding for anything slightly more 'bold' and 'experimental' content and production-wise even for the established filmmakers.

The situation appears to be even more problematic for documentary cinema, as documentary films do not get cinema distribution as often as fiction films. This makes documentary filmmakers even more dependent on Yle than the fiction filmmakers (Virtanen 2019). As an example, director and script writer Mia Halme considers the lack of [documentary film] distributors as a major problem (ibid.). Halme says that "[i]f we wish to preserve Finnish documentary film also as a form of art, it cannot solely be something Yle has a fixed program slot for" (ibid.).

Some of the interviewees mention the lack of diversity regarding which filmmakers get financed in the first place, for example, how age, gender and ethnicity imbalances are visible in the final support decisions. Especially how young women are practically invisible in the industry is often repeated in both the interviews and media articles. Gender imbalance cannot be explained with education, for example, Helsingin Sanomat[2] wrote that despite the fact that 70% of the documentary film students in film schools are female (and the percentage is even higher when looking at the numbers of examined students), only one-third of the full-length documentary films that get into the spotlight (which I assume means, e.g., prime-time broadcasting or something similar) are made

---

2   A Finnish newspaper formed in 1889, back then going by the name 'Päivälehti', and currently with approximately 690,000 daily readers (paper subscriptions as well as readers online).

by women (Virtanen 2019). Reportedly women also get much smaller budgets for their films (ibid.). However, according to the recently published report "Elokuvavuosi 2018/Facts & Figures 2018" [online], in 2018, films with female directors received larger sums on average than their male counterparts, and often female directors were more successful with their applications.

In the same Helsingin Sanomat article, the blame for the imbalance in documentary film financing and exhibition is put on Erkko Lyytinen, who is currently in charge of documentary projects on Yle (Virtanen 2019). Additionally Lyytinen refused to give any comments for the article in Helsingin Sanomat (ibid.).

The imbalance issues further reflect also on what eventually is seen on the screen – what are considered as the 'important topics' to make films about, and who are the main characters in a story. One of the interviewees explains that, for example, romantic comedy is often seen less valuable than a story about war, or that a story about a man is considered a universal story about humanity whereas a story about a woman is merely a story about one particular individual. However, the interviewee continues, these are deeply rooted ideas or ideals in society and things will probably not change just by adding a couple of more women in the decision making and financing.

As mentioned earlier, Finland has two national languages and further some 150 small language minorities. The problem according to practically all interviewees is that this diversity of Finnish society does not reach the cinema screens. Either the filmmakers are not able to make films in Swedish language because the financers will not grant money for films in other languages than Finnish, or the filmmakers decide to make films in a language that they think 'will sell'.

The current CEO of the Film Foundation Lasse Saarinen claims that it would be intruding the artistic freedom if one starts to guide language choices to a specific direction, yet, for example, one of the interviewees claim that the people in charge of, for example, short films in the Film Foundation are Finnish speaking (assumably not that fluent in Swedish) and thus this may affect the language chosen by the filmmakers as well as the eventual financing decisions.

Lately the language aspect has gotten much attention in Finnish media as there are plans of making a historical film about painter Helene Schjerfbeck – in Finnish – yet Schjerfbeck did not know more than a few words in Finnish language. Among the arguments for choosing Finnish over historical accuracy has been that Finnish language film has a broader audience and possibilities for funding. The film is going to be directed by Antti J. Jokinen, and he explains the language decision by claiming that Finnish language films have more success in Finland (Hällsten 2018). Erkki Astala, former head of production at the Finnish

Film Foundation and current commissioner of Finnish Yle, further says that forcing someone to make a film in a certain language would "be close to censorship" (Sahlgren-Fodstad 2018). However, Yles' attitude or statements towards language choices appears peculiar if not self-contradictory as Astala also says that "as I only work for the Finnish side of Yle, it would have been strange if I would have said 'you need to switch language and the contact person on Yle if you wish to make the film' [in Swedish], referring to that there is another commissioner on the Swedish language side of Yle" (ibid.). Further more, one of the filmmakers interviewed says that he/she was forced to add Finnish language into a film which this filmmaker had intended to be completely in Swedish precisely as (Finnish) Yles' condition for participating in the production was to have "some, or preferably half of the film in Finnish language".

A researcher interviewed explains that historically in the silent film era language was no problem. The "natural bilingualism" disappeared from the films in Finland (and additionally in other parts of the world) when sound films came along, and that the bilingualism was gone for a long time. If Swedish language was heard in the Finnish films, it was often ridiculed or portrayed in comical way. Additionally, if a film was intended to be exported to Sweden, the actors had to speak 'proper Swedish', not the Finno-Swedish dialect. One interviewee says that even in the recent past, if a film was meant to be exported to Sweden, it sometimes had to be 'translated' into 'proper Swedish'. However as some of the interviewees say, unfortunately the Finnish films – regardless of being in Finnish or Swedish language – are very seldom exported to Sweden or other Nordic countries for that matter.

The problems are not only with reaching audiences over national borders, as to reach the domestic audiences in Finland is far from unproblematic too. Not only are there issues because distribution companies are acting as gatekeepers,[3] but there are also too few screens.[4] Additionally the majority of film theatres can be traced to foreign ownership. As an example, Finnkino cinema theatre chain, which can be traced to Chinese ownership, owns approximately one-third of the roughly 300 screens in cinemas, and Finnkino possesses 70% of the market share. The second biggest chain owning roughly 10% of the film theatres is Bio Rex, which is currently in Swedish ownership. And as one interviewee says, these bigger theatre chains nowadays have little or no interest in preserving

---

3   See e.g., chapter by Heidi Grundström in this book.
4   According to Elokuvauutiset (online) there were 321 screens and according to Elokuvavuosi 2018 / Facts & Figures 2018 (online) 355 screens in 2018.

cultural diversity by adding domestic films into their program, and that they are merely after profit and thus prefer to show Hollywood blockbusters. One interviewee says that just a decade or so ago, the smaller local film theatres had to wait for the latest blockbuster film releases (their physical copies), and meanwhile these theatres may have screened more local productions. Now with the digitalization and digital distribution of films there is not really any need to wait, and thus the exhibition of the local productions suffers. On another token, digital distribution may also be beneficial for some local productions. We need to remember that the number of screens also strongly connect to how much volume is put into marketing and how much visibility a film gets.

In 2018, the box office gross was 90.4 million euros (Elokuvavuosi 2018 / Facts & Figures 2018 [online]). As the deals between distribution companies and film theatres are veiled in business secrets there is little or no information available on how the revenues are shared, but one interviewee estimates that the film theatres take roughly half, then the distributors take their share, and if there is anything left, that goes to the production company. "Making films is not profitable, screening them is", as one of the interviewees states.

Overall, my interpretation is that censorial actions in contemporary Finland come in forms of, for example, lack of transparency in the decision making (by the ones in control of the resources for filmmaking), which further reflects on *who* gets financed in the first place (filmmakers and production companies), and *what* are the stories that are regarded by the decision-makers important enough to make (and *how*), and what then becomes a film. Additionally censorial actions come from distribution and exhibiting companies, namely through which films get to be screened and how much or often, and with what volume they are marketed to audiences, making it even more difficult for small-nation cinema to be sustainable and self-reliant. Censorial reactions are often linked to all of these, yet often they are viewed as norms or 'just the way things are'.

Conclusions

Censorship may take many different guises. Widening the concept of censorship from its 'traditional' conception offers the possibility to better understand various forms of exercises of power and control, and the relationships and dependencies between different actors.

Müller proposed that we can use the classical model of communication in which there are six factors to take into account when we analyse censorious actions and reactions: the sender of the message, the receiver, the message itself, the code employed, the channel or medium, and the [socio-political] context (Müller 2004, p. 15). Thus I will now try to summarise my conclusions according to this model.

1. Context

Albeit the notion of 'free speech' in the Finnish legal context consists of the right of free expression without any prohibitions in advance, this does not extend to the cinematic field as the resources are in practice regulated by governmental institutions as well as private corporations. The power over public subsidies in Finland are in the hands of few, and at least until now there has been a lack of transparency in the decision making.

Traditional forms of censorship were perhaps most clearly visible (even if also then in an indirect way) in the interviews and media texts, for example, when Yle demands certain languages to be used.

It must however be said that concrete governmental policy guidelines and laws have been made and changed very recently – also with the purpose of supporting a more diverse cinematic cultural expression, yet only time will tell what the practical effects of these will be, or perhaps what the new forms of censorship eventually will be.

2. Message

The cinematic representation of the world and society, be it in fiction or non-fiction form, appears to be very homogeneous or biased. This can be traced back to the financing of productions and namely *which stories are regarded as important,* and further *who* gets funding in the first place.

3. Author

Despite the fact that students studying in film schools have approximately a 50–50 gender balance, or in some cases the majority of students are female, something peculiar happens between studies and getting into the industry and gaining funding for films. Ethnicity is another aspect which was brought up in some interviews, yet it is an issue that is seldom discussed in the media.

The diversity aspect in relation to film education was not further discussed with the interviewees in the MEDA-Cinema project, yet some of the interviewees mentioned that it may be easier for people with ethnic backgrounds to be able to make documentary films than fiction films, and I connect this with the situation that typically the production budgets for documentary films are smaller than in fiction films. In any case, the question *who* gets funding in the first place is a big question, as well as what are the ways or platforms for gaining visibility.

4. Code

Linguistic diversity is not regarded as an asset, albeit, for example, films made in Swedish language or other language minorities could perhaps reach wider audiences in other Nordic countries[5] and beyond. Very often the claim is that films made in other languages than Finnish 'will not sell', which leads us closer to 'market censorship'.

5. Medium and receiver

The film theatres are in the hands of foreign owners, and this seems to affect which films get screened and the volume they are marketed to audiences. Eventually this has consequences on how audiences will find access to films. Foreign ownership also implies that most of the revenues from screening local films flow outside of Finland, and this has (negative) consequences on the sustainability of Finnish cinema. This may lead to an 'evil cycle' in which the Finnish filmmakers are or become dependent on the Film Foundation and Yle for the 'wrong reasons'. In other words, instead of their support helping to preserve expressions of local cultural and the societal diversity, the subsidies indirectly flow towards supporting foreign corporations who get to decide what should be produced and screened. As far as I am aware of, there is no governmental policies and regulations regarding the ownership of film theatres nor distribution companies. If this is the case, in the long run, the public subsidies eventually benefit the foreign corporations – not the Finnish film industry, the local filmmakers nor the local audiences.

How internet and, for example, the various forms of video-on-demand (VOD) services will 'change the game' regarding both the marketing films to audiences and the ways of viewing films remains to be seen. As Jansen says (2010, p. 25), "while the internet does allow us all, if we have the time and inclination, to transmit our views to the world, it does not ensure that anyone will pay attention to what we have to say. Voices in the wildness may be expressive but we must also ask whether they are consequential"

Finally – the awareness of the various softer forms of censorship (even though not all would directly articulate them as forms of censorship) may sometimes

---

5   More on this in forthcoming MEDA-Cinema and Identity book.

lead to self-censorship. Especially when certain things are internalized as 'norms' or 'just the way things are' – for example, in the Finnish case the perceptions on language choices or what are perceived as the important stories to tell – they have an effect already during the creative process (Müller 2004, p. 24). As Müller writes (2004, p. 25) "the internalization of norms cannot easily be overcome, let alone reversed", and

> Consequently, self-censorship can prevent [...] from writing daring texts, an indirect form of silencing that is the ultimate goal of censorship: policing the mind rather than the product. (Müller 2004, pp. 24–25)

References

Aromaa, Jouni and Tuominen, Stina. "Yle Uutiset selvitti: Ohjaaja Saara Cantell sai eniten julkista rahaa elokuvilleen – katso miten muut pärjäsivät" Yle [online] 8.12.2017, retrieved 12.3.2019, from https://yle.fi/uutiset/3-9965801.

Bar-Tal, Daniel. "Self-Censorship as a Socio-Political-Psychological Phenomenon: Conception and Research." *Political Psychology 38.S1* (2017): pp. 37–65. 2017.

Bourdieu, Pierre. *Language and Symbolic Power*. Cambridge: Polity, 1991.

Burt, Richard. *The Administration of Aesthetics: Censorship, Political Criticism, and the Public Sphere*. Minneapolis, MN: University of Minnesota Press, 1994.

Dahl, Robert A. *On Political Equality*. New Haven, CT: Yale University Press, 2006.

Elokuvauutiset [online]. *Suomen elokuvateatterit 2018*, retrieved: 13.3.2019, from https://www.elokuvauutiset.fi/site/sf-2011/muut-tilastot/7878-suomen-elokuvateatterit-paikkakunnittain.

Elokuvavuosi 2018 / *Facts & Figures 2018* [online], retrieved: 29.4.2019 from http://ses.fi/fileadmin/dokumentit/Elokuvavuosi_Facts_Figures_2018.pdf.

FFF [online], http://ses.fi/en/home/.

Finlex [online], retrieved 29.3.2019, from https://www.finlex.fi/fi/laki/ajantasa/1999/19990731.

Holquist, Michael. "Corrupt Originals – The Paradox of Censorship." *Pmla-Publications Of The Modern Language Association Of America 109.1* (1994): pp. 14–25.

Hällsten, Annika. "Helene Schjerfbeck pratar finska på film". *Hufvudstadsbladet* [online] 12.10.2018, retrieved 14.11.2018, from https://www.hbl.fi/artikel/helene-schjerfbeck-pratar-finska-pa-film/.

Institute for the Languages of Finland [online], retrieved: 8.3.2019, from https://www.kotus.fi/en/on_language/languages_of_finland.

Jansen, Sue Curry. "Ambiguities and Imperatives of Market Censorship: The Brief History of a Critical Concept." *Westminster Papers in Communication and Culture 7*.2 (2010): pp. 12–30.

Mankkinen, Jussi. "Näin Yle käyttää rahasi", *Yle [online]*, retrieved: 19.3.2019, from https://yle.fi/uutiset/3-7855922.

Ministry of Education and Culture [online]. *Selvitys: Elokuvien tuotantotuki alalle elinehto*, retrieved: 20.6.2018, from https://minedu.fi/artikkeli/-/asset_publisher/selvitys-elokuvien-tuontatotuki-alalle-elinehto.

Müller, Beate. *Censorship & Cultural Regulation in the Modern Age.* Amsterdam/New York: Rodopi, 2004.

Pesonen, Mikko. "Ehdotus: Elokuvasäätiö pysyy vallankahvassa – lakkauttamistakin pohdittiin", *Yle 26.9.2017*, retrieved: 19.3.2019, from https://yle.fi/uutiset/3-9850507

Sahlgren-Fodstad, Silja. "Svenskspråkiga Helene Schjerfbeck talar finska på film för att språket inte ens diskuteras när stöd beviljas." *Svenska Yle 25.10.2018*, retrieved: 13.3.2019, from https://svenska.yle.fi/artikel/2018/10/25/svensksprakiga-helene-schjerfbeck-talar-finska-pa-film-for-att-spraket-inte-ens

Sironen, Jiri. *Videolaista elokuvien aikuissensuurin poistumiseen: sensuuripuhunnat ja kuvaohjelmien kulttuurinen sääntely 1980-luvulta nykypäivään* (Master's thesis) Jyväskylä, 2006.

Smythe, Dallas W. *Dependency Road: Communication, Capitalism, Consciousness, and Canada.* Norwood, NJ: Ablex, 1981.

Virtanen, Leena. "Suurin osa dokumenttielokuvan opiskelijoista on naisia, mutta tekijöistä vain murto-osa – Ohjaajat syyttävät tilanteesta Yleä." *Helsingin Sanomat* [online] 30.1.2019, retrieved: 31.1.2019, from https://www.hs.fi/kulttuuri/art-2000005982736.html?fbclid=IwAR2YXi4L-AGUgtlFpsi2ksCSLCk006j17utRyXCH-_eleOXtR5YIhDZurEc.

Westerlund, Elin. "Finland ett tvåspråkigt land – men har inga tvåspråkiga medborgare." *Ylen historia* [online], retrieved 12.3.2019, from https://yle.fi/aihe/artikkeli/2015/01/11/ylen-historia.

Argelia Muñoz Larroa[1]

Sustainability as a framework of analysis and a guide for policy-making: The film industry in Wellington, New Zealand

Abstract Cultural policy-makers worldwide have expressed the desire to promote local 'sustainable' cultural industries, including film industries. While well intended, this has been somehow problematic as what 'sustainable' entails has remained unclear. This paper suggests a definition of a sustainable film industry and develops a framework to study and leverage it by drawing on two approaches: the political economy of culture and geographical industrialisation. The framework is used to analyse the case of the film industry in Wellington, New Zealand, where a qualitative analysis of interviews, documents, and media reports informed the empirical study. The research identified localised 'vertical' blockages along the value chain relations and 'horizontal' blockages among the interdependencies of industry stakeholders. Those blockages undermine five key areas to enable sustainability: financial capacity, ability to maintain labour pools, to feed from creative sources, to develop infrastructure, and the opportunity to reach audiences. The Wellington case showed constraints in all five areas which also suggest potential paths for policy-making to overcome those challenges.

Keywords: film industry, sustainability, cultural policy, New Zealand, political economy

Introduction

Some of the reasons why governments and international organisations support cultural industries are their contributions to generate jobs, tourism, trade, income, "cultural enrichment, social empowerment and cohesion" (UNCTAD 2010, p. 26). Government and international organisation's reports worldwide have expressed the desire to promote local 'sustainable' film industries.[2] While well intended, this has been somehow problematic as what 'sustainable' entails has remained unclear. Even though the film industry has been widely

---

1 Many thanks to Dr. Deborah Jones and Dr. Geoff Stahl for their valuable advice and input into this research.
2 For examples in New Zealand see NZFC: *Statement of Intent 2013–2016*. Wellington: New Zealand Film Commission, 2013; SPT: *Taking on the World. The Report on the Screen Production Industry Taskforce*. Screen Production industry Taskforce, Ministry of Industry and Regional Development: Wellington, 2003.

researched, studies have only indirectly dealt with its sustainability and further steps could be taken to transfer such knowledge into more applicable policy solutions. However, as David Throsby observed, before the concept of cultural sustainability "can become operational in […] empirical terms […] [it needs] to be rescued from the wilderness of vagueness and generality […] and given a precise interpretation" (Throsby 2017).

This chapter addresses the question of how a film industry can be made sustainable, socioeconomically speaking. It explores a definition of a sustainable film industry and develops a framework to study and leverage it by drawing on the political economy of culture and geographical industrialisation approaches. The framework consists of identifying localised 'vertical' blockages along the value chain relations and 'horizontal' blockages among the interdependencies of industry stakeholders.

Underlying this work is the idea that the cultural aspect of films is the most relevant as it provides a space for people to communicate, create and generate a sense of community. Nonetheless, films have an industrial component; therefore study of the socio-economic factors that enable film production is necessary in order to develop such an important cultural space. Furthermore, the chapter's aims are aligned with UNESCO's ethical imperative to consider cultural diversity as the right for all cultures to "express themselves and make themselves known" (2002) through a powerful medium such as films. The idea is to move towards Throsby's set of principles[3] by which cultural sustainable development outcomes can be judged. These are: (a) *intra* and *inter-generational equity*, that is, the capacity for present and future generations to access cultural resources, cultural production, participation and enjoyment; (b) the value of *cultural diversity* for maintaining resilience as a human species; (c) *precautionary principles*, which protect cultural heritage and valued cultural practices from disappearing; and (d) the *interconnectedness* among economic, social, cultural and environmental systems. These principles enable the operationalising of cultural sustainability outcomes and transform a theoretical concept into a desirable background for making cultural policy (Throsby 1997, 2017).

However, this essay steps back to place emphasis on the socio-economic aspects of the film industry but hoping to be a starting point to develop in the future more holistic frameworks that could incorporate Throsby's aforementioned principles such as wider desirable cultural and environmental aspects

---

3   Extrapolated from environmental sustainable development.

(i.e., film heritage, wider social access to production and consumption of films, minimising the environmental impact of film production, etc.).[4]

The framework suggested here will be used to examine the film industry in Wellington, the capital of New Zealand. New Zealand, a country of 4.4 million people, has a small national film industry. There is a strong tradition of public funding for arts and culture and public service broadcasting, which has recently transitioned into a market-driven model (Volkerling 2001). The New Zealand Film Commission (NZFC), created in 1978, is the main government agency that provides funding to film projects. New Zealand on Air (NZOA), although focused on television programming, occasionally provides funding to feature films.[5] Wellington, described as "the coolest little capital" (Lonely Planet 2010), has a film district that has been driven by post-production activities since the 2000s when it became a satellite production centre for Hollywood, notably via the productions of Peter Jackson and Weta Digital (e.g., *The Lord of the Rings* and *The Hobbit* trilogy). Satellite and domestic productions have benefited from government's grants and tax incentives; however, both models struggle to be stable and profitable. These challenges provide a good arena to examine the sustainability of the Wellington film industry.[6] The blockages to sustainability identified here are also opportunities for policy-makers and business strategists to leverage sustainability. Even though the outcomes of this analysis are unique to the film industry in Wellington, the framework itself could be transferred to examine other film industries.

The chapter is organised as follows. First, it situates itself within a wider debate on culture and sustainability and provides a definition of sustainability in the film industry. Second, it draws on two theoretical traditions to propose an analytical framework to study sustainability in the film industry. Third, it outlines the methodology of the empirical study. Finally, it discusses the research findings against the framework of analysis and suggests main areas of policy intervention.

Sustainability and cultural industries

The term 'sustainable' has been widely applied to environmental and economic fields but more recent efforts to apply it to culture have come from

---

4   See Jonathan Victory, "Green Shots: Environmental Sustainability and Contemporary Film Production," *Studies in Arts and Humanities* 1, no. 1 (2015): 54–68.

5   For more information on funding in New Zealand see Ferrer-Roca (2018).

6   The scope of analysis is the Wellington film industry as a whole as opposed to individual films or companies.

international organisations such as the United Nations and the European Union, which called for more research on the link between culture and sustainability (Throsby 1997). Since then, an emerging body of literature has made important developments.[7] This chapter sits within such literature, particularly within: (1) 'culture in sustainability',[8] that is, work around the idea that culture as a dimension of human life can be sustainable (Dessein et al. 2015); and (2) 'cultural policy', where policy plays the role of regulator and protector to sustain cultural heritage, practices, and rights as ends in themselves (Duxbury, Kangas, and De Beukelaer 2017).

As an approach, sustainability implies that specific conditions should be preserved/self-perpetuated amid change[9] but the challenge to build a bridge with culture was to pin down the abstract and polysemic notion of culture from anthropological and sociological traditions (i.e., culture as civilization) into more specific operational concepts.

The work of sociologist Bourdieu on cultural capital has been key in allowing theorists to build the link culture/sustainability as he provided an economic – but not economistic – lens that grounds culture to more concrete concepts such as labour. That is, Bourdieu did not propose a reduction of all cultural aspects to the economic dimension, nor did he adhere to an economic ideology/theory (i.e., neoclassical economics) as a way to understand culture. Instead, he provided an explanation of culture through a set of concepts and practices that are more familiar with the economic language, which are useful in order to think on its sustainability.

Bourdieu defined *cultural capital* as a form of accumulated labour that could be embodied — incorporated in the "dispositions of the mind and body" (1986, p. 243) such as through education — or objectified, in cultural goods. In both cases, such accumulation took time and resources, as do other forms of labour. Cultural capital, observed Bourdieu, could be appropriated by individuals or social groups both "materially — which presupposes economic capital— and symbolically — which presupposes cultural capital" (1986, p. 246). But in any case individuals would be appropriating "social energy in the form of reified or

---

7   In the areas of international policy (UNCTAD 2010) and social theory (Throsby 2017).

8   Rather than within: 'Culture for sustainability' in which culture is seen as a vehicle to achieve economic, social and ecological sustainability; or 'Culture as sustainability', the idea that culture is the overarching concept that contains economic, social and ecological dimensions, and therefore is essential to the paradigm that could achieve their sustainability. See Dessein, Soini, Fairclough, Horlings (2015).

9   From the Latin roots 'to sustain' or 'to hold up' see Lewis and Short (1969, p. 1822).

living labour" (1986, p. 241). Bourdieu's concept of cultural capital sheds light on understanding the important interplay between culture and socio-economic resources, and the relevance of one of them to the long-term maintenance of the other and vice versa.

Building on this line of work, Throsby (1997) suggested that cultural capital could take the form of tangible assets or services, from art works to cultural heritage. But it can also be intangible, as found in art works like music or, as it embodies knowledge, values, beliefs and ideas shared with some community groups and even humankind. Both tangible and intangible cultural stocks, he remarks, carry a symbolic value that can vary across different social groups and which can also "decay through neglect or increase through new investment" (1997, p. 15). This remark echoes Bourdieu's observation that the creation and the maintenance of cultural capital require resources such as labour, time, symbolic and material resources. This chapter suggests that it is precisely within this foundation that the concept of cultural sustainability becomes relevant as it encapsulates the availability of such factors/resources and their functional and structural relationships among them. Therefore, the presence or absence of sustainability underpins cultural growth, preservation or deterioration, all of them being potential scenarios. In tune with the cultural-economic logic of this linkage, Throsby argued that cultural systems could be sustainable, defining sustainability as "the long-term supporting viability of any type of system" (1997, p. 10).

In applying these contributions to the film industry and its double cultural-economic component, this chapter suggests that addressing sustainability in the film industry would mean *ascertaining the long-term endogenous viability of the cultural aspects of film and the economic aspects of its industry*. Nonetheless, this definition could remain hollow unless the question of how to achieve this *long-term endogenous viability* is addressed by a set of dynamics and variables. The next section pinpoints general theoretical constructs that shed light on this query.

Theorising sustainable film industries

Sustainable cycles

Research on how film industries work have carried the use of metaphors such as 'cycles' and 'spirals', which display a sense of sustainability even though the term has not been necessarily employed.

Within the political economy of culture (PEC) approach, Garnham (1990; 2005) focused on the distribution and dissemination of feature films and observed that in capitalist societies, economies of scale in the film distribution phase – such as low marginal costs per unit distributed – have facilitated large capital concentration (that is, the creation of oligopolies such as Hollywood's), and political influence over regulation.

As Mosco (2009) notes, PEC has focused on the power relations among the phases of the film industry's value chain such as: (a) production—content creation, (b) distribution—administration of promotion and dissemination of films, and (c) commercialisation—the consumption outlets for films, such as cinemas, physical and online retail, and television broadcasting. Garnham (1990, p. 183) observed that the relations among these phases underlie important outcomes such as the possibility to reinvest in producing more films. He argued that in order to facilitate the articulation of the circuit – that is, "to establish a viable linkage between production on the one hand and exchange [commercialisation] on the other", there was a need to pursue "making the flow of money from the widely scattered box-offices [and other outlets] back to production as efficient and rapid as possible (thus accelerating the turnover time of capital)" (1990, p. 185). Similarly, Pendakur (1990) argued that for film production to be sustainable, production and distribution companies needed to be integrated. PEC's contributions are widely accepted; economic geographer Scott (2002, p. 969) remarks, "the distribution system disseminates the industry's products on wider markets, pumps revenues and information back to [...] [producers], and hence is a basic condition of the sustained economic well-being of the [...] [industry].". It can be inferred from the work of political economists that the articulated cycles of the value chain, called here *vertical relations*,[10] are decisive for the sustainability of the film industry (see Fig. 1).

Furthermore, the geographic industrialisation approach (GI) focused on the Smithian concept of the division of labour inside or outside production companies, such as the work of Young (1928), who suggested that production activities are *primary economies* that generate opportunities for other secondary economies or organisations to get involved. In Scott's (2005) analysis of film districts, secondary economies include mainly services to production or film-related players. For example, a film production company might require the work of a special effects company, and in doing so, it will

---

10 *Vertical* refers to the diachronic relations occurring at different moments in time along the value chain of the film industry (i.e., relations between production and distribution).

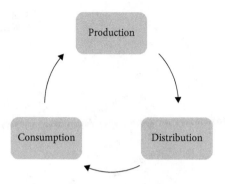

Fig. 1: The value chain of the film industry. Source: Author

create an opportunity for special effects businesses to be involved. In the same way, the special effects company might need the services of a software development company, and so on. With each round of investment at the core, the secondary players and economies might benefit and, in turn, the core benefits as well. Secondary players could be government bodies such as location offices or film archives that depend on the core film production activities.

The more frequently primary and secondary players relate to each other, the more the trust and communication increase among them. As one generates particular needs and the other provides customised services, they might generate a competitive advantage that is unique to those organisations (Scott 2005). The relationships by which diverse agents learn from the experience and interaction among them are called *interdependencies* (Nelson and Winter 1982). Markusen (1996) argued that interdependencies in an industrial district generate the ability to initially attract and then maintain the attraction among the district's components. In other words, interdependencies, a type of *horizontal relations*,[11] become sustained as they propel new rounds of production into spirals of increasing returns (see Fig. 2).

In sum, both cyclical models represent the ability of the film industry to reproduce capital and in turn, self-perpetuate; one through vertical relations, and the other one, through horizontal relations.

---

11   *Horizontal* refers to the synchronic relations occurring at the same time or during the same value chain phase (i.e., during the production phase).

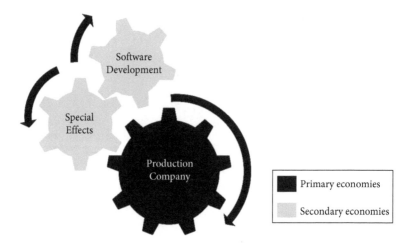

Fig. 2: Spirals of increasing returns. Source: Author

Criteria for socio-economic sustainability

The literature on film industries has observed certain standards that are present in the viable industries it has studied. This is systematised below as socio-economic conditions for sustainability (see Muñoz Larroa 2015). They are:

(1) *Financial capacity for reinvestment to increase economic returns and social rewards*. Following the work from Garnham (1990) and Pendakur (1990) it is expected that part of the box office and sales revenue from other commercialisation windows (i.e., DVD, Video-On-Demand (VOD), TV, etc.) will be reinvested to maintain the value chain cycles. Even in publicly funded film industries within market economies, there is a widespread expectation that films will return money as well as social recognition, although expectations vary among regions and schemes. Returns from the ownership of other audio-visual industries – such as videogames – can also increase the financial capacity of film production companies and the industrial district in general.

(2) *Pools of specialised workers and a production system that can guarantee the generation and maintenance of quality jobs*. Maintaining jobs allows workers to acquire know-how, that is, the "relevant skills, experience and knowledge needed for competent performance" (Rowlands 2009). The inability to maintain the production system could result in losing labour pools through emigration as well as raising unemployment. A pool

of workers shared with other cultural industries – whose skills often overlap – can facilitate the maintenance of jobs and knowledge transfer. However, as Scott (2006, p. 15) argues, importing a creative and technical workers from other regions for specific projects (i.e., hosting runaway productions) is not enough to generate industrial development. On the contrary, specialised pools of labour "must be organically developed through the complex interweaving of relations of production, work and social life in specific urban contexts".

(3) *The capacity to feed from creative sources.* The *cultural milieu* is "the matrix within which the social machinery of production is entrenched and the main repository of the diverse cultural resources that are both consciously and unconsciously mobilised in the conceptualisation and execution of cinematic projects" (Scott 2000). Film workers' acculturation gives films their distinctiveness; it infuses creative work with concrete character drawn from the frames of reference, visual styles, stories, and so on, which provide a "cinematic background vocabulary" (Scott 2006, p. 26). Synergies with other cultural industries also propel the existence of creative resources. A vibrant cultural environment can generate competitive advantages; however, "as important as these assets may be, they are apt to be inert until energised and reproduced through an actually working production system" (Scott 2000, p. 105).

(4) *The appropriate infrastructure and productivity levels.* Having adequate levels of yearly film production helps to maintain jobs and to create spillovers for infrastructure such as film services and facilities, which can also be shared with other cultural industries (TV, videogame/animation, and even music recording). There is also a film-related institutional infrastructure coming from the public sector, the civil society, and academic and private organisations. As GI researchers argue, face-to-face contact, exchange of information, and short and long-term outsourcing as well as input and output flows are key to the creation of interdependencies in industrial complexes and their spirals of increasing returns (Scott 2000).

(5) *Captive local and international audiences.* The film industry depends on economic returns and social rewards from consumers to maintain production cycles. Expanding captive audiences is one of the conditions of existence of the film industry as they represent the demand required to generate economies of scale (Graham 2005). Even though places with limited populations have difficulties generating economies of scale, small markets "can often find sustainable niches for themselves on world markets provided they

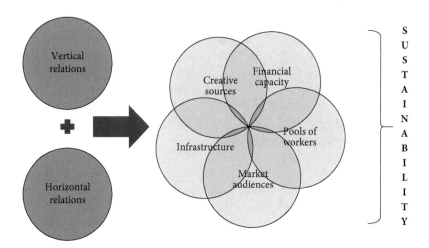

Fig. 3: Analytical framework of sustainability. Source: Author

offer sufficiently distinctive" products (Scott 2006, p. 13). Furthermore, cross-media promotion and spin-off products (among different cultural industries) can take advantage of the social momentum and help to expand audience awareness.

A framework to analyse and foster sustainability in the film industry

Based on the theory revised above, the framework suggested here (see Fig. 3) is a tool for analysis and a normative guide to canalise policy intervention. The framework is based on the principles that relations that are vertical (along the phases of the value chain) and horizontal (interdependencies among interlinked organisations) are key aspects of sustainability as they underwrite outcomes in five main areas: financial capacity, ability to maintain labour pools, ability to feed from creative sources, ability to develop productivity and infrastructure, and the opportunity to reach audiences. By mapping the constraints to vertical and horizontal relations that shape those five areas, they could become opportunities to overcome (Muñoz Larroa 2015).

The framework establishes a bridge between the theory discussed in this section and its application to the sort of policy-making concerned with sustainable outcomes discussed in the Introduction (see Fig. 4).

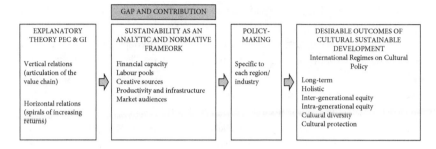

Fig. 4: Gap and contribution. Source: Author

However, the framework is not intended to impose a universal definition on what a sustainable film industry consists of, which is rather a field of flexible and contesting positions that communities should discuss.

Self-sustainability: Local versus transnational and private versus public funding

The term *self-sustainable* has been used to refer to systems that fend for themselves. It is important to address whether the *self* refers to the local, national, regional, or transnational spatial dimension because such *communities* are the units of collective interrelatedness into which film industries have immediate impact on people's lives through jobs, economic development, cultural enrichment, and social empowerment (UNCTAD 2010, p. 26). This book shows plenty examples of flexible boundaries among different communities that go beyond the local and the national, such as Finnish Swedish cinema (see chapter "In the Land of Finnish Swedish Cinema: A Look into the Political Economy of Local Cinema in Finland", by Daniel Lindblom) or Arab Gulf cinema/Khaleeji cinema (see chapter "The Political Economy of the Khaleeji Cinema: Historical Developments of Arab Gulf Film Industries", by Abdulrahman Alghannam in this volume).

The framework proposed here cannot replace the sovereign process of each community to define itself in those terms. Nonetheless, it is based on the idea that some general boundaries are justified by the film industry's endogenous socio-economic dynamics and its socio-cultural implications to communities. For instance, the film industry in Hong Kong has historically relied on foreign capital and foreign markets (Lim 2006). The question is, does that make it at odds with being self-sustaining? Based on the theory, there could be a self-sustainable industry in Hong Kong provided that it incorporates those foreign links into internal positive productive cycles.

In addition, self-sustainability should not be framed purely in commercial terms but also incorporate public-funded industries. For example, the film industry in France has significant public funding and regulation as well as synergies with television to complement private investment (Scott 2000). For instance, there are screen quotas and shares from cinema and television revenue allocated to film funds. Can the French film industry be seen as self-sustaining? An interpretation based on the theory would suggest that we could think of it as self-sustainable only if it canalises public subsidies to generate internal positive cycles of production and dissemination of films.

Methodology

According to the framework developed in the sections above, relations among film industry stakeholders enable or constrain sustainable outcomes. Therefore, the empirical research analysed the industrial and institutional relations of the Wellington film industry in order to evaluate its sustainability. The empirical research conducted during 2011–2015 involved in-depth interviews with thirty film industry stakeholders such as producers, service providers, distributors, exhibitors, guild representatives, public servants and policy advisors. The majority were based in Wellington although others, whose activities influenced the region, lived somewhere else in New Zealand. Interviews were analysed thematically by coding patterns found in the data using NVivo 10. These findings were compared with data from other sources such as statistics, public and media reports as well as previous academic studies. Research after 2015 followed up the development of online VOD as a new window of dissemination.

The film industry value chain in New Zealand

In New Zealand, film distribution and exhibition sectors have been geared to the supply of foreign, mainly Hollywood films, since the 1920s (Churchman 1997). Today, both sectors are highly concentrated in a few transnational companies. Hollywood major distributors Paramount, Universal, 20th Century Fox, Disney, Sony and Warner Bros. concentrate a share of 73% of the box office approximately whereas the remaining 27% corresponds to smaller Australian and New Zealand companies (Muñoz Larroa 2017). Similarly, the country has high levels of market concentration in the cinema exhibition sector where three major chains, Event Cinemas (owned by Australian Amalgamated Holdings Ltd.), Hoyts Cinemas (owned by Australian Pacific Equity Partners) and Reading Cinemas (owned by US

Reading International) shared 70% of the New Zealand box office (Huffer 2012). The high concentration has created a barrier to opportunities for new business entries and to the growth of smaller businesses that cannot compete on that scale. Other windows of commercialisation have dramatically changed in the last decade. For example, revenue from video rental and retail went from being above cinema box office to suffering massive closure of businesses due to competition from online VOD services. The latter developed slowly as they were disincentivized due to the data cap of Internet Service Providers. Some people have seen the potential of online distribution to open markets for independent producers (see Lobato 2009) as it has further decreased costs of reproduction/distribution to almost nil – although administrative and promotional costs are still high. However, emerging online players are forming new oligopolies that do not deal with single-title producers but with content aggregators who decide which titles are distributed – usually integrated upon the traditional commercial infrastructures (Lobato 2009). This is the case in New Zealand where there are around fifteen platforms dedicated to disseminating movies; among them are US-based global players such as Google Movies, Microsoft Movies, Amazon Prime, iTunes and Netflix. The latter entered relatively late, in 2015, but already dominated the market by 2016 along Neon, a regional player owned by Sky Television (Drinnan 2017). As Ian Huffer's study concluded, "given the dominance of US content in the majority of the legal catalogues, New Zealand-specific content struggles for visibility" (Huffer 2016). It is local public funded platforms such as New Zealand on Screen and New Zealand Film on Demand or regional private sites such as Quickflix (Australian owned) that provide a space for local content. However, they have a limited international reach and the first two "require the user to have a pre-existing interest in looking for titles as they are specific niche portals" (Huffer 2016).

The market structure as per above is facilitated by New Zealand's international free trade deals (Kelsey 2003) whose regulations have fenced in New Zealand's audio-visual trade deficit and fixed New Zealand's role as a net consumer of foreign screen products. For instance, approximately 97% of the films released in New Zealand were foreign and 68% of the television screen time was foreign as well (NZOA 2012). Current trade regulations have also facilitated the establishment of audio-visual transnational companies and their flow of capital to overseas headquarters (Huffer 2012). This in turn has hindered the articulation of the local value chain at the commercialisation phase affecting its sustainable cycles of reinvestment.

The historical disenfranchisement of the local production sector from the distribution and commercialisation sectors – which are oriented to transnational products – explains, among other factors, why the local production sector in the country continues to be unable to disseminate products and to participate in reinvestment cycles.[12] This situation has also favoured the dependency of local production on state subsidies to produce films that otherwise would not be made.

The Wellington film district

Filmmaking in Wellington is shaped by the city's density, walkability, thriving street life, culinary and café culture, which are "part of its identity" (MCH 2012) and facilitators of networks of socialisation and cultural consumption (Stahl 2011). These imprinted specific filmmaking aspects based on experimentation, technical and creative collaboration.

From 2012 to 2015, there were approximately thirty-nine screen production companies in the Wellington region and there were at least two main models and one sub-model of film production coexisting in Wellington:

(1) The local or independent model. Ninety percent of the companies were small, locally owned, and produced films that were more directly linked to New Zealand culture.

(2) The satellite model. Ten percent of the companies dedicated mainly to work-for-hire services to *runaway productions* from Hollywood studios – looking for lower production costs and local incentives. They were mainly located in Miramar, a cluster of companies, facilities, and services co-owned by director Peter Jackson and his closer collaborators.

Both models were dependent on state funding and unfortunately had been unable to canalise those resources into inward sustainable reinvestment cycles (Jones, Barlow, Finlay, and Savage 2003; Rothwell 2010).

(3) There was, however, a sub-model of production: international co-ventures.[13] That is, international co-productions established between local and overseas producers (including those outside official treaties). This model was less prominent than the others but no less important. International co-productions are mechanisms that allow producers to attract funding and film workers, and gain access to wider audiences from other regions while extending "state funding, tax incentives or distribution arrangements available in either country" (Crewdson 2014).[14]

---

12 For an analysis on the power relations and market failure of the New Zealand film distribution industry see Muñoz Larroa and Ferrer-Roca (2017).

13 Considered here as a sub-model of production as local or satellite companies can also be involved in co-productions with international companies.

14 These three models coincide with Ferrer-Roca's (2017) study of New Zealand's development of a three-tier feature film industry structure considering the challenges of a small domestic media market.

Tab. 1: Comparison of the spillovers by production model. Source: Author. Major (√√), minor (√), or absent () spillovers

	Primary economies	Secondary economies	Below the line	Above the line	Film services	Financial pools
Satellite		√√	√√	√	√	
Local	√√	√√	√√	√√	√	
International co-ventures	√√	√√	√√	√√	√√	√√

Tab. 1 summarises the advantages and shortcomings of each model to produce spillovers that, according to the theory of geographic industrialisation, could enable sustainability in the rest of the district.

An important characteristic of the satellite model based in Miramar is that its key investment decisions are made externally, by Hollywood majors. This meant that Miramar's satellite activities entailed mainly secondary economies or services such as post-production, visual and special effects. Unlike primary economies, secondary economies have less capacity to generate the spirals of increasing returns by themselves, which the theory used here considers essential for sustainable cycles. For instance:

- Satellite activities generated spillovers to general services, like catering and car rentals, but film services such as film equipment were outsourced from overseas because they exceeded the capacity of local service providers.
- With important decisions made in Hollywood, above-the-line workers – the top creative talent like top producers and main performers – were from overseas. The exception was writer/director Peter Jackson and his writing team, who did not collaborate with other local screenwriters (limiting positive spillovers to the rest of the district).
- Although Miramar participated in major studios' blockbusters with successful box office worldwide, the majority of revenue flew to the headquarters of overseas studios and did not translate into local financial pools. Even though Peter Jackson's hold on intellectual property meant there were returns to Miramar, there were no co-financial relations with local production houses.

There is, however, the potential that Miramar production companies like WingNut films or Pukeko Pictures engage in more in-house productions and reach out to the local creative talent and companies.

It was local productions and co-ventures that ticked most of the boxes for the positive spillovers that could enable sustainability in the district. They entailed primary economies, they spanned secondary economies, and they hired below and above the line workers. However, as mentioned before, it was difficult for local producers to find distribution and commercialisation deals to generate financial pools. Therefore, local producers were undercapitalised (see more below) and could not afford local film services. Nonetheless, international co-ventures tended to be better capitalised and were able to afford local film services. Unfortunately, international co-ventures were not that common in Wellington despite the official co-production deals established with many countries, which were not being used at their full potential (Gibson 2014).

The analysis of the industry's relations, as above, partially explains why the satellite model, although the most successful, had been limited in sharing its success with the rest of the district. Other regions have experienced similar outcomes, see discussion on 'parallel industries' – local vs international production – in Alghannam's chapter "The Political Economy of the Khaleeji Cinema: Historical Developments of Arab Gulf Film Industries". The satellite model in Wellington generated below-the-line jobs and allowed local producers to use some of their facilities at a discount price, thereby increasing the technical quality of films made in the district. However, as a model to develop sustainability, it showed limitations. This was unlike the other two models, which were more worthy of support for being more capable of producing sustainable outcomes.

Mapping constraints to sustainability

Financial capacity

A generalised constraint in the film industry in Wellington has been the undercapitalisation of domestic producers (see also Jackson and Court 2010). The distribution sector is a channel of dissemination and a source of financing. However, independent producers from Wellington expressed difficulty in dealing with distributors based in Auckland and Australia. Producers lacked resources and expertise in establishing networks with them, and their low-budget films were unappealing to large and medium-sized distributors.

Even local films that achieved national and international distribution deals with successful sales and box office figures, struggled to recoup due to presale financial structures. Producers were at the lower end of the recoupment position after the exhibitor took its share of the box office (starting at 55%), the distributor took its commission (20% of the remaining 45%) and covered the operational and marketing expenses (a percentage depending on each film), and, after film investors[15] were paid, if there was any remaining return.[16] This is a world-wide trend exemplified also in Rajala's Chapter on 'market censorship' in the Finish industry.

Another potential source of finance in New Zealand was public funding from NZOA, under the condition that a TV channel would be committed to broadcasting the film. However, broadcasters often preferred buying more commercial, cost-effective international programmes (Thompson 2011). Even when producers were able to obtain NZOA funding, the amount received was close to the cost of making the film, thus producers were unable to generate returns to reinvest.

Despite their financial struggles, local production companies were literally 'independent'; they hardly ever collaborated with each other on joint efforts. Neither were there collaborations with better-financed satellite-oriented companies.

In the light of the analytical framework proposed here, undercapitalisation is a vertical constraint that signals a hindrance to capital flow from markets back to producers. It reflected broken relations between local independent producers on the one hand, and investors (including public funding bodies), sales agents, distributors, exhibitors and broadcasters on the other (see Fig. 5). The imbalance of power allowed the latter to dictate the terms of the revenue streams, which were disadvantageous to producers. The government support via public funding for local producers, though necessary, was still partly misallocated as it failed to break dependency cycles.

---

15 Including public funding agencies such as the NZFC.
16 For a deeper analysis on revenue redistribution see Ferrer-Roca (2015) and Muñoz Larroa and Ferrer-Roca (2017).

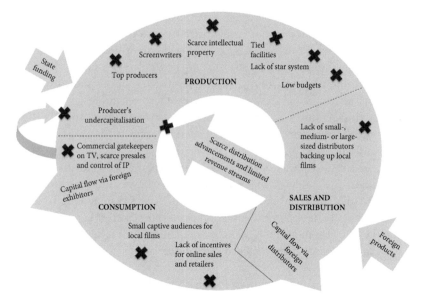

Fig. 5: Mapping constraints to sustainability. *Source: Author.* _____ = *articulation;*
- - - - - = *disarticulation.*

There are, however, policy areas that have the potential to tackle the constraints to financial capacity:

• Fostering collaboration and amalgamation strategies between local production companies to leverage their position to negotiate access to capital or dissemination deals. This is a strategy already fostered by the government in China (see Keane 2013).

• Engaging more in international co-ventures and distribution deals with other independent players (as opposed to major corporations) that offer access to financial pools and markets from other regions without compromising control over revenue. Some of these business strategies are direct distribution or self-distribution as described by Grundström in her chapter "Film Distribution in Finland: Gatekeepers of Local Cinema" in this volume.

• Policies, legislation or funding mechanisms could also establish minimum standards regulating contractual relations between dissemination channels and producers to guarantee the latter a better cut and recoupment position. For instance, Peter Jackson and David Court suggested the creation of a Box

Office Incentive Scheme, which would reward local box office films with "$1 per each $10 of the gross box office" (2010, p. 69).

Ability to feed from creative sources and pools of specialised labour

Screenwriters

One constraint to the Wellington film district's ability to feed from creative sources was the lack of good professional screenwriters (see also PC & NZIER 2003). Although there were professional writing courses in New Zealand, there was no ongoing work to offer a career path, a training ground to develop the skills and craft of professional screenwriters.

In view of the analytical framework, this issue is a vertical blockage in the value chain that impedes good storytelling from becoming an input into film development and, further down in the value chain, to engage with audiences. It is also a horizontal disconnection between the pool of screenwriters and producers (see Fig. 5).

A policy path worthy to be explored by funding agencies is to develop screenwriting careers by increasing the number of projects that writers can participate in, so they can get trained, gain exposure to audiences, and learn from project to project, even if that means making lower-budget films or TV programmes. This has been a successful strategy in Denmark (see Collins 2012).

Top creative producers

Another constraint identified in the Wellington film industry was the lack of creative producers with enough expertise in marketing overseas (see also Barnett 2013). Market intelligence and co-production knowledge are time consuming and expensive, and the district had a dearth of high-level business and marketing skills (see also PC & NZIER 2003, p. 28).

This is another horizontal blockage during the phase of production, indicating the disconnection of producers with financiers/buyers due to producers' lack of capital and continuous production (see Fig. 5).

A similar suggestion to the screenwriters above is to increase producers' exposure to subsequent projects to gain expertise. Although government agencies have funded producers' trips to international markets to get savvier and acquire social connections, those resources have been used for producers' own projects but not transferred to others (Campbell and Hughes 2003). This is one of the disadvantages of the project-based model in film production, which is unable to retain and transfer the specialised knowledge to the whole film district (Davenport 2006).

Intellectual property

Another shortcoming identified was the lack of generation and exploitation of intellectual property (IP), which is essential to receiving returns for cycles of rein-vestment. There are high costs involved in the management and exploitation of rights, which require specialised intermediaries such as accountants, lawyers, sales agents, and collecting societies. Consequently, right holders were often vulnerable in New Zealand where "ownership of copyrights [...] [was] often lost with for-eign money driving the deal" (PC & NZIER 2003, 27). This is true for the satel-lite movies whose vast copyright revenue belonged to the US-based transnational company (SPT 2003). But also in public-funded films, government funders claimed the rights, leaving residuals "in the hands of people with limited moti-vation and abilities to exploit them" (PC & NZIER 2003, vii). By the same token, when funding bodies encouraged producers to search for third party investment, investors had "a powerful negotiation position, which often weakens the position of the owner of the residual and other IP rights" (PC & NZIER 2003, vii).

The lack of intellectual property or IP is a vertical blockage that prevents the film industry from transforming ideas into products that reach audiences. It is also a horizontal blockage that reflects disarticulation and unequal relations between content creators on the one hand, and financiers and investors on the other (see Fig. 5).

A policy path for increasing IP management and creative producers' expertise (mentioned on the previous section) could be to support local inter-mediary organisations (public or private) that are specialised in those activities so they can accrue and transfer that knowledge in the long-term more effec-tively than single individuals (Grant 1996). For example, the NZFC outsourced the marketing of its films to overseas sales agents (with reported little success). Having a sales agency within the NZFC would require capital investment and the generation of expertise (maybe hiring some savvy overseas sales agents) but with the possibility of accruing that knowledge and sharing it with many local projects.

Productivity and appropriate infrastructure

Another constraint identified in the production sector was that most of the projects were polarised on either large-scale satellite operations or small-scale independent productions. Middle-tier productions such as international co-ventures, television productions and medium-sized film budgets were scarce. This created a disproportionate effect; firstly, the small domestic producers lacked the capacity to absorb large numbers of workers during the satellite blockbuster downtimes. Secondly, neither large nor small-scale producers could provide the industry with the continuity of the work it required to maintain film services. As large satellite productions drove up costs of labour, facilities and general services (PC & NZIER 2003), the domestic industry had to stretch its already-thin budgets. In fact, interviews showed film service providers had to offer numerous discounts in order to accommodate local producers' needs, despite being unviable in the long-term (see also *Onfilm* 2008). Furthermore, some high-quality facilities built with government support were tied up to a single top producer, which made them expensive for independent producers to use.

Budgetary mismatches between independent and large satellite productions are another set of horizontal blockages in the film production phase (see Fig. 5).

On this issue, policy-makers could support: (1) building facilities of a modest scale that can guarantee that most customers will be able to use it (Kenworthy 2013); and (2) middle-tier screen budgets such as international co-ventures or television series and programmes to breach the gap and increase ongoing production.

Captive local and international audiences

Another constraint for the Wellington film industry was the small domestic market share. For instance, from 1993 to 2012, it represented an average of 2.5% of the box office (NZFC 2014). There are no data available to estimate the volume of international audiences for New Zealand films but interviews indicated that it was very modest. Big disparities were found in the distribution sector between large or medium but internationally owned distributors that dominate the New Zealand market and a few small local distributors; this also contributed to a budget scale mismatch. Firstly, large and medium distributors were not interested in disseminating small-budget local films, and tended to bring in larger budget international films. Secondly, small local distributors who were striving to survive depended on highly publicised medium or large-budget international films. This, in turn, inhibited symbiotic relations between small local distributors and local films.

This is another vertical blockage located in the dissemination phases of the value chain, which prevents local producers from obtaining economic and social rewards through expanding market audiences and economic returns (see Fig. 5).

Policies in New Zealand have focused mainly on subsidising film production, yet they have left the area of distribution and exhibition aside. However, policy paths in those sectors would be worth exploring, such as:

- Audience-development strategies. Denmark, a small population country similar to New Zealand, has been quite successful in this regard, achieving a steady 30% of domestic market share (Scoffier 2014). Some of the strategies in Denmark entailed the joint efforts of local cinema theatres with local producers to support Danish films until they actually became very popular. Other strategies included attracting young audiences, showing films for school children, and creating promotions for groups of family or friends to socialise the experience of cinema-going (Schramm 2002). Similar strategies have also been fruitful in China as discussed by Han in chapter "Production of Main Melody Film in Post-socialist China: A Deconstruction of Wolf Warrior 2" in this volume.
- Fostering alternative channels of distribution and commercialisation, which are not already dominated by mainstream distribution, for example, through online outlets as well as supporting local independent distributors and exhibitors with interest in showing local films (such as art-house, community cinemas already successful in Wellington, similar to CineCiutat in Mallorca, see Bergillos', chapter "The Political Economy of Participatory Community Cinemas: CineCiutat as a Standpoint of Resistance" in this volume). A very important development is the introduction of NZ Film on Demand in 2014, an online platform offering content funded by the NZFC and available for rentals and purchases. The effects of this new platform and other online VOD sites' capacity to provide returns to right holders should be a topic for further studies.
- Establishing synergies with other screen and cultural industries (such as TV, gaming, music, and publishing), to develop properties, spin-off products, exploit IP, and take advantage of cross-media promotion to expand markets. See in this book Ferrer-Roca's chapter on some successful business strategies of NZ films' exploiting different windows of commercialization.

Conclusions

A self-sustainable film industry – socio-economically speaking – is one with the ability to fend for itself in the long-term, and support the viability of its cultural and socio-economic aspects. In Wellington, mapping the constraints in the five key areas for sustainability revealed limitations that could become opportunities if addressed by policy-makers and business strategists.

As the New Zealand case showed, the right for cultures to express themselves and make themselves known has become more relevant as economic globalisation has strengthened the dominant position of transnational companies and consequently the unilateral flows of audio-visual services. However, globalisation has also seen the rise in digitalisation and its potential to expand markets and make diverse screen content more available. The essay, however, has discussed that online film distribution is liable to be integrated into mainstream distribution business models; therefore, more holistic policies are needed to support alternative channels of dissemination – including digital platforms. Further research in this emerging market is needed in order to make the most of its potential to contribute to independent film industries' sustainability.

The framework suggested here could be applied to other film industries as a tool to design policies that target specific issues that are structural, overarching and long-term driven. It hopes to establish a link between academic theories and international organisations' call for cultural sustainability by offering a set of variables that allow more concrete analyses and applicable policy solutions to leverage the socio-economic sustainability of film industries. However, more work is needed to pursue Throsby's principles for cultural sustainability laid out in this chapter's Introduction.

Research: The chapter's research was conducted as part of the author's PhD studies at the School of Management, Victoria University of Wellington in New Zealand.

References

Bourdieu, Pierre. The Forms of Capital. In: Richardson, John (ed.) *Handbook of Theory and Research for the Sociology of Education*. Greenwood: New York, 1986, pp. 241–258.

Campbell, Grant, and Hughes, Owen. *Film Focus Group Response to the Screen Production Industry Task Force Report*, 2003, p. 15, retrieved 17.9.2014, from www.spada.co.nz/documents/Sub-SPITFFG.pdf (no longer available online)

Churchman, Geoffrey. *Celluloid Dreams : A Century of Film in New Zealand*. IPL Books: Wellington, 1997, 146 p.

Collins, Lauren. "Danish Postmodern". *The New Yorker* 31.12.2012, retrieved 17.1.2015, from http://www.newyorker.com/magazine/2013/01/07/danish-postmodern

Crewdson, Patrick. "China Film Deal: The Great Fast Forward". *Stuff* 3.7.2010, retrieved 22.5.2014, from http://www.stuff.co.nz/business/3881051/China-film-deal-The-great-fast-forward

Davenport, John. "UK Film Companies: Project-Based Organizations Lacking Entrepreneurship and Innovativeness?". *Creativity and Innovation Management*, 15(3), 2006, pp. 250–257.

Dessein, Joost, Soini, Katrina, Fairclough, Graham, and Horlings, Lummina. *Culture in, for and as Sustainable Development: Conclusions from the COST Action IS1007 Investigating Cultural Sustainability*. University of Jyväskylä: Finland, 2015, 73 p., retrieved 4.3.2017, from http://www.culturalsustainability.eu/conclusions.pdf

Drinnan, John: "Sky TV's Big Battle". *The New Zealand Herald*, 1.8.2016, retrieved 7.4.2017, from http://www.nzherald.co.nz/business/news/article.cfm?c_id=3&objectid=11570900

Duxbury, Nancy, Kangas, Anita, and De Beukelaer, Christiaan. "Cultural policies for sustainable development: four strategic paths". *International Journal of Cultural Policy*, 23(2), 2017, pp. 214–230.

Ferrer-Roca, Natàlia. "Multi-Platform Funding Strategies for Bottom-Tier Films in Small Domestic Media Markets: *Boy* (2010) as a New Zealand Case Study". *Journal of Media Business Studies*, 12(4), 2015, pp. 224–237.

Ferrer-Roca, Natàlia. "Three-tier of Feature Film Productions: The case of New Zealand". *Studies in Australasian Cinema*, 11(2), 2017, pp. 102–120.

Ferrer-Roca, Natàlia. "Feature Film Funding Between National and International Priorities. How Does New Zealand Bridge the Gap?". In Murschetz, Paul Clemens, Teichmann, Roland and Karmasin, Matthias (eds.), *Handbook of State Aid for Film – Finance, Industries and Regulations* (Media Business and Innovation Series). Cham, Switzerland: Springer. 2018, pp. 383–401.

Garnham, Nicholas. "From Cultural to Creative Industries". *International Journal of Cultural Policy*, 11(1), 2005, pp. 15–29.

Garnham, Nicholas. *Capitalism and Communication. Global culture and the economics of information*. London: Sage, 1990, 216 p.

Gibson, Dave. *Dave Gibson's Speech to the Industry*. New Zealand Film Commission, 13.3.2014, retrieved 15.7.2014, from http://www.nzfilm.co.nz/news/dave-gibsons-speech-to-the-industry

Grant, Robert. "Toward a Knowledge-Based Theory of the Firm". *Strategic Management Journal*, 17(S2), 1996, pp. 109–122.

Huffer, Ian. "NZ Film on Demand: Searching for National Cinema Online". *Journal of Media & Cultural Studies*, 30 (6), 2016, pp. 697–705. p. 773.

Huffer, Ian. "Wellywood's Cinemas: Theatrical Film Exhibition in Post-Industrial Wellington". *Studies in Australasian Cinema*, 5(3), 2012, pp. 251–264.

Jackson, Peter, and Court, David. *Review of the New Zealand Film Commission.* Wellington: Ministry for Culture and Heritage, 2010. Retrieved 6.9.2012, from http://www.mch.govt.nz/projects/culture/100628NZReport.pdf

John Barnett. "Film Industry Needs More Top Producers". *New Zealand Herald* 12.11.2013, retrieved 2.2.14, from http://www.nzherald.co.nz/business/news/ article.cfm?c_id=3&objectid=11155871

Jones, Deborah, Barlow, Jude, Finlay, Steven, and Savage, Helen. *NZ Film. A Case Study of the New Zealand Film Industry.* Wellington: Victoria University of Wellington. 2003. 88 p.

Keane, Michael. *Creative Industries in China: Art, Design and Media.* Cambridge: Polity Press. 2013. 192 p.

Kelsey, Jane. *Lessons From New Zealand: The Saga of the GATS and Local Content Quotas.* Paper presented at the Conference on Cultural Diversity, Paris, 2003.

Kenworthy, Andy. "All the World's a Stage". *Idealog*, 53, 6.2013, pp. 48–53, retrieved 16.9.2013, from http://idealog.co.nz/venture/2013/08/ all-worlds-stage.

Lewis, Charlton, and Short, Charles. *A Latin Dictionary.* Oxford: Oxford University Press. 1969, p. 1822.

Lim, Kean Fan. "Transnational Collaborations, Local Competitiveness: Mapping the Geographies of Filmmaking in/through Hong Kong". *Geografiska Annaler: Series B, Human Geography*, 88(3), 2006, pp. 337–357.

Lobato, Ramon. "The politics of digital distribution: Exclusionary structures in online cinema". *Studies in Australasian Cinema*, 3(2), 2009, pp. 167–178.

Lonely Planet. *Lonely Planet's Best in Travel 2011.* Victoria, Australia: Lonely Planet Publications. 2010. 208 p.

Markusen, Anne. "Sticky Places in Slippery Space: A Typology of Industrial Districts". *Economic Geography*, 72(3), 1996, pp. 293–313.

MCH (Ministry for Culture and Heritage). *Wellington Cafe Culture.* 20.12.2012, retrieved 19.7.2014, from http://www.nzhistory.net.nz/culture/ the-daily-grind-wellington-cafe-culture-1920-2000

Mosco, Vincent. *The Political Economy of Communication.* London: Sage. 2009, 268 p.

Muñoz Larroa, Argelia. *Sustainability in the Film Industry: External and Internal Dynamics Shaping the Wellington Film District* (PhD thesis). Wellington: Victoria University of Wellington. 2015.

Muñoz Larroa, Argelia. "Film Distribution and Delivery Outlets in New Zealand: A Transnational Phase and Some Implications for Local Films and Diversity". *Studies in Australasian Cinema*, 11(3), 2017, from DOI 10.1080/17503175.2017.1397235.

Muñoz Larroa, Argelia, and Ferrer-Roca, Natàlia. "Film Distribution in New Zealand: Industrial Organisation, Power Relations and Market Failure". *Media Industries*, 4(2), 2017, from DOI 10.3998/mij.15031809.0004.201. 2017.

Nelson, Richard, and Winter, Sidney. *An Evolutionary Theory of Economic Change*. Cambridge: Harvard University Press. 1982, 454 p.

NZFC (New Zealand Film Commission). *New Zealand Feature Films Share of New Zealand Box Office*, retrieved 30.12.2014, from https://www.nzfilm.co.nz/resources/new-zealand-feature-films-share-new-zealand-box-office

NZFC. *Statement of Intent 2013–2016*. Wellington: New Zealand Film Commission, 2013.

NZOA (New Zealand On Air). *2012 Local Content New Zealand Television*, retrieved 6.6.2013, from http://www.nzonair.govt.nz/document-library/local-content-report-2012/

Onfilm. "Service and a Hire Calling". *Onfilm*, February, 2008, pp. 19–29.

PC & NZIER. *A Capability Study: The New Zealand Screen Production Industry*. Wellington: Industry New Zealand. 2003, p. 28. Retrieved 7.10.2013, from http://www.nzte.govt.nz/common/files/exec-summarycapability.pdf

Pendakur, Manjunath. *Canadian Dreams and American Control: The Political Economy of the Canadian Film Industry*. Detroit: Wayne State University Press. 1990, 330 p.

Rowlands, Lorraine. *The Life of Freelance Film Production Workers in the New Zealand Film Industry* (Masters thesis). Wellington: Massey University. 2009, p. 31.

Schramm, Mette. "Essays on Denmark". In *European Cinema Exhibition, a New Approach*. Ebeltof, Denmark: Media Salles, Danish Cinema Association, The European Film College. 2002, pp. 71–74, retrieved 4.1.2014, from http://www.mediasalles.it/training/report.htm

Scoffier, Axel. "Denmark: A Small Film Industry with Great Shape". *Ina Global* 4.1.2014, retrieved 3.6.2014, from http://www.inaglobal.fr/en/cinema/article/denmark-small-film-industry-great-shape-7515

Scott, Allen. "A New Map of Hollywood: The Production and Distribution of American Motion Pictures". *Regional Studies* 36, 2002, pp. 957–975.

Scott, Allen. "Creative Cities: Conceptual Issues and Policy Questions". *Journal of Urban Affairs*, 28(1), 2006, pp. 1–17.

Scott, Allen. *On Hollywood: The Place, the Industry*. Princeton: Princeton University Press. 2005, 216 p.

Scott, Allen. *The Cultural Economy of Cities: Essays on the Geography of Image-Producing Industries*. Thousand Oaks: Sage. 2000, 256 p., p. 104.

SPT. *Taking on the World. The Report on the Screen Production Industry Taskforce*. Wellington: Screen Production industry Taskforce, Ministry of Industry and Regional Development. 2003.

Stahl, Geoff. "'DIY Or DIT!' Tales of Making Music in a Creative Capital". In *Home, Land and Sea: Situating Music In Aotearoa New Zealand*. Auckland: Pearson Education. 2011, pp. 145–160.

Thompson, Peter. "Show Me the Money: Funding Possibilities for Public Television in New Zealand" (Unpublished conference paper). Presented at the SPADA Conference, Wellington, 2011.

Throsby, David. "Culturally Sustainable Development: Theoretical Concept or Practical Policy Instrument?". *International Journal of Cultural Policy*, 23(2), 2017, pp. 133–147.

Throsby, David. "Sustainability and Culture, Some Theoretical Issues". *International Journal of Cultural Policy*, 4(1), 1997, pp. 7–19.

UNCTAD. *Creative Economy Report, 2010. Creative Economy: A Feasible Development Option*. Geneva: United Nations Conference on Trade and Development, United Nations Development Programme. 2010.

UNESCO. *Universal Declaration on Cultural Diversity*. Paris: United Nations Educational, Scientific and Cultural Organisation. 2002.

Victory, Jonathan. "Green Shots: Environmental Sustainability and Contemporary Film Production". *Studies in Arts and Humanities*, 1(1), 2015, pp. 54–68.

Volkerling, Michael. "From Cool Britannia to Hot Nation: 'Creative industries' policies in Europe, Canada and New Zealand". *GCUL*, 7(3), 2001, pp. 437–455.

Young, Allyn. "Increasing Returns and Economic Progress". *The Economic Journal*, 38(152), 1928, pp. 527–542.

List of Figures

List of Tables

Index